Eugene O'Neill's Last Plays

Eugene O'Neill's Last Plays

SEPARATING ART
FROM AUTOBIOGRAPHY

Doris Alexander

THE UNIVERSITY OF GEORGIA PRESS

ATHENS & LONDON

© 2005 by the University of Georgia Press
Athens, Georgia 30602
All rights reserved
Set in Electra by G & S Typesetters, Inc.
Printed and bound by Thomson-Shore
The paper in this book meets the guidelines for
permanence and durability of the Committee on
Production Guidelines for Book Longevity of the
Council on Library Resources.

Printed in the United States of America
09 08 07 06 05 C 5 4 3 2 1

Library of Congress Cataloging-in-Publication Data

Alexander, Doris.
Eugene O'Neill's last plays : separating art from
autobiography / Doris Alexander.
p. cm.
Includes bibliographical references and index.
ISBN 0-8203-2709-3 (hardcover : alk. paper)
1. O'Neill, Eugene, 1888–1953 — Criticism and
interpretation.   2. Dramatists, American — 20th century —
Biography.   3. O'Neill, Eugene, 1888–1953.
4. Autobiography in literature.   5. Self in literature.
I. Title.
PS3529.N5Z5555 2005
812'.52 — dc22   2004026982

British Library Cataloging-in-Publication Data available

Contents

Preface   vii

Introduction. The Last Plays of Eugene O'Neill   1

The Iceman Cometh

1 · Riddle in *The Iceman Cometh*   7
2 · The Proxy Suicide   16
3 · The Anarchist Contingent   29
4 · Ward Heelers, Pimps, and Prostitutes   45
5 · The Vital Impulse for *The Iceman Cometh*   53
6 · Broadway — On and Off   62

Long Day's Journey into Night

7 · The "One-Day Play"   67
8 · The False in the True   70
9 · James Tyrone   92
10 · Mary Tyrone   120
11 · Jamie Tyrone   133
12 · Edmund Tyrone   144
13 · The Black Widow   149

A Moon for the Misbegotten

14 · The Epitaph   157

Abbreviations Used in the Notes   165
Notes   167
Index to Literary Works of Eugene O'Neill   239
Index   241

Preface

A lifetime of research on Eugene O'Neill went into this book. Every new fact presented here rests on extensive original research into Eugene O'Neill and his family in ways that have not been approached before. For instance, I took complete notes on all references to and interviews with Eugene's actor father James O'Neill in the two great theatrical weeklies, the *New York Dramatic Mirror* and the *New York Clipper,* from the time James O'Neill began his career at the Cincinnati Theatre and was reported in their pages in 1866 to the time he ceased acting and died in the summer of 1920. As a result, I could have him speak for himself throughout this book and I knew where he was and what he was doing, and so could also place Eugene at times such as the months when he acted in his father's company. Thus when biographers came up with a recent dating of O'Neill's attempt at self-murder, as taking place in the middle of March 1912, I had only to open my notes to see at once that during that time Eugene O'Neill was in Denver, Colorado, snowed in with his family, and not committing suicide at Jimmy the Priest's in New York as asserted. Those same notes yielded tips for other research in local newspapers all over the country. For instance, I learned from the obituary of Eugene's grandfather Thomas J. Quinlan that he could not possibly have died of tuberculosis, as Mary Tyrone's father did in *Long Day's Journey into Night*. Also, from another obituary, I discovered that Jimmy Byth's death was officially considered accidental, although Eugene always believed that he had killed himself.

Among the richest sources of information on the boyhood of Eugene's father were the city directories of Buffalo and Cincinnati, in which I traced James O'Neill and his family through the first years after they arrived from Ireland. From them I derived the extraordinary story of the machinist O'Neills, John and William, who came to the rescue of James's family when his father, old and sickly, abandoned them to return to Ireland. Other stories too, such as that of James's first mentor "Pop" Seaman, came from the directories and also from Chicago newspaper articles at the time of the scandal after James's marriage.

I was also fortunate to begin my researches while a number of people who had known both James and Eugene intimately were still alive. I transcribed their valuable recollections in detail. Particularly enlightening on James O'Neill were those of Thomas Dorsey Jr., the son of James's closest New London friend, and of Judge Troland, who knew all James's associates in New London. Equally valuable sources on the life of Eugene and James were the recollections of Eugene's New London friends from boyhood, Arthur McGinley and Ed Keefe. I also received excellent information from Eugene's cousin Philip Sheridan and his wife; from Carlotta Monterey O'Neill, Eugene's third wife; and from Carlotta's daughter Cynthia and her husband. I learned from Max Wylie much about the relationship between O'Neill and his second wife, Agnes, who had shared information while she was writing a memoir of her marriage with O'Neill and Wylie was writing *Trouble in the Flesh*, his novel based on O'Neill. There were also quite a number of others I interviewed cited in notes here and in my earlier books on O'Neill.

Finally, I relied upon the great depositories of unpublished letters both to and from O'Neill at Yale, Harvard, Princeton, and the University of Virginia, as well as other collections. I also found information in the correspondence of people associated with Eugene, such as Saxe Commins's letters to his Aunt Emma Goldman. All of these sources allowed me to correct the biographical record of Eugene and his family and to compare that record to their portrayals in the so-called autobiographical plays, *The Iceman Cometh*, *Long Day's Journey into Night*, and *A Moon for the Misbegotten*.

By this date many of the librarians who assisted me, and most of the people who gave me information on O'Neill and his family, are no longer living. I thanked them in earlier books on O'Neill and I remain grateful to them always. For this work, I wish in particular to thank Yale University, which holds the rights, for permission to quote from unpublished notes and letters of Eugene O'Neill. I also wish to thank Patricia C. Willis, Elizabeth Wakeman Dwight Curator of the American Literature Collection, Beinecke Rare Book and Manuscript Library, Yale University, from which a great many of those quotes come.

I also wish to thank all of the other libraries housing the collections I have quoted, in particular, gratitude to the Department of Rare Books, Cornell University; to the Houghton Library, Harvard University; to the Henry W. and

Albert A. Berg Collection of the New York Public Library; the Astor, Lenox, and Tilden Foundations; and to the manuscript collection at the Princeton University Library. For quotes in letters and diaries about the O'Neills, I also thank the Fales Library of New York University and the International Institute of Social History in Amsterdam, the Netherlands.

I owe a great debt to my good friends Professor Edward Margolies (Emeritus from the City College of New York), with his wife, Claire, and Professor Robert E. Proctor (of Connecticut College) for checking certain sources unavailable to me from my home in Venice to resolve late queries during the writing of this work. To them and all my friends I give thanks for unfailing encouragement and advice.

Because this book compares the facts of the plays with the documentary evidence of the historical record, it offers what is really a first study in biography based on knowledge of what in a work are the facts of its author's life and what are not. From the publication day of *Long Day's Journey into Night*, books on Eugene O'Neill (up to Stephen Black's *Beyond Mourning and Tragedy*, which perhaps leans on it most heavily) have taken the play as a reliable source for the facts of O'Neill's life and a guide for interpreting the meaning of his life. So perhaps this study will alert O'Neill biographers — and all biographers — of the dangers in confusing the artistry of a work with its raw materials and of taking a great revelation of an aspect of human life as literally the life story of its author.

Eugene O'Neill's Last Plays

Introduction

THE LAST PLAYS OF EUGENE O'NEILL

O n June 6, 1939, Eugene O'Neill woke up with a strong feeling that time was running out for him. He had been devoting himself for the last four and a half years to a great cycle of interconnected plays about several generations of an American family. What had started as four plays swelled to nine, and almost all of those for which he had done first drafts had come out double size. He felt, he said, "fed up and stale," and hungry to turn to plays he knew he could finish. Two plays that he had long wanted to write came to him at once. He set about writing them.

It was no coincidence that both plays were set in 1912. That had been a crucial year, for it had both started and ended as if it were going to be the year of Eugene's premature death, but instead became the magical year that transformed him from a chronic n'er-do-well into an entirely committed playwright. He had most probably timed his attempted suicide to take him out of life on New Year's Day 1912. Its failure to kill him brought him back to his family and into his first real attempt to adopt a congenial career as a journalist. But in December 1912 the threat of death returned with the frightening diagnosis of tuberculosis, at that time frequently fatal, and that, in turn, brought him at last to his true profession with the realization that his lifelong knowledge of the theater and drama equipped him, as few would ever be equipped, to become a playwright. So by choosing 1912 for the settings of his plays, he returned to his most crucial year, the year of his rebirth into his life work.

The first of these plays written took up the people who had influenced his development most decisively and who had created the theater in which his earliest plays found production. These people figured most prominently in his life in 1915 and 1916, but they were so essential to his viability and growing reputation as a playwright that they were to him an intrinsic part of his transformation in 1912. The second (*Long Day's Journey into Night*, 1941) dealt with his nearest and dearest youthful influences, those people who had given him his remarkable grasp of theaters — acting, directing, lighting — and of plays: his father, mother, and brother.

As soon as he had finished both these plays, Eugene O'Neill set to work on a third that seems almost an extension of *Long Day's Journey into Night*. With his brother Jamie again at the center of the play, it focuses on the days shortly before Jamie's death in 1923. Like the first two plays, then, *A Moon for the Misbegotten* appears to be intimately associated with his life. His personal distress over Pearl Harbor and America's entry into World War II knocked O'Neill off his creative stride, so he turned from it to see what he could salvage from his unfinished cycle of eleven plays. The first of these was the idea for a miniature cycle of eight one-act plays, only one of which, *Hughie*, he was able to finish. Inevitably it carried on some of the ideas of *The Iceman Cometh* and *Long Day's Journey into Night*, such as the need for a pipe dream to render the reality of the past palatable and to illuminate the future with hope. The projected title, "By Way of Obit," for the miniature cycle also resolved the questions of looming death and loss in the way the pipe dream of a romantic gambler is reborn to save the new night clerk Hughie from fear of death, as it saved his predecessor. O'Neill also took time to salvage the only full-length cycle play, *A Touch of the Poet*, that had come close to normal play time so that he could cut it easily and shape it so it could stand alone if the rest of the cycle were never written. Only after he had done both was O'Neill able to revise and finish the third intimate play about the people formative in his own youthful dream as an artist: *A Moon for the Misbegotten*.

That play took up his brother's character from *Long Day's Journey into Night* and also the comic story told in that play of his father's tenant Dolan. In the ultimate rewriting, Eugene O'Neill created an epitaph for himself as well as for the brother he loved, and also achieved an acceptance of his own loss of power and of the death that would liberate him from all suffering only ten years after the death of his creative life.

These three intimate last plays — *The Iceman Cometh, Long Day's Journey into Night*, and *A Moon for the Misbegotten* — are the subject of this book. The first two in particular have intrigued a very wide public who have read them or seen one of their many performances in a multitude of languages all over the globe since O'Neill's death in 1953. Written as they were in the final four years of his creative life, and redolent as they are of the people significant in his development as an artist, they tell the moving story of a mature artist looking back on and evaluating his creative life. He was only fifty when he began to write these final plays. His mind teemed more richly than ever in original ideas, but his bodily powers — even his capacity to guide a pencil over paper — were giving out under the devastation of a frightful neurological disease. Inevitably O'Neill's biographers and critics have grasped these plays as sources for his early years.

As a matter of fact, from the time his family play *Long Day's Journey into Night* was published many years before O'Neill had wanted it to be and with an inscription never intended for it by its author, O'Neill's critics and admirers have been convinced that it represents a deliberate and accurate revelation of his intimate family, his childhood, and his youth, as well as of his early friends, so that it can be used as a source for O'Neill biography.

As a result, a good deal of misinformation has found its way into the story of Eugene O'Neill's life. If there was anything O'Neill himself was clear on, it is that a literal following of the historical facts in a case will never add up to a tragic revelation of the meaning of human life or a moving reliving of another person's emotional experience. No one can achieve emotional truth, much less philosophical truth, by reporting everything irrelevant or contradictory that falls within a particular set of facts. An artist of necessity selects his materials.

One of the absolute necessities of understanding and evaluating these three last plays of Eugene O'Neill, as well as for appreciating the artistic shaping that makes them indelible emotional experiences to those who know them, is that of being clear on the overwhelming difference between the historical records of what took place in the lives of O'Neill, his family, and his friends, and the view of it offered up in his literary work. Both for accurate biography and a real appreciation of artistry, it is far better not to muddle the two.

As for the differences between the two, they came about for many reasons. The most elementary, of course, was that in some cases Eugene O'Neill simply did not know what had actually taken place, particularly to his mother and her family before he was born. Another was that over the years events related to him as disparate facts had merged as a single episode in his memory, making for errors. Yet another source of differences was the confined time scale of a play, and most particularly of *Long Day's Journey into Night*, in which the events of the play take place on a single day from morning to midnight in the summer of 1912. Nevertheless, Eugene O'Neill used in it materials from a good number of years. Events taken from one set of historical circumstances assume a totally different significance placed in another. As a result, many of the fictional father's actions are contradictory and misleading because historically they took place during Prohibition times, but in the play they take place a good seven years before Prohibition was even a coming threat, much less an actuality.

More important differences occur because a dramatist is present in all of his characters; so, Eugene O'Neill had to be as present in the personalities of the mother and father in the family play as in the character representing his youthful self. In a number of instances the mature Eugene O'Neill, himself a father as he wrote, entered into and took over the play father, and his dearest companion and love as he wrote, his wife Carlotta, entered into the play mother. In fact, all along the way, events in the play took on for O'Neill a special meaning that they would not have for any other person assessing the facts.

Finally, there are all of the many reasons why O'Neill found that what actually took place did not contribute to the emotional build of a scene or to its meaning. He never hesitated for an instant in those cases to adopt an event from another person's life and attribute it to the character, or to invent a situation better suited to the needs of his story. So in separating fiction from fact and by going to the actual sources of events, this book offers a documented history of much hitherto unknown biography of O'Neill's father, the very popular actor James O'Neill, his mother Ella, his brother Jamie, and O'Neill himself, as well as the true stories of a number of the people important in his life. All of this fresh biographical information allows for greater insight into the artistry that shaped these final plays and brought them to life.

The need for new biography in O'Neill's case arises from the fact that so many of the major facts about him remain in error — such as the chronology of which year he first found Jimmy the Priest's saloon, which month he attempted suicide, and which event set it off, or of when he and his family moved into the house celebrated in *Long Day's Journey into Night*. Also in confusion are such questions as how and with whom O'Neill reached Cape Cod in the summer of 1916, and major uncertainties such as at which periods his mother was or was not suffering from an addiction to morphine — and even if there are no easy or exact answers to all such questions, they are susceptible to more accurate answers than the indeterminate fatality pictured in the play. So this book functions as a fresh biography of O'Neill, his family, and his friends with much new, well-documented evidence in the text and thoroughgoing notes keyed to page and phrases.

The Iceman Cometh

CHAPTER ONE

Riddle in *The Iceman Cometh*

□ ▣ ◰

Aunique blend of memories (plucked out of diverse places and widely separated years) flavors a great work of literature. Sometimes an author takes a memory from one time and blends it with memories from an altogether different period, so that one wonders by what link it was drawn in. A riddle like that arises among the memories that nourished Eugene O'Neill's *The Iceman Cometh*. Why was it that Al Adams — known to New York reporters as the "Policy King" — joined his tragic fate to those of people O'Neill came to know in later years for its cast of characters? Furthermore, how on earth was it that Eugene — a schoolboy at the time — came to know that seasoned old rogue Al Adams during his days of crisis?

O'Neill himself declared that he had once known all the originals for the characters in *The Iceman Cometh*, and they came out of three former hangouts of his. His very first note for the play calls it "the Jimmy the Priest — Hell Hole — Garden idea," naming those three haunts of his youth. But biographers disagree on when the haunting took place. They assume that Eugene must have discovered Jimmy the Priest's saloon on Fulton Street in New York City after he worked his way back from Buenos Aires as a common seaman on the S.S. *Ikala* in April 1911. Their timing comes from O'Neill's first talk of Jimmy the Priest's as a hangout of his seafaring days (placing it squarely in 1911). O'Neill was speaking of it in interviews arranged to publicize his play *Chris Christopherson* in the spring of 1920 when George Tyler gave it a brief and unsuccessful out-of-town try-out, and again late in 1921 when Arthur Hopkins produced a completely rewritten second version called *Anna Christie* with great success. In both these versions O'Neill was doing a character study of an old Swedish deep-water sailor actually named Chris Christopherson. (O'Neill had learned the correct spelling for his name — rather than an odd Danish form he had improvised — from the American Scandinavian Foundation in a reply to his letter of inquiry by Hanna Astruf Larsen of May 5, 1919, now at Yale, well in time for these productions.) O'Neill had roomed with Chris in Jimmy the Priest's during 1911, and act 1 of both were set in Jimmy's saloon, called fictionally "Johnny the Priest's." So everything O'Neill said of the place implied 1911, when he had roomed there with Chris.

Nevertheless, there is every reason to believe that O'Neill discovered Jimmy the Priest's saloon as early as the fall of 1907, after his debacle at Princeton. Eugene's father, James O'Neill, had then seen to it that Henry L. Brittain, in whose New York–Chicago Supply Company he was a major investor, gave Eugene a job at his New York office in Room 33 of a building at 194 Broadway between Dey and Fulton Streets. Early in his work there, during lunch breaks Eugene O'Neill probably came upon Jimmy the Priest's at 252 Fulton Street right around the corner from the office and directly opposite the Washington Market and very popular because a nickel schooner of beer there included free lunch. In the year or so that Eugene worked for Brittain, he seems to have become an habitué. If he chose to room at Jimmy's when he returned to New York from Buenos Aires in 1911, he did so because it offered cheap lodgings in which he felt very much at home.

Sometime during 1908 he came to know the bar of the Garden Restaurant in the Garden Hotel on the northeast corner of Madison Avenue and Twenty-seventh Street. By the end of 1911, Eugene O'Neill knew it as well as he knew Jimmy the Priest's. When he participated in the witnessed adultery for his divorce from Kathleen Jenkins on December 29, he made the Garden Restaurant one of the places he casually stopped for drinks before arriving, seemingly without design, at the house of prostitution on Forty-fifth Street.

Eugene and his brother Jamie's heavy drinking there probably took place at that time. At any rate, by the end of 1921 he was looking back at them as their "old drunken Garden days." Eugene and Jamie went on patronizing the Garden hotel and its restaurant for years after that, both of them often staying there during trips to New York into 1918. As late as the end of 1919 when Prohibition had started, Eugene was looking into the Garden Restaurant hopefully, only to find it "dry as dry."

The "Hell Hole" came later than Jimmy's and the Garden. Its actual name was the Golden Swan, and it stood on the corner of Fourth Street and Sixth Avenue in Greenwich Village. O'Neill began spending evenings there soon after his return to New York from his year at Harvard, where he had taken Professor George Pierce Baker's playwriting class. Some of the poems O'Neill was writing that fall are dated "Hell Hole 1915." O'Neill's letters to his wife Agnes during his visits to New York speak of nights at the Hell Hole as late as December 1921 when the saloon was staggering to extinction after Prohibition.

Al Adams came into Eugene O'Neill's life well before these three haunts and their denizens — in fact, during his last year at Betts Academy in Stamford, Connecticut, when he was seventeen. During the Christmas holidays of that year, 1905, Eugene's father, James O'Neill, was playing matinees and evenings to packed houses in his perennial favorite *Monte Cristo* at New York's West End Theater. According to the address Eugene gave his girlfriend Marion Welch as he left Stamford for New York, he would be joining his parents at the Lexington Hotel on Forty-seventh Street between Sixth Avenue and Broadway. After the New Year, James O'Neill would be performing nearby in New Jersey, culminating in another week in New York City at the Harlem Theater, so the O'Neills may have moved at that time to the more conveniently located Hotel Ansonia on Broadway and Seventy-third Street. At any rate, they certainly were established at the Ansonia by the beginning of May 1906, when they were back in New York at the end of the theatrical season.

O'Neill and his wife were preparing for a trip to England and Ireland, setting sail on the *Caronia* May 22, 1906. Since they would therefore not be opening their New London, Connecticut, summer home on Pequot Avenue, James arranged with his good friend John McGinley for Eugene to stay with McGinley's large family in their house on Ocean Avenue. The youngest son Arthur was Eugene's age and like him had just graduated from secondary school. The two boys could go swimming and boating together and watch all the baseball games.

Art McGinley was hoping to become a sports reporter, if possible, on one of the large New York newspapers. In the first days of August when Eugene's parents returned to the Hotel Ansonia, both boys joined them in their suite there so that Art could go job hunting during the weeks James O'Neill would remain in New York rehearsing his company in *The Voice of the Mighty* until his tour opened in Chicago on August 27.

It was during this visit in 1906 that Art McGinley developed a lifelong admiration for James O'Neill, whom he always spoke of thereafter as a "magnificent man." By that August James knew everyone at the Hotel Ansonia from the manager, W. E. D. Stokes, down to the porters — so Art recalled — and was always ready for a friendly chat with all of them. Gregarious as he was, James must have very quickly become friendly at the Ansonia bar with the hotel's most noteworthy resident, Al Adams, who lived in a luxurious suite on the fifteenth floor and was lonely in those days and drinking heavily. This was by no means the first time in James's life that he had been kindly to a man "under a cloud." He was criticized a number of times throughout his life for associating with tarnished characters.

Ever since his release from Sing Sing prison in October 1904, Al Adams had been living in the Ansonia rather than in his mansion at 23 West Eighty-fifth Street because he wanted to spare his wife and children the disgrace of his indictment and incarceration. While his six children — four boys and two girls — had been growing up, Adams kept them in the best schools money could buy and completely ignorant of the source of his wealth. So his conviction came as a hideous shock.

As a young man, Adams had been a "runner" for Zachariah Simmons, who invented the policy racket, a lottery that had virtually all the cigar stores in the city taking bets of as little as a penny or a nickel on numbers that could win a hundred times as much. As Simmons conducted it, the drawing of the winning numbers had been an honest gamble, but when Adams took over the lottery early in the 1880s, he saw at once that he could make even more money if he studied the reports of bets and chose the winning numbers from those that had the least money on them, so that payments would be minimal. With New York's chief of police liberally in on Al's profits, and openly a great friend of his, Al Adams could go on fleecing the poor for decades.

Trouble did not come to him until 1901 when reformers succeeded in abolishing the office of chief of police, wiping out in that one blow Adams's police protection. Even so, he persisted in business until he fell into serious trouble in 1903. As Lawrence, one of Adams's two lawyer sons, put it: "The governor wasn't half as bad as he was painted. The trouble was he was stubborn and self-willed, and nobody could tell him anything. He ought to have been out of that policy game long before he was." As Lawrence saw it, his father served as "scapegoat" for a lot of others, and besides, he never really had had to go to prison. The district attorney's office had offered him a settlement with only a thousand-dollar fine if he would plead guilty. "We all wanted him to accept the settlement," Lawrence said, but Adams, who did not see himself as guilty, wanted to fight, "and so" — Lawrence summed up — "they got him." Sentenced on April 21, 1903, Adams was released in October 1904, months before his sentence terminated, because Dr. Irvine, the prison doctor, diagnosed him as having diabetes, tuberculosis of the right lung, and hardening of the arteries — and therefore likely to die at once in prison.

When W. E. D. Stokes, manager of the Ansonia, had visited Adams in Sing Sing, Adams confided that "the disgrace and grief" brought upon his family by his conviction "were killing him." He was distraught because his children were suffering under "the shame he had tried to hide from them." Because of his disgrace — so Adams revealed — "his daughters did not make friends at the seminaries they attended" and "his sons were not allowed to enter college societies."

All that had sustained Al Adams at the time of his conviction, he said, was his former "happy life with my family." He and his children, he said, had "dwelt together in mutual love and respect." Even in his disgrace his older sons had stood by him. As he was being dragged off to prison, Adams bragged to reporters that if he "were paupered tomorrow," his two lawyer sons "college-bred" — so he announced — would "carve their way to prominence." His eldest son, Albert J. Adams, acted as his private attorney throughout his troubles, and during Al's days at the Ansonia would breakfast with his father every few days in his rooms to confer on their business projects.

When released from prison, Al Adams had told reporters that his past was a "sealed book" and that he intended to devote himself to the stock market and real estate. In fact he had thought up a brand-new scheme for making further millions through the passion of the poor for gambling. With his son Albert's aid, he set up a series of fly-by-night investment offices for gambling on the stock market — what were known in the slang of the day as bucket shops — under such titles as Boardman and Company and M. J. Sage and Company. During the summer that James O'Neill and his son Eugene came to know Al Adams, his bucket shops had already been raided by police and he was once again being threatened with a prison sentence. To everyone he talked with in those days, Al Adams complained of being "hounded" unfairly by police and reporters.

As to his younger sons, Al sent Walter off to Mexico to look after his mining properties there, and he put Louis in charge of the real estate office he set up at 42 West Thirty-fourth Street. Probably tipped off before his troubles by his friends in high places, Al Adams had bought a lot of property west of Seventh Avenue between Thirtieth and Thirty-fourth Streets, and it was now booming with the announcement of plans to build the Pennsylvania Railroad Terminal in that area.

Louis seems to have been the son most severely disturbed by the discovery of his father's crookedness, and certainly the one most torn by ambivalence thereafter. On an evening when both he and his father had had a great deal to drink, they quarreled so fiercely in the office over policy that Louis became frantic and threatened his incorrigibly crooked parent with the office revolver. Soon the New York newspapers were treated to the scandalous disclosure that the jailbird Adams had placed his own son under arrest.

As Eugene O'Neill understood it, the son was convicted and sentenced to six months for assaulting his father. At the time, the newspapers made it clear that Louis had been held only a few days on Blackwell's Island until his father withdrew charges. This episode, typical of the whole lurid story of Al Adams and his sons, probably was the chief memory that impelled Eugene so many years later to put a character into *The Iceman Cometh* based on "Al Adams's son" among the people from later years. Apparently, Eugene never came to know personally either Louis or the other sons. Except for Albert with his early morning breakfast conferences in his father's suite, Adams's family — at his own wishes — never came near the Ansonia. Since O'Neill gave no first name to any particular son of Adams for his character, he was probably thinking of all four sons, rather than the personality of any one. He compounded the character from what he knew about the sons from Adams himself, whom he met with his father at the bar of the Ansonia, from the talk of the manager (Stokes), and others in the hotel, and also from the steady gossip about them in the newspapers while fate was closing in on the crooked millionaire.

What pulled the character of Willie Oban, son of Bill Oban, the Bucket Shop King, into *The Iceman Cometh* came from the meaning Adams and his sons took on as a tragic forecast of Eugene O'Neill's years of rebellion and ambivalence that were about to begin that August of 1906. Somewhere in the years following that summer, memory had inextricably mingled for Eugene his position as the son of a well-known father for whom he felt warring emotions and the ambiguous notoriety of Adams's sons after their father's disgrace. Eugene could identify with the lawyer sons of whom Adams was so proud, who had been educated, as he well knew, "at Harvard and at Heidelberg." In 1906 Eugene himself was just about to enter the equally expensive Ivy League university, Princeton, that his father had chosen for him, to study, as his father had advised, law.

Certainly once he got there, he found — as he had been finding all his life — that everyone knew his father as the Count of Monte Cristo because he had been starring in that role all over the United States (with other plays in repertory) for as many years as Al Adams had been policy king in New York City. By 1906 Eugene had begun to suspect that his father had sold out his talents and potential greatness as an actor for the lure of easy money and easy fame that came to him from that wildly popular melodrama he had been starring in for so many years. So Eugene took a queasy view of his father's fame and of his own inevitable notoriety as "the son of Monte Cristo" — by which title reporters would still be calling him long after he had come into his own fame as a playwright, and after the Count of Monte Cristo had been lying in his New London grave for years.

As for the ambivalence that had sparked the almost fatal follies of his youth, Eugene O'Neill had had it all explicitly diagrammed in his mind by 1926 when he sketched it out for Dr. Gilbert Van Tassel Hamilton, at the beginning of his counseling on his alcoholism. He explained to Hamilton how his exile to boarding school had curdled his childhood love for his father into "hatred and defiance of father," and "resentment." By the time he began writing *The Iceman Cometh* in 1939, he had the whole picture, including his return during his father's last year of life to the love, comradeship, and identification with him he had felt as a child. When Art McGinley reminded him of some of the cruel things he had said of his father in his rebellious years, O'Neill told him, "In the days you speak of I was full of a secret bitterness about him — not stopping to consider all he took from me and kept on smiling."

So it was out of self-knowledge that he could depict Willie Oban waking from an alcoholic nightmare at the start of *The Iceman Cometh* full of love and grief for his "Papa" and a refusal to believe in his guilt — only to be torn by rage against that "crooked old bucket-shop bastard," who had been, he knew, "guilty as hell." O'Neill made Willie's father "King of the Bucket Shops" because it was Adams's guilt in running them, rather than his earlier guilt as policy king, that hung over him during that summer of 1906 at the Ansonia.

To create the rather strange history of Willie Oban's career at Harvard, O'Neill blended his contradictory recollections of his debacle at Princeton with his brilliantly successful term, eight years later, at Harvard in Professor Baker's playwriting class. Because of his father's disgrace, Willie has been treated, as were Al Adams's sons, as an outcast, and that trauma in his freshman year has brought about his wasted life of chronic alcoholism. But cause and effect are strangely separated. Willie goes on to become a brilliant law student, graduating at the top of his class. Only then does he collapse completely into vagrancy and perpetual drunkenness.

This odd hiatus points to an intrusion of O'Neill's own strange Ivy League story into the history of Al Adams's sons. O'Neill was exiled from his prestigious university, not by any reflected disgrace because of his position as the Count of Monte Cristo's son, but rather by his own folly. In April 1907, near the end of his freshman year at Princeton, when his father's advance man was announcing to newspapers that James O'Neill's "younger son is at college, studying law," Eugene was getting himself suspended indefinitely from Princeton and from any career in law. Returning from an alcoholic binge with classmates in Trenton, New Jersey, too late to catch the last trolley at Princeton Junction, he and his friends had amused themselves on the ten-mile hike to college by shying stones at and breaking the glass insulators of the trolley line. Dean Fine of the disciplinary office punished them all by suspending them until further notice. Eugene made it a permanent exclusion by declaring his withdrawal then and there from the class of 1910.

Nevertheless, after this debacle, Eugene O'Neill did go on—although only after eight years of dangerous adventures—to become, as he had Oban become, a brilliant student at Harvard (in his case, in Professor Baker's playwriting class). He even was granted a degree a decade later when Yale University, having lured Professor Baker from Harvard, honored him through his most prestigious former student by awarding Eugene an honorary doctorate of letters. This astonishing finale to his disgrace at Princeton apparently went into Oban's story to give him his strange success between the trauma that destroyed him and his resulting collapse into alcoholism.

The rest of Willie Oban's story is really an adaptation of all O'Neill knew of Al Adams. He had Willie explain, as Lawrence Adams explained of his father, that he was really a "scapegoat" for others equally guilty, who got off free. Lawrence's summation, "they got him," is echoed in Oban's dictum on his father's imprisonment, "Remember, they get you in the end." Willie's pipe dream that the district attorney will give him a job in his office, in gratitude for the graft his father dispensed, comes from what O'Neill knew of the offer by the real district attorney of a "settlement" with a fine of a thousand dollars if Adams would plead guilty. Given the public outcry, that was clearly the lightest penalty he could exact.

Also O'Neill was working, apparently, with what he knew of Al Adams's friend, the grafting police chief—whose office had to be abolished before Adams could be prosecuted—when he created Willie's second futile dream. Willie and his fellow alcoholic, former Police Lieutenant Pat McGloin, share the pipe dream that Willie will, as his attorney, institute a case to get him reinstated on the force, from which he was ejected long ago for graft.

Although O'Neill used all these elements of Adams's real story, he did not use his sensational finale, which came a month after O'Neill had left his room at the Ansonia for 30 University Hall, Princeton. In *The Iceman Cometh* Willie tells us that his father died in jail, as the Sing Sing doctor had thought Adams would die, and as he certainly would have died had he been sentenced all over again for the chicaneries of his bucket shops. O'Neill chose this subdued death, rather than the shocking reality, because he wanted to highlight the son's tragedy, rather than that of the father. Although Adams's ultimate tragedy had no part in the play, it seems to have been a decisive force in bringing the rest of Adams's story into the play. In a curious way, Adams's finale foreshadowed the crucial episode of O'Neill's rebellious years, which very nearly was as fatal as that of the former policy king.

Early in the morning of October 1, 1906, at the luxurious suite in the Hotel Ansonia, Al Adams, still in his pajamas, placed one of his large revolvers against his right temple and pulled the trigger. Thus in an instant he put an end to the worry, the insomnia, the indelible stigma of his past, by blowing his brains out. The suicide made headlines in all the local newspapers on October 2, and there were long accounts of his entire career in the policy racket and the bucket shops. In the days afterward came reports of the inquest, funeral, and Adams's testament, which left one-third of more than eight million dollars in loot to his wife and the other two-thirds to be divided equally among his four sons and two daughters. Editorials such as the one in the *New York Times* summed him up as a "contemptible swindler" whose fortune came out of "the organized theft of pennies and nickels and dimes from the very poor." Certainly, Eugene read many of these accounts. With his ambivalence toward his own father that helped him identify with Adams's sons, and with his later intuition into the way Adams's suicide foreshadowed the most desperate of his own follies to come, O'Neill had every reason to associate Adams's story with the people from his years of rebellion whose lives gave him the theme and atmosphere of *The Iceman Cometh*.

Suicide — his own suicide, luckily abortive — seems to have been the chief memory that triggered the writing of this monumental work at this time. Both consciously and unconsciously this play is saturated in memories of O'Neill's own attempted suicide at Jimmy the Priest's, in ideas of what allows life to be livable and what makes death an acceptable, even desirable, alternative. At the heart of this play was O'Neill's own need to come to terms with death, not only as it touched him in 1911 when he was twenty-three, but as it presented itself to him in 1939 when he was fifty. The climax of this play is a suicide, and O'Neill was perfectly conscious that the "Iceman" in his title *The Iceman Cometh* is only on its surface a reference to the old joke about the iceman in bed with the wife when her husband is away. "In a deep sense the iceman is death" — O'Neill explained — death that "cometh like a thief in the night."

CHAPTER TWO

The Proxy Suicide

Eugene O'Neill had no intention of revealing in *The Iceman Cometh* the absolutely lowest point he reached in his years of rebellion. He had always tried to keep hidden his ridiculous involvement with Kathleen Jenkins, which had sent him, just as he reached his twenty-first birthday, into flight first to Honduras and then to Argentina with the sympathetic help of the father he had been obliquely fighting — most self-destructively — during all those desperate years. He was even more anxious to put behind him the ultimate episode of all that folly — his attempted suicide two years later, after providing the evidence of adultery for his divorce from what had been his own style of self-impelled shotgun marriage.

One of the additional mistakes of his later years as an apprentice playwright consisted of letting that skeleton out of the closet by way of one of the crudely autobiographical one-act plays he was writing in those years merely to stay on the bill of the Provincetown Players, his first producers — an indiscretion that he grasped and tried to push back into the closet within a year of letting it out. In this two-scene comedy, *Exorcism: A Play of Anti Climax*, O'Neill had used fairly truthfully — just suppressing its origins in a ruinous sexual involvement — the attempt he had made to kill himself at Jimmy the Priest's because he had failed, he thought, in both love and in work. Right after the production of *Exorcism* — March 26 through April 8, 1920 — came O'Neill's realization that as autobiographical revelation it made for the very last kind of publicity needed by an up-and-coming young playwright. Barely six months after *Exorcism* came the first of his successes, financial, not merely artistic, of a full-length play with uptown productions of *The Emperor Jones* and *Anna Christie*, the rewritten *Chris Christopherson*. From then on, O'Neill was careful to exorcize *Exorcism*, destroying all copies of it, even the copyright scripts in the Library of Congress.

So successful was this suppression of the literal expression of O'Neill's suicide attempt that little is known about this crucial episode of his life. The only sources for it are the reviews of *Exorcism* and two farcical fairy tales, both told afterward by those two reckless fictionalizers George Jean Nathan and Agnes Boulton (O'Neill's by-then long-divorced second wife). Nathan's account is far from reality: he assumed O'Neill's days at Jimmy the Priest's took place more than a decade after they actually did, and that they took place during Prohibition times starting in 1919. As a result, Nathan derived much of his humor from accounts of the wildly improbable substitutes for alcohol the denizens of Jimmy's imbibed, such as diluted varnish or wood alcohol flavored with sarsaparilla and benzine. As for Agnes, she invented a mythical resort to Bellevue Hospital in which the interns mistook the drunken companions of O'Neill for the patients, and he, the resuscitated suicide, as their chaperon.

That experience remained in Eugene's memory as profoundly tragic, as demonstrated clearly by all he had to say later about Jimmy the Priest's. But the actual details of when and why he tried to kill himself remain murky. His surviving note for the suicide play *Exorcism* places the action on a "miserable foggy" evening "in the middle of March." Recently biographers have given the date of O'Neill's attempted suicide as mid-March of 1912 because the action of his early short story "Tomorrow" takes place then. But indisputable facts about O'Neill at that time contradict this. In all the literary works in which O'Neill dealt directly or in disguised form with that near tragedy, and in all that he confided to his wife Agnes or his friend George Jean Nathan about it, one detail remained unalterably the same. The suicide was attempted in his room at Jimmy the Priest's during the months he lived there.

After his lucky revival from the overdose of Veronal he had taken, we know that he stayed in New York through January 20, 1912, because on that day—according to testimony for *Kathleen O'Neill v. Eugene O'Neill*—Eugene went to the American Surety Building at 100 Broadway, where Kathleen's attorneys Van Schaick and Brice had their office, and there James C. Warren served him, as previously arranged, with the summons for the divorce. Eugene must have left New York City and ended his residency at Jimmy the Priest's forever in the next few days or he would have been unable to reach his family in New Orleans when his father opened at the Orpheum Theater there the third week of January in a reduced forty-minute vaudeville version of *Monte Cristo*.

All that Eugene O'Neill told reporters later of his brief acting career with his father's vaudeville company was clearly meant to hide from publicity the negotiations for the divorce, the attempted suicide, and the fact that—just like the revived suicide of his play *Exorcism* — he was making a prodigal son return, after years of self-imposed exile, to family love and protection when he joined his father, mother, and brother in New Orleans. To the reporter Hamilton Basso, he declared that he had simply woken up one morning on a train with a ticket for New Orleans he did not remember buying and "by chance" his father was also in New Orleans when he arrived. To Kyle Crichton, who interviewed him, he related more elaborately a legend of how he had turned "five bucks" into a "thousand" by gambling at faro and decided to blow it at New Orleans drinking champagne and eating oysters. After two months and enough oysters to wipe out his funds, he learned unexpectedly that his father had "arrived in town," and so went to him for more money.

In contrast, there is no doubt that Eugene O'Neill, as a touring actor's son, always had a copy of his father's dates ahead from the time he first went to convent school at the age of seven. He could always refresh it in later years at Liebler and Company when he made his regular trip there to pick up his allowance. If he did not get there, he had only to buy one of the "in" theatrical weeklies, the *New York Dramatic Mirror* or the *New York Clipper,* to read in their Dates Ahead columns where his family were at the moment and where they would be on every day of the months to come. So it would have been no surprise to him that his father and family were at Memphis on January 20, 1912, and would arrive at New Orleans within a few days after that. Indeed, he was counting on finding them when he went there.

As for the suicide, there is every reason to believe that the traumatic night Eugene O'Neill spent providing the witnessed adultery that would allow Kathleen to divorce him was the culminating disaster of all those self-destructive years of his youth, and it filled him with unbearable self-loathing. Years afterward, contrasting the excellence of Eugene Jr., the offspring of that unfortunate marriage, when the boy reached approximately the age his father had been when he begat him, Eugene told his friend George Jean Nathan on August 31, 1929, "When I survey his merits and think of the rotten mess of a life I was at his age, I have no superiority assumptions, believe me!"

It was that condemnation of his "rotten mess of a life" that brought him to the despair of self-murder, and it must have come directly after the night of December 29, 1911, when with Edward Mullen, Frank Archibold, and James C. Warren, Eugene went to the brothel at 140 West Forty-fifth Street for the prearranged adultery. There he went upstairs with one of the women and later, when his friends sent up word that they were about to leave, he had a maid invite all three up to the room for a parting drink where they could observe and later testify that Eugene was in bed with a prostitute, both "undressed." According to Warren's testimony, Eugene "left there with me about six o'clock in the morning."

Exhausted by being up all night, Eugene probably slept all through December 30, 1911, and it was perhaps the following night of New Year's Eve that he took the Veronal, expecting to go out with the year. The exact date is unknown, but he must have done so before the meeting at the attorneys' offices on January 20 with Warren to receive the summons that he was to ignore so he would be in default by February 10, 1912, and the divorce could go through without him. (The case was tried and divorce granted at the Supreme Court, Westchester County, White Plains, New York, on June 10, 1912.)

So we know definitely that a day or two after January 20, 1912, Eugene O'Neill ended his residency at Jimmy the Priest's and, except for visits to the bar there from time to time in the following years, never again took it up. He therefore could not have ever tried to commit suicide in his room there at any time after that day.

By the last week in January 1912 Eugene O'Neill was back with his family taking small parts in his father's vaudeville *Monte Cristo* until his brief acting career ended a few weeks later. On February 14 James O'Neill was already announcing that although he was contracted for eighteen more weeks, he found this "mangled" version of *Monte Cristo* in the "two-a-day," seven days a week, so "soul-crushing" that he intended to close his tour "after the next week." A month later — on March 17, 1912 — the *Denver Times* reported that James had been "in town last week," held up by "snow blockades" of the railroads. So in the middle of March 1912 when a recent biography has Eugene O'Neill committing suicide at Jimmy the Priest's, he was with family members, either snowbound in Denver or having embarked with them on the long train trip back to New York.

Eugene celebrated his return to his family and New London by swimming across the Thames River from Scott's wharf, at one side of 325 Pequot Avenue, to the Watson estate at Eastern Point, about a mile away, on July 22, 1912, as reported in the *New London Day*. For the first time in his life, Eugene O'Neill tried for a job in line with his real proclivities. James O'Neill got him in as a reporter for the *New London Telegram* in mid-August through his good friend the editor, Frederick P. Latimer (by secretly repaying the newspaper for Eugene's salary in what worked out as a kind of apprenticeship, according to Charlie Thompson, the business manager). Besides reporting, Eugene could begin to publish in the *Telegram*'s Laconics column some of the verse he had been writing during his rebellious years. When a second brush with death came to him with a diagnosis of tuberculosis that December, he was already on the way to becoming reborn as a dedicated writer, as he said he became during the months he spent recovering at Gaylord Farm.

Far from the farce he made of it in talks with George Jean Nathan and his wife Agnes, the suicide attempt was a major redirecting force in Eugene's life. And in the years that followed, he came to associate Jimmy the Priest's more and more powerfully with the death that almost met him there. In the six years after his suicide attempt came the deaths of three friends — one of them very dear — who had roomed at Jimmy the Priest's when he did. Those tragic deaths colored his recollections of Jimmy's and blended inextricably with his own near death. All three deaths inspired his early writing, and one of them became almost a proxy for his own suicide attempt. The second of these deaths chronologically was that of J. Driscoll (who may have been called "Jimmy"). As Eugene explained on March 11, 1941, Driscoll had been "a friend of mine, a Liverpool Irish stoker, who lived, when ashore, at the same waterfront dump — Jimmy the Priest's — that I did, and who was on the *New York* [an American Line ship] when I sailed on her." As a deckhand, Eugene would never have met a "fireman" or "trimmer," as the stokers were called, on ship, but he did meet him at the bar at Jimmy the Priest's. Whenever Driscoll was ashore during Eugene's residency there, they would carouse together. In one of his later returns to the bar there, Eugene learned with shock that Driscoll had committed suicide by jumping overboard in midocean (on August 12, 1915, according to the Register of Deaths at Sea at the Public Records Office, Surrey, England).

Eugene O'Neill was amazed that Driscoll would kill himself, for he always "thought a whole lot of himself" and was proud of his ability, being "a giant of a man" and "absurdly strong," to do "more work than any of his mates." As O'Neill saw it, Driscoll "loved life" and was not at all one who would "just give up."

The puzzle of what had broken Driscoll inspired him to try a short story, "The Hairy Ape," in the fall of 1916. Five years later, during two weeks of December 1921, the question of Driscoll's death arose again in his mind, this time integrated with all his own former suicidal desperation and alienation from life, along with all he had just experienced of the warfare factory owners had unleashed on their striking workers in the American steel industry. Thus one of the greatest of his early plays, *The Hairy Ape*, came to life with the protagonist based on his friend J. Driscoll. A psychologist could have solved for O'Neill the puzzle of the stoker's total change of character. Driscoll was clearly manic-depressive: manic and megalomaniac during the months that O'Neill knew him; and depressive when he threw himself overboard. But a diagnosis does not make a great play. By bringing his protagonist, Yank, into a larger vision that included O'Neill's own search for a place and a meaning in life, he could arrive at a theme more hauntingly universal in human significance than any mere diagnosis of chemical imbalance.

The tragic aura of Driscoll's suicide was emphasized two years later by another death of a former roomer at Jimmy the Priest's, O'Neill's roommate for a few weeks, Chris Christopherson, who left to captain a barge. Chris's body had been found floating near the Statue of Liberty a week after he accidentally fell overboard on October 15, 1917. Whatever Eugene O'Neill was told of Chris's death in what had actually been a spell of warm autumn weather, later he always thought of it as taking place, like his own suicide attempt, in the middle of winter. When he told Charles Sweeney of Chris's death, he seems to have blended it with his own admission to a tuberculosis sanitarium on Christmas Eve of 1912. O'Neill told Sweeney that after a drunken Christmas Eve party at Jimmy the Priest's, Chris had staggered back to his barge at two o'clock in the morning, missed his footing trying to board, and fell into the water. The next morning he "was found frozen in a great cake of ice between the piles and the dock." Thus Chris, like Driscoll, joined his own midwinter brush with death as "one of many" tragedies engendered at Jimmy the Priest's.

Those two deaths in 1915 and 1917 were preceded by one in 1913 that associated Jimmy the Priest's with self-destruction in Eugene O'Neill's mind forever. He had always been very familiar with his father's press representatives, most particularly with A. Toxen Worm, who had worked with James O'Neill through all the years of Eugene's growing up. Worm was not only a graduate of the University of Copenhagen and the former dramatic critic of the *Pittsburgh Dispatch*, but he had also been, as he was fond of telling, a tutor to the grandsons of Christian IX, King of Denmark, who later became rulers themselves. When Worm took a promotion to a higher position as business manager at Liebler and Company, his place as James O'Neill's advance man was taken by James Findlater Byth in September 1907.

In the years following that fall of 1907—that is during 1908, 1909, 1910, and 1911—Jimmy Byth became a close friend and drinking companion of James O'Neill's son Eugene. During those years in New York, Eugene came to know many of Jimmy Byth's friends. In fact, when Eugene incorporated Byth into *The Iceman Cometh*, he also brought in two of Byth's friends from South Africa. In the play these two, a Boer and a Briton, are said to have met when both came to the United States "to work in the Boer War spectacle at the St. Louis Fair." (The actors at the fair landed in New York in March of 1904.) As a British citizen and a former press correspondent of the Boer War doing theatrical publicity in New York, Jimmy Byth met a great many of the actors at once, and he kept up his friendship with them in the years after the St. Louis Fair when they came to perform the spectacle in the New York area.

Drinking with Jimmy at the Garden Restaurant, Eugene O'Neill met many of them too. He became so fascinated with their talk of South Africa that later, in Buenos Aires at the start of 1911, he signed on as a seaman on a cattle steamer taking mules to Durban in the hope of landing and seeing South Africa at last. To his chagrin, he was prohibited from landing because he lacked the requisite hundred-pound entry fee. As late as July 1928, Eugene O'Neill was still thinking he might achieve that dream of his youth. As he told Terry Helburn of the Theater Guild, he had always had "a strong yen" to go to South Africa "because in the distant past I was pals with so many of its people, both British Africanders and Boers and really know a lot about it for one who has never been there."

He no doubt told Jimmy Byth—who was doing odd jobs for Liebler and Company—about his frustration when he landed back at New York in the spring of 1911 and looked up Tyler for money and news of his family. Thus when Chris Christopherson left Jimmy the Priest's, Eugene asked Byth to share his room there at the economical rental of three dollars a month. If *Exorcism* was historically correct on this—and both Eugene's wife Agnes and his friend Nathan believed that it was—it was his roommate Jimmy Byth and a Major Adams who succeeded in reviving Eugene from his suicide attempt.

A few days after Eugene O'Neill was released from Gaylord Farm on June 3, 1913, and had rejoined his family in New London, he was unutterably shocked to learn that Jimmy Byth was dead in New York. Almost, he felt that he himself had succeeded finally in killing himself. The *New York Times* was perfectly clear that Jimmy's death was accidental, not suicide. On June 8, 1913, the *Times* reported that "James Findlater Byth, 46 years old, for many years connected with newspaper and theatrical work, died yesterday at the New York Hospital of injuries sustained last week when he fell from the window of his house at 252 Fulton Street." Of course, 252 Fulton Street was Jimmy the Priest's, where Byth had remained after Eugene left to join his family in New Orleans. Although nothing could have been more natural than the fact that a man who drank himself comatose nightly might lose his balance at an open sash window, particularly if he were leaning out, and fall, Eugene O'Neill became instantly and unshakably convinced that, in that fatal room, Jimmy Byth had followed his own appalling example, only more disastrously than he had, and deliberately killed himself.

Why a man bent on killing himself should decide—in a city full of accessible ten- and fifteen-story windows—to throw himself from a little low-ceilinged edifice with only three stories and a half-attic over the bar on the ground floor, Eugene O'Neill apparently never asked himself. A jump like that would certainly hurt a man but could not be counted on to kill him. Nevertheless, Eugene remained completely convinced that Jimmy's death had been suicide.

As he told Charles Sweeney, Byth had reached the "depths" at Jimmy the Priest's. "But always my friend — at least always when he had had several jolts of liquor — saw a turn in the road tomorrow. He was going to get himself together and get back to work. Well, he did get a job and got fired. Then he realized that his tomorrow never would come. He solved everything by jumping to his death from the bedroom at Jimmy's."

From that time on, Byth's death, which Eugene continued to read as a suicide, became in O'Neill's mind virtually a proxy for the actual, but abortive, suicide he had attempted a year and a half earlier at Jimmy the Priest's. Nothing makes this as clear as does the short story called "Tomorrow," which he wrote in the fall of 1916 along with his stories "The Hairy Ape" and "The Web." Since, through John Reed's help, "Tomorrow" was published in the *Seven Arts* magazine in the June 1917 issue, it has survived, and it probably tells us even more than *Exorcism* would have.

Although it is the character based on Jimmy Byth, called "Jimmy Anderson," who kills himself in the story, the suicidal despair of it comes through his young roommate who is called "Art" after the nickname of O'Neill's boyhood friend Arthur McGinley. Art is a self-portrait of Eugene himself at the time he attempted suicide (on New Year's Eve 1911, or the first two weeks of January 1912). His age, the story tells us, is "twenty-three," the age of Eugene O'Neill at the time of his suicide attempt, and in a crossed-out passage of the manuscript we are even told that Art had just returned several months ago as a sailor from Buenos Aires, where he had been "broke and on the beach." Echoing O'Neill, Art, who tells the story, declares that he has "run the gamit" and has not merely failed, but he never "even cared enough about it all to want to succeed." He confesses that he is "sick in body, brain, and soul," and he is filled with "suicidal melancholia." In his gray alcoholic state, he feels that "all worldly hopes are as naught and the great longing one for annihilation. Ah, to fall quietly asleep and never wake again to cower before the fetish of life!"

In this way O'Neill attributed to the young man telling of Jimmy's suicide his own intentions when he took an overdose of sleeping pills in order "to fall quietly asleep" and never awake. Another curious aspect of the story lies in the fact that O'Neill surrounds Art with "lungers," with one in the room next to his dying of consumption, coughing and groaning so that the place is more like a tuberculosis sanitarium than a rooming house. Art is ready to accept infection, thinking "'Con' or something else, today or tomorrow, it was all the same—the end. What did I care?" Apparently O'Neill was blending both of his consecutive brushes with death: the near-suicide at Jimmy the Priest's and the diagnosis of consumption a year later that put him into a sanitarium full of "lungers" on Christmas Eve 1912. In O'Neill's mind the death of Jimmy Byth had become a proxy for the death he had narrowly escaped.

And so both Byth and his proxy suicide entered *The Iceman Cometh* just as it had entered the story "Tomorrow" twenty-three years earlier. At first O'Neill was even going to call the play "Tomorrow," but the very next day he found, he said, the "fine title 'The Iceman Cometh.'" Even the basic situation at the start of "Tomorrow" inspired him. In it Art tells us he is "sick and penniless," "hunched up" on a chair in the back room where he and his fellow roomers look up "hopefully" whenever anyone enters, in search of a "Good Samaritan" who will dispense "hospitality." In *The Iceman Cometh*, too all the denizens of the house are holed up in the backroom "sick and penniless," waiting in hope that the salesman Hickey will arrive on his usual periodical drunk and treat them all to drinks.

The hero of "Tomorrow," James Findlater Byth, is also in the play, this time called "Jimmy Cameron," and nicknamed "Jimmy Tomorrow" because he is—so Larry Slade announces—"leader of our Tomorrow Movement." In fact, he is identical to his depiction in "Tomorrow" as "Jimmy Anderson," who "lived in a dope dream of tomorrows." Thus Jimmy Byth entered *The Iceman Cometh* bringing with him its theme of the saving pipe dreams that revise the past and illuminate the future with hope. He also brought with him his significance for O'Neill as a proxy for his suicide. Clearly then, James Find-later Byth was pivotal to the genesis of the work.

Unfortunately, very little is known about that "dear personal friend" of O'Neill's and that little has been grossly misunderstood. This much is clear. If Blyth was really forty-six when he died in June 1913, he must have been born in 1867. At twenty-five (that is, by 1892), he was already in the United States working as a theatrical advance man and publicity agent, for in August 1895 he was advertising in the *New York Dramatic Mirror* that he was "at liberty" after being employed for the "past three seasons in advance of The Devil's Auction company." After that he worked as "booking representative of the Hopkins Theatre Circuit" in Chicago. So he revealed in the *Mirror* of June 1898 when he announced that he was opening a theatrical agency and exchange in partnership with David Carpos at 51 West Twenty-eighth Street in New York. When the Boer War broke out, he left America to go to South Africa as a reporter.

Luckily, one of the best publicity feature articles that Jimmy Byth brought about back in February 1908 was written up by Richard M. Little in the

Chicago Record Herald and gave a brilliant portrait, not only of James O'Neill, but also of his press representative, Jimmy Byth, as he took Little about introducing him to important members of the company. Little's portrait is our main source of information about the real man, even to his name, which O'Neill suppressed from interviews about him — apparently because Byth was so much closer to him than Driscoll or Chris Christopherson whose names he used freely. (O'Neill did give Byth's last name to his good friend George Jean Nathan in talk. Never having seen it spelled, Nathan used a Germanic spelling, "Beith," which made him untraceable.)

Little's portrait of Byth actually quotes repartee among him and James O'Neill's stage manager Edgar Forrest and his business manager John G. Nagle as an example of how Byth was loved and teased by everyone, that he was already drinking heavily, and that he was clearly of Scottish origin and highly educated. In one of these exchanges, Nagle referred to the fact that Byth had been a war correspondent with the Boer army throughout the Boer War, adding, in mock disapproval, "And you are a loyal subject of the King." Byth replied:

"But I was not fighting, old chap. I was a war correspondent for Reuters. I was not a beastly pro-Boer; [I was there] merely because duty put me among them, don't you understand?"

"But weren't the English soldiers going to tie a rope around your neck and fasten you to a tree until the coroner arrived?"

"Oh yes," answered J. Findlater Byth carelessly. "They did have a bit of a rope and there was a bit of a tree somewhere abouts, and the beggars made no end of a row when they captured me. But they thought I had been fighting, which I jolly well hadn't."

From this exchange has come both the major misunderstanding of biographers and critics of Byth — promulgated by Louis Sheaffer — and the information needed to correct it. Using Little's quote of Byth saying, "I was a war correspondent for Reuters," Sheaffer checked but found, he said, no record of a "career as a wartime Reuters correspondent." So he concluded that Byth was a "fraud, an innocent harmless one, yet still a fraud."

But Sheaffer should have doubted the accuracy of Richard Little's report. If Jimmy Byth had actually said he was a correspondent for Reuters, he would have been far worse than a fraud; he would have been a lunatic. In the history of warfare, when has there been a belligerent nation that could openly send its official reporters into the enemy ranks? Reuters was strictly an English agency and pro-British. Byth made it clear that he was marching with and reporting from the Boer army. He certainly would have known better than to assert that he worked for Reuters right in the midst of talking about how the British — who

went in for summary execution of nationals found fighting with the enemy —
had been ready, until they had proof he was a correspondent, to hang him
when he was captured among Boers near the close of the war.

In the years after Byth's death, O'Neill was as clear as Byth himself would
have been that he had not worked for a British syndicate. In "Tomorrow,"
O'Neill described Jimmy as having been a "correspondent on the continent"
who represented "some news service" during the South African War. In his interview with Sweeney, about the real man — without naming him — Eugene
O'Neill declared that his friend had been a "highly valued correspondent of
one of the greatest news agencies" and "covered the South African War."
Reuters correspondents marched with the British army and reported from the
British imperialist point of view. Byth could only have worked for a continental agency, for only the European agencies sent their reporters into the Boer
army and slanted their reports — whether French, German, or Dutch — in favor of the embattled farmers who were mainly Dutch or French Huguenot in
origin. The European news agencies needed English-speaking reporters for
their dispatches to such of the newspapers in the United States that were pro-
Boer and anti-British-imperialist. Apparently the prestigious continental syndicate for which Byth reported had a difficult non-English title that slipped
past O'Neill, for he never named it, and also slipped past the *Chicago Record
Herald* reporter, Little. What seems to have happened is that Little, recalling
no name for the agency when he wrote up his interview, filled in the blank
with the familiar English agency Reuters, which looked right for the obviously
British Byth. As for Byth himself or O'Neill in the days of their friendship,
neither would have given Reuters as the name of his employer. Naturally
Sheaffer found no record there.

Thus evolved the myth that Jimmy Byth's knowledge of the Boer War came
not from "firsthand experience in Africa" but from doing publicity for a theatrical extravaganza, the Great Boer War Spectacle. This supposition was
probably set off by O'Neill's explanation in *The Iceman Cometh* that the two
former combatants, General Piet Wetjoen and Captain Cecil Lewis, met
when they came to America to "work in the Boer War Spectacle at the
St. Louis fair." Since Jimmy Tomorrow shares their table, Sheaffer assumes
that Byth worked there with them. But there is no direct evidence that he did.
The program for the reenactment of the Boer War at the St. Louis fair lists
H. C. Duce as the man in charge of press and publicity. Of course, it is possible that Byth did some publicity for the spectacle, qualified as he was as a former Boer War correspondent. If so, it most likely would have been when the
former fighters arrived in New York in March of 1904 or after the St. Louis fair

closed when the show transferred to New York City. Nevertheless, Byth might just as easily have met the Boer and British actor-soldiers, to whom he introduced O'Neill, at the British Consulate in New York or at the Garden Restaurant on Madison Square when they performed there, for it was probably there that O'Neill became, as he said, "pals with so many" of them.

At any rate, O'Neill put in one from each side, along with Jimmy. As for the Jimmy of the play, he differs little from the Jimmy of "Tomorrow." Although his eyes have changed from the "blue" of the story to "big brown friendly" ones in the play, he is the same affectionate, lovable, teasable character of the short story and of Richard Little's interview.

Since O'Neill needed accurate facts for the reminiscences of Wetjoen and Lewis, he refreshed his knowledge by reading and taking notes from histories of the war. Apparently these readings alerted him to the fact that he had made a gaffe in "Tomorrow" when relating the great tragedy to which he attributed Jimmy's alcoholism. For the story is one that could not have taken place for a correspondent of a European news syndicate as Jimmy is in the story and the real James Findlater Byth had been.

In "Tomorrow" Jimmy reveals this destructive experience and then immediately kills himself. He tells of having married a pretty English girl named Alice "just before the war — took her to South Africa with me" and "left her in Cape Town when I went to the front." Called back unexpectedly to Cape Town, he found her in "flagrante" with a "staff-officer — dirty swine!" Whether O'Neill picked up this story from one of his British South African pals and used it for Jimmy, or whether he simply invented it, he realized, by the time he wrote *The Iceman Cometh* that it could not have happened to a correspondent like Jimmy who marched with the Boers. Pretoria, not Cape Town, was headquarters for the Boers, accessible to correspondents from Europe by way of the port of Lorenço Marques in the Portuguese protectorate of Mozambique, from which a long train journey was necessary to reach Boer-held South Africa and Pretoria. No one would have left a newly wedded English wife alone among the hostile Afrikaans-speaking Boers in Pretoria. Nor would anyone marching with the Boers have stationed his bride in Cape Town, considering the difficulties and time required to reach it from Boer Territory. Certainly, after his readings, O'Neill corrected this mistake by changing Jimmy from a correspondent of a continental news agency in "Tomorrow" to a reporter for "some English paper" in *The Iceman Cometh*.

The untrustworthy bride in the play is called Marjorie, and her adultery in Cape Town is perfectly plausible once she has become the wife of a reporter for an English newspaper. For this play populated with characters from the years after Jimmy Byth's death when the Hell Hole in Greenwich Village was his hangout, O'Neill endowed Jimmy's mythical bride with traits of his own lost love of that time, Beatrice Ashe, as well as with a touch of the archetypal betrayer of his life, his drug-addicted mother. Apart from her adultery, we learn of Marjorie only that she was "beautiful and she played the piano beautifully and she had a beautiful voice." The piano-playing was a central attribute of O'Neill's mother, who had once studied to become a professional, though not a concert, pianist, and the beautiful voice is a chief attribute of his fiancée Beatrice, who sent him into a tailspin of desperate alcoholism by breaking her engagement to him in 1916. Also, in the play the betraying bride is no longer meant to be truly the trauma that ruined Jimmy's life, but more an excuse for his drinking, which was already under way before the adultery and indeed itself a cause of it.

The greatest change in Jimmy Byth for *The Iceman Cometh* emerged from the plot O'Neill created for it. "The suicide really happened pretty much as shown in the play," O'Neill told George Jean Nathan, but the play character who kills himself is not based on the real man who "bumped himself off that way." As in "Tomorrow," in *The Iceman Cometh* O'Neill put in a suicidal young man who represents O'Neill and his suppressed suicide, for which the suicide he attributed to Jimmy was a proxy. This desperate young man of the play no longer appears, like Art in "Tomorrow," as an exact portrait of O'Neill at the time, but emerges out of a blend of two people quite unlike him who impinged on his life in 1916. Curiously enough, the suicide he had ascribed to Jimmy Byth in 1913 by contagion from his own is detached in the play from the Jimmy character and becomes the finale for the desperate young man, almost as if some part of O'Neill knew what his conscious mind did not know: that the only suicide at Jimmy the Priest's had been his own abortive one, and the real Jimmy had never lost his faith in a glorious tomorrow.

At any rate, Jimmy regains, at the end of the play, as do all but one of the denizens of Harry Hope's saloon, his saving pipe dream. In fact, in *The Iceman Cometh*, both his dream and his life are still flourishing when the play is over. The only converts to death are the young man — ostentatiously divided from O'Neill's personality and history — and his mentor, Larry, a real person from O'Neill's past and blended with himself as he wrote, a man twice as old, looking back at and reevaluating the Eugene O'Neill of his wild youthful follies.

CHAPTER THREE

The Anarchist Contingent

In 1906 when the eighteen-year-old Eugene O'Neill discovered Benjamin Tucker's anarchist bookstore in New York, the term *anarchist* covered a wide range of left-wing positions. Not until the 1920s did the various components break apart into socialists, communists, nihilists, and anarchists—the last were against all forms of government. Whatever the word meant to those who called themselves anarchists in 1906, they included some of the foremost creative thinkers in America. No wonder the youthful O'Neill, with his inquiring mind, was attracted to them and graduated quickly from reading the books Tucker was publishing to acquaintance with the people who were reading them and even to a number of those writing them.

In fact, O'Neill had already entered creative anarchist circles as early as the fall of 1909, when he moved out of his father's hotel suite in New York to share the rental of a studio in the Lincoln Arcade building at Broadway and Sixty-fifth Street with his New London artist friend Ed Keefe and two other young painters, George Bellows and Ed Ireland. Keefe and Bellows were both studying with Robert Henri, whose studio was down the corridor from theirs, and Henri brought the four young men directly into contact with the radical anarchist world. As the newspaper critics derisively called him, Henri was the leader of the Ash Can School of painting. His work was so labeled because Henri delighted in depicting the vivid life of New York's slums, crowded with workers, immigrants, and the poor. So impressed by Henri's idealism and humanity was young Eugene O'Neill that only four years later, when he attempted to write one of his first full-length plays called *Bread and Butter* about a tragically destroyed young artist, he added a wise master artist based on Robert Henri. The character bore O'Neill's own first name (suggesting his identification with him), plus the obviously French last name "Grammont."

By the fall of 1915, when O'Neill returned to New York after his year at Harvard, he found Robert Henri and George Bellows at the anarchist Ferrer School, jointly teaching an evening class in painting on Mondays and Fridays and charging a tuition of "two dollars a month," as they declared in an advertisement in the December 1915 issue of Emma Goldman's anarchist monthly, *Mother Earth.*

The Ferrer Center also saw much of Eugene O'Neill at this time, for he had become an unpaid volunteer worker helping to put out the weekly anarchist magazine *Revolt,* which aspired to be, as its masthead declared, "the stormy petrel of the labor movement." O'Neill had just assisted in getting together the first issue, to appear on New Year's Day 1916, when their office was invaded by the New York police, who were powerless to arrest the staff at this point but managed to frighten their landlord into evicting them at once. They took refuge in the Ferrer Center at 63 East 107th Street. In the following months, O'Neill frequently saw his old artist friends and also came to know the remarkable anarchists who would transform his life later that summer. A number of these would shape the plot and pose for several central characters of *The Iceman Cometh* twenty-three years later.

The editor of *Revolt* was Hippolyte Havel, a half-gypsy from Bohemia who for years had edited a German-language anarchist paper in Chicago, the *Arbeiterzeitung.* Early in life, probably while a student, for he knew classical Greek, Havel was caught in revolutionary activities and incarcerated in a prison for the criminally insane, where he might have remained for life as the sentence could be prolonged indefinitely. But by luck the great psychiatrist Baron Richard von Krafft-Ebing came there, examined him, and, deciding that he was sane, had him transferred to a regular jail, from which he was ultimately released.

Later Havel found Emma Goldman lecturing in England, and she brought him with her to the United States, docking on December 7, 1900. By 1915, Havel was prominent in American anarchist circles, and through him O'Neill came to know the anarchists who would, along with Havel, model for the anarchist contingent of *The Iceman Cometh.* They also led O'Neill that summer of 1916 to Provincetown on Cape Cod and to just those creative writers, scene designers, theater directors — all loosely designated "anarchists" — who would give him his chance as a playwright, first with their Wharf Theater in Provincetown and then, that fall, as the Provincetown Players in Greenwich Village, New York.

Certainly O'Neill's friendship with the seething, explosive editor of *Revolt* survived the brief life of the periodical itself. Not fully three months after

Revolt began, its office at the Ferrer Center was raided by federal agents and closed down (just after the appearance of the February 19, 1916, issue). As O'Neill later told Beatrice Ashe, he and the rest of the staff "narrowly escaped" ending up in the "Federal pen." In the following years O'Neill saw much of Hippolyte Havel in Greenwich Village during the time of Havel's tempestuous love affair with and partnership as chef in the restaurant of Polly Holladay, sister of O'Neill's friend Louis Holladay, a woman calculated to incite Havel's jealousy because, as George Cram Cook saw it, her name should have been "Polyandrous," rather than Polly Holladay.

No wonder O'Neill could re-create Hippolyte Havel accurately in Hugo Kalmar of *The Iceman Cometh*. But it was not the young Havel whom O'Neill knew at *Revolt* or during the years right after its demise who went into the character, but the battered man in his sixties that he became, at the point when he was ready to retire to a shack in the anarchist colony at Stelton, New Jersey. The hard years in prison and his reckless later alcoholism turned Havel into the battered relic O'Neill depicted in Hugo Kalmar of *The Iceman Cometh*. Of course, during all the years that O'Neill knew him, Havel was a periodical drinker. As Hapgood explained, "To drink much and often was part of his code of honor. It was limited only by the fact that although he had many friends, he couldn't always count on their treating him." Often, after Havel had left Dobbs Ferry in upstate New York—where he was cook for the Hapgood family—for a debauch in Greenwich Village, Hutchins Hapgood would have to retrieve him, finding him in a pitiable state, even sometimes with his thick glasses smashed, although without them he was virtually blind.

Nevertheless, the Havel whom O'Neill knew at *Revolt* was a very different person from the alcoholic Hugo of the play. For one thing, he was certainly not the pathetic figure whose comrades are through with him and only he does not know it. When O'Neill first knew him in 1916, Hippolyte Havel was immensely active. He not only edited *Revolt,* he was one of four leaders conducting the Anarchist Forum for Current Topics on Sunday evenings at the Ferrer Center. Also, during January 1916, Havel spoke on the twenty-second at the Harlem Casino in the Commemoration Meeting for Japanese revolutionaries "murdered," as the announcement in *Revolt* declared, five years earlier by "the Japanese ruling class." Havel spoke again on the thirtieth at an International Protest Meeting against War and Preparedness at the Star Casino. In those days Hippolyte was not, like Hugo, a mere "old drunken has-been."

Also in those days Havel was never totally destitute, as is Hugo of the play. He was never one of the anarchists who refused to work under capitalism. He was always ready to apply his skill as a chef for income. In O'Neill's play, no reference is made to such a resource for Hugo, and he is clearly destitute from O'Neill's description of him as "dressed in threadbare black clothes" and with his white shirt "frayed at collar and cuffs," but everything about him "fastidiously clean," and even "his flowing Windsor tie" tied "neatly." Actually, this dandified getup—only not in the least shabby—was Havel's typical holiday attire throughout his life. As Hutchins Hapgood described him, Havel would set out for Greenwich Village from Dobbs Ferry with "a stick, conventional black clothes, a flowing black tie, and even spats with his patent leather shoes." In a photograph taken in July 1916, Havel appears with the stick, very trim even wearing informal clothes, observing the setting up of the scenery for the production of *Bound East for Cardiff*, the first New York performance of an O'Neill play. So Hugo is certainly a faithful portrait.

O'Neill's description of Havel's physique is as accurate, according to extant pictures, as of his clothing, although again O'Neill did not have in mind the man of 1916 whose "crinkly long black hair" had just begun to be "streaked with gray," but the more grizzled figure of later years. Mabel Dodge Luhan, who knew Havel in the years before 1916, talked of the anarchist's "long black hair" and of how "very small" he was. Similarly, O'Neill's Hugo is a "small man" with "tiny" hands and feet and a head too large for his body. Mabel Dodge Luhan too was impressed by Havel's broad and "intelligent brow." Hutchins Hapgood thought that Havel's small nose accentuated his "high and imaginative forehead." O'Neill's Hugo too has a pug nose and a "high forehead."

Just as accurate was O'Neill's capture of Havel's talk and behavior. Hutchins Hapgood saw Havel as a "wild little man" in a "perpetual state of vituperative excitement," often "mean, vindictive, or jealous" (at least during his liaison with the promiscuous Polly Holladay) and always "irrationally condemnatory of almost all the world." So Hugo's first words in *The Iceman Cometh*—addressed absurdly enough to the bartender Rocky and the philosophical anarchist Larry—are "Capitalist swine! Bourgeois stool pigeons!" Hugo's most affectionate epithet is "leedle monkey-face!"

As Mabel Dodge Luhan reported, Havel burst out after listening to a discussion by no lesser people than Emma Goldman and the redoubtable labor leader Big Bill Hayward, "They talk like goddam bourgeois." Later that same evening Havel exclaimed to Mabel Dodge Luhan in a "sweet whining voice" with tears running over his spectacles: "My little sister! My little goddam bourgeois capitalist sister!" Art Young recalled Hippolyte Havel with "glasses bigger than the moon" suddenly crying out during a meeting of the *Masses* staff, when they had just voted on whether to include a poem in their next issue: "Bourgeois! Voting! Voting on poetry! Poetry is something from the soul. You can't vote on poetry."

O'Neill also caught for Hugo Havel's typical chant when demanding a treat: "Don't be a fool! Loan me a dollar! Buy me a trink." Apparently, Havel had fixed upon a dollar as, once and for all, the amount of money for his requests. He even set the price of a year's subscription to *Revolt* at a dollar and his expenses for editing *Revolt* at "a dollar a day." As Hutchins Hapgood recalled, whenever he met the wild little anarchist in later years, Havel "would ask me for a dollar." Once Hapgood found Havel riding on a Fifth Avenue bus, which at that time offered a more expensive and luxurious ride than other buses. Not at all embarrassed by his aristocratic choice, Havel, Hapgood said, "characteristically asked me for a dollar, which I dutifully handed over to him."

The only aspect of Havel that O'Neill could not depict with literal accuracy in Hugo was Havel's knowledge of languages. He could have Hugo sing the revolutionary "Carmagnole" in French because he himself had studied French at Betts Academy and Princeton. But unfortunately he had never studied Havel's native German. If Havel, like Hugo, ever quoted the poet Ferdinand Freiligrath, he must have done so in his own and the poet's native German. O'Neill's Hugo always quotes Freiligrath in English translation, and in particular the translation of his poem "Revolution" that Emma Goldman published in the March 1910 issue of *Mother Earth*. Himself an exiled revolutionary poet, in his poem, Freiligrath sees the exile and captivity in Babylon of God's chosen people as similar to the exile and imprisonment of Europe's revolutionaries after the suppression of the uprisings of 1848. The final line of the poem suggesting the inevitable fall of the Babylonian oppressors is the one Hugo is given to quoting: "The day grows hot — oh, Babylon! 'Tis cool beneath thy willow trees." Certainly the English translation of this line — epitomizing as it does Hugo's principal pipe dream — was better for the American audience and readers for whom the play was written than the German, which only a few would have understood. Although O'Neill subtly changed "The day grows hot" of both original and translation into "The days grow hot," his version sounds the inevitable doom of Babylon's rulers, as does the original. It also conveys the ambiguity of Hugo's pipe dream, in which rage and hatred of humanity battles with and sometimes overpowers the loving-kindness that first conceived the dream.

If O'Neill was peculiarly sensitive to the ambiguities in Hippolyte Havel, he became so through his insight into his own conflicting emotions. Not six years after O'Neill had devoted himself to putting out *Revolt*, he was telling Oliver Sayler that life was a struggle, and often an "unsuccessful struggle, for most of us have something within us which prevents us from accomplishing what we dream and desire." That, he told Sayler, was "one reason why I have come to feel so indifferent toward political and social movements of all kinds." He did not think human beings could be made better "by tinkering with externals or by legislative or social fiat," but only by inner struggle to become better within themselves. A few years after that, O'Neill was saying that he no longer had fixed opinions about anything because "there are too many things to consider from which opinions are derived." He still felt that the most significant theme for his plays was "man's rebellion against his environment," but his hopes lay in each person's struggle to arrive within himself at higher values and better behavior, rather than in dreams of setting up a perfect society that would abolish greed for money and power.

So he made Hugo's most tragic moment in *The Iceman Cometh* the one in which he recognizes, in a devastating flash, his own inner scorn and rage against the human beings for whom he supposedly wants to construct his better society, and also his real reluctance for any revolution to come in which he will no longer be in a position to play a grandiose role.

The three other anarchists who shaped *The Iceman Cometh* came into O'Neill's life, as did Havel, through the short-lived publication of *Revolt*. One of them O'Neill never knew personally but he heard much about. The New York anarchists at the time were in a turmoil over the capture, trial, and condemnation to life imprisonment of Matthew Schmidt, because Schmidt had been betrayed by a stool pigeon among them to the William J. Burns detectives.

The crime Schmidt was charged with had happened five years earlier. On the morning of October 1, 1910, an explosion of dynamite in Ink Alley of the Los Angeles Times Building had killed twenty *Times* employees. It was quickly discovered to be an act of reprisal by James B. McNamara and his brother John — not anarchists, but devoted union men — against the publisher of the *Times*, Harrison Gray Otis, who was conducting an all-out campaign to destroy and render illegal the unions. The bomb had been set for one o'clock in the morning, when the building would have been empty, and McNamara was heartsick to discover that it exploded much later, killing people. He regretted so bitterly "that these unfortunate men lost their lives" that, he said, he would freely give his own life if doing so could "bring them back." After James B. had been sentenced to life imprisonment and his brother John to fifteen years, it became known that the Burns detectives were seeking to bring Matthew Schmidt in as an accomplice, so he, anticipating being railroaded, disappeared underground.

When Donald Vose, using his mother's name, not his father's, "Meserve," appeared at Emma Goldman's New York center for *Mother Earth* in May 1914, he was taken in immediately as the son of Gertie Vose, for his mother was an old friend of Emma Goldman and had stood by Alexander Berkman during the terrible time of his imprisonment for assaulting Frick. In 1914 Gertie Vose was living in the anarchist Home Colony at Lake Bay, near Tacoma, Washington, and she gave her son Donald a letter to Emma Goldman in New York begging her to look after him and full of pride that at last he was taking an interest in the movement.

Eleanor Fitzgerald and Alexander Berkman, who were running *Mother Earth* for Emma Goldman while she was in Los Angeles that May, gave Donald a room in the building, and Emma herself visited him when she returned to New York. He was then (September 1914) twenty-two years old. Later Emma Goldman recalled that her impression of Vose was "not agreeable," because she had been repelled, she thought, by "his high pitched, thin voice and shifting eyes."

Emma Goldman was then in difficulties that forced her to give up the large house that sheltered *Mother Earth*, where anarchists could rent inexpensive rooms. She told Vose that he could transfer to a derelict farm on the Hudson River at Ossining that had been lent to her by a comrade a few years before. Just before the move, on the last Saturday in September, Matthew Schmidt emerged from hiding to meet with friends and advisors at Emma Goldman's New York house. Lincoln Steffins, Hutchins Hapgood, Alexander Berkman, Eleanor Fitzgerald, and Emma Goldman spent an afternoon conferring with Schmidt on his continued incognito. As he was about to leave, Emma Goldman recalled that Vose had told her he had an urgent message from Washington for Schmidt, so she sent for Vose and another roomer, Terry Carlin, whom Schmidt had known on the West Coast and wanted to see before going back underground.

Thus for about ten minutes Vose saw Schmidt and was able to get the name he went by, Moe Hoffman, as well as the address of his hideout supposedly so the message could be gotten to him. Later, when Schmidt was arrested, suspicion as an informer immediately fell on Vose because there had been warnings from the anarchists staying at Ossining that, despite his apparent poverty, Vose somehow always had money to buy drinks for everyone around him — so many drinks that he was holding real carouses. Suspicion became certainty with Schmidt's trial, for Donald Vose Meserve was the chief witness for the prosecution. He testified that William J. Burns had hired him, coached him to pose as a radical, and sent him with the letter from his deceived mother to spy on the New York anarchists.

O'Neill must have heard much about Vose's treachery by the time Terry Carlin came to the *Revolt* office with an open letter dated January 20, 1916, denying some of the false testimony involving him that Donald Vose Meserve had given at the trial. Carlin wrote that "the perjured Burns' spy" had testified "that M. A. Schmidt, and myself were in the Woodstock Hotel Bar, where Schmidt made a 'confession' to us. Now I have never been in that place with either one or both of them, nor have I ever been there. Furthermore, I am more than anxious and willing to make a sworn affidavit to that effect." (At this time there was hope — quickly shattered — for a retrial and the letter had been corrected by Schmidt's defense attorney.)

Never having met Meserve, O'Neill at first had no idea of including him in the cast of characters of *The Iceman Cometh*. As his pencil notes show, he meant to put among his characters the personality of Robert Minor, who was listed as "illustrator" on the title pages of *Revolt*. Minor had been in Europe with the reporter John Reed and the illustrator Boardman Robinson, drawing and writing articles on the appalling butchery of World War I, which had just begun in Europe. *Revolt*'s first issue had included a letter from the trenches by Minor conveying the full horror of the slaughter taking place. Undoubtedly *Revolt*'s strong stand on keeping America out of the massacre was what inspired federal agents to silence it at once, along with other antiwar anarchist publications. When Minor returned from Europe in January 1916, he had already sickened with one of the diseases then decimating the trenches along with the shells and bullets. So he never did the cartoons for *Revolt*, and most likely O'Neill did not come to know Minor until that spring after its suppression.

Minor was one of the few anarchists for whom O'Neill felt no comradeship. As Saxe Commins wrote his Aunt Emma Goldman ten years after these events, when she was lecturing on modern drama, O'Neill had "a complete hate" for "the sort of thing Bob M stands for." O'Neill, Commins added, "clearly saw through him from the beginning. The overzealous theorist has been his bete noir these many years; the intellectually curious, the man anguished by his doubts, harassed on all sides by the caprices and cruelties of life, ever questioning, ever seeking and tireless, his sought companion." What put O'Neill off Minor was his faith in the philosophic theories of Karl Marx and his belief that answers to most political questions could be found through a careful — even rigid — application of theory.

At any rate, listing the real names of his characters and their traits in his first sketches for *The Iceman Cometh*, O'Neill noted, "Bob M — Anarchist — incorruptible fanatic — coldly pure, no women, no booze — passionate idealist — in hiding — suspicion wanted on Coast for bombing activities with Wobblies — savagely intolerant weakness — about 30 —." From this note, it appears that O'Neill meant at first to use Minor in the position of Matthew Schmidt the betrayed, rather than Donald Vose, the betrayer. It is possible that O'Neill meant to have the betrayal, the treachery, an event of the play and to make it, perhaps, one of the shocks that shatter the pipe dream of the anarchist contingent in the play.

By the time O'Neill sketched a scenario for the play, this character (whom he was then calling "Potter") had moved from Minor and Matthew Schmidt back to the Burns spy Donald Vose. Clearly, O'Neill had not yet latched onto the plot of the betrayed mother or of her old love affair with the major anarchist of the play, Larry. In the scenario, Potter has not, as in the final play, found Larry's address from the letters his mother kept. Instead, Potter, having come "from Coast drunk," has stopped off to get the address from the "Farm school," showing that O'Neill was very familiar with the progressive anarchist Ferrer "Modern School" for children at Stelton, New Jersey, which taught them farming and crafts, according to their interests, as well as abstract subjects, so they could participate in the real world — printing and distributing, as well as writing, for instance, their own newspaper.

So the Bob Minor character disappeared from the final play, but a few of his traits, such as a touch of his purity, migrated over to the character based on Donald Vose, who is called in the play "Donald Parritt." Like Minor in 1916, Parritt has "no women" (later on, Minor did marry) and like Minor in 1916 and ever after, "no booze." Both Donald Vose and Bob Minor came from pioneer American stock rather than from recent immigrants, as did many of the anarchists. Gertie Vose was, as Emma Goldman declared, "one of the few unusual American characters in the radical movement." Minor was even more American, hailing from San Antonio, Texas, and related on his mother's side to General Sam Houston of Alamo fame and on his father's to an aunt of George Washington. In the finished play, Parritt, seeking rationalizations for his treachery, declares he became fed up with a movement that was full of foreigners: "After all, I'm from old American pioneer stock."

In the end, O'Neill gave Parritt only the two traits that Emma Goldman had seen in Donald Vose: his "shifting eyes" and his "not agreeable" personality. While introducing the character of Parritt in his play, O'Neill specified that his "personality is unpleasant," and he has "a shifting defiance and ingratiation" in his eyes. Most surprising, O'Neill transferred the hiding-out of Matthew Schmidt, which originally he had meant to use for the Bob Minor character, to the character of Donald Parritt, so that elements of the real story for both the stool pigeon and the man he betrayed are strangely coupled to shape Parritt in the final play.

Nothing could illustrate more dramatically the manner in which the actual facts that feed into fiction can lose all sequence in time and all connection to person. A writer may use all the details of a real story with such wild freedom that they come to mean the opposite of their original significance. Nor is there anything mysterious about the way in which the creative impulse behaves. There is a logic to how an author selects and transforms his materials. In O'Neill's case for *The Iceman Cometh* — and very likely in the case of all writers — what transforms and rearranges the facts he has taken from reality is very simply the demands of the story he needs to convey his meaning.

The force that transformed Donald Vose's story into Donald Parritt's was the necessity of having the full treachery and the arrest of the betrayed anarchists take place before Donald Parritt appears on the scene at the start of the play. O'Neill needed to surround the boy with suspicion from the start, but to delay the clear revelation of his guilt to the climax of the play, when it provokes a moral crisis in Larry Slade that awakens him to a terrible truth and converts him to an acceptance of reality in contrast to all the other characters in the play who end, as they began, hiding behind a lie.

To achieve this effect, O'Neill needed to give Parritt an explanation of why he has not been arrested with his mother and the other betrayed anarchists other than the actual reason that it was he who betrayed them. So O'Neill had Parritt represent himself as having gone underground just as Matthew Schmidt actually had done. Schmidt certainly had not been a stool pigeon, and he seems to have been innocent of any complicity in the McNamara bombing of the Times building. Thus in O'Neill's play, Donald Parritt appears at first to be innocent but with a growing taint of suspicion until he, like Donald Vose, stands fully revealed.

To create this, O'Neill had to erase Vose's testimony at the trial and the trial itself from his play. But he aroused suspicion of Parritt in the same way it was aroused for Vose, because although he is not working, he somehow has money. In fact, O'Neill went beyond giving Parritt a roll of bills; he also dressed him in flashy new clothes and had him explain that they were a kind of disguise. In reality, William Burns had Vose looking as poor as possible, and even had the boy go without an overcoat so that he could give needing to keep warm as the excuse for hanging around the heated *Mother Earth* office.

The rest of Parritt's story came to O'Neill by combining these details with all that he knew of the chief anarchist of the play, Larry Slade, whom he modeled on his lifelong friend Terry Carlin, met all those years ago through his work with *Revolt*. When O'Neill first heard of the old anarchist, Terry Carlin was being strongly coupled with the Burns spy Donald Vose so that some of Vose's guilt became attached to him. Both Carlin and Vose had been transferred, along with a few other anarchists whom Emma Goldman had been sheltering at the time, to the dilapidated upstate farm she had been lent when *Mother Earth* moved to smaller quarters at 20 East 125th Street.

In those days when Donald Vose was treating the anarchists to drinks on instructions from Burns, Terry, an alcoholic, was often seen drinking with him. Thus some anarchists jumped to the conclusion that Terry, like Vose, must also have been a Burns detective. Hippolyte Havel, an old friend of Terry's from their Chicago anarchist days, instantly printed in *Revolt* an article by Hutchins Hapgood defending Terry Carlin and deploring these accusations based on nothing more than guilt by association.

Hapgood explained that Terry's entire life was a refutation of such a charge. Terry could not be bribed because he cared for nothing in the world but the integrity of the soul. Years earlier Benjamin Tucker had told Hapgood that Terry Carlin, who preferred to starve rather than work for capitalism, was "the only uncompromising Anarchist he knew in America." In his defense, Hapgood declared that Terry had talked to him about Donald, and had "evidently warmly liked the boy, but wondered from what source he got his money." As suspicion of Donald became widespread, Terry "clung to the idea of the boy's innocence," so that the proof of his treachery came as a "terrible shock to him." *The Iceman Cometh* depicts a similar reluctance on the part of Larry to recognize his own growing suspicion of Donald Parritt.

Most probably Eugene O'Neill made friends with Terry Carlin during the brief life of *Revolt.* Perhaps Terry was one of the volunteers working, along with O'Neill, to get the paper out. At any rate, O'Neill felt warmly enough toward the old philosopher by that spring to room with him in the flat on Fourth Street in Greenwich Village that O'Neill always called the Garbage Flat because Terry — adroit as he was in hobo-style survival — furnished it entirely with cast-off crates and sacks, using discarded newspapers as bed linen. So unswept was the place that — so O'Neill would "fondly" recall — it developed "a nice even carpet of cigarette butts, reminding one of the snow scene in an old melodrama."

When warm weather came, Terry took O'Neill with him for another lesson in tramp-style living at Truro on Cape Cod, where he knew of the "hulk of a wreck" on the beach that could serve as shelter. At once they were joined by Hippolyte Havel, who was working in nearby Provincetown as cook in the cottage full of John Reed's guests. As Jack Johnson reported, "the trio were inseparable." Soon after their arrival, Terry took O'Neill to see Hutchins Hapgood in Provincetown in order — so Hapgood later recalled — to "put the bite" on him for ten dollars, which, "it will probably amuse Gene to know has never been repaid." Harry Kemp the poet (who had published in *Revolt*) recalled afterward that O'Neill had come to Cape Cod "trampishly with an older man for companion and mentor," that is, the "remarkable" anarchist philosopher, Terry Carlin.

By July 1914 Terry and O'Neill had transferred to Provincetown, renting one of John Francis's apartments across the street from John Reed's cottage, because at last O'Neill's chance as a playwright had come. The summer before, Hutchins Hapgood, his wife Neith Boyce, Susan Glaspell with her husband George Cram Cook, John Reed, and several others had begun performing their own one-act plays in a theater they had fashioned in the old fish house on the wharf in Provincetown. They had selected O'Neill's one-act sea play, *Bound East for Cardiff*, for their program on the evenings of July 28 and 29, 1916. As Hapgood wrote Mabel Dodge, who had been with them the summer before, "Terry Carlin and O'Neill (son of James O'Neill) have taken Bayard's studio."

The friendship begun that spring and summer between Terry Carlin and O'Neill endured to the old anarchist's death in September 1934. In fact, later, when O'Neill's parents bought for him the abandoned lifeguard station on the shore outside Provincetown (remodeled by Mabel Dodge), O'Neill took Terry into his home with his wife Agnes and baby Shane. Once O'Neill had money, he supported Terry financially for the rest of his life. Thus when O'Neill chose Terry as the model for the central character, Larry Slade, in *The Iceman Cometh*, he had close to eighteen years of intimate memories to draw on for his portrait.

Nevertheless, O'Neill reinforced those memories with accounts written by others about Terry Carlin and also about Donald Vose and Matthew Schmidt. In June 1937—two years before he began *The Iceman Cometh*—O'Neill sent an SOS to his friend Saxe Commins asking him if he knew of any English translations of Bakunin or Kropotkin or any book by his Aunt Emma Goldman giving a picture of the kind of "Utopia" envisioned by the anarchists. O'Neill wanted these materials because he was thinking of having one of the characters in the cycle of plays he was then writing to "dope out" an ideal society similar to the anarchist or syndicalist dream. In response, Commins outdid himself by gathering what O'Neill referred to as a "library of Anarchist-Syndicalist literature"—so that, as O'Neill joked, he hoped "we don't both get pinched for conspiring to pollute the mails with seditious propaganda." No inventory survives, but most probably, among the materials Commins sent would have been back copies of Saxe's Aunt Emma Goldman's anarchist monthly *Mother Earth*. (O'Neill had already read her autobiography.) So it is hardly a coincidence that the two points O'Neill gave to describe Donald Parritt in *The Iceman*

Cometh — his shifty eyes and disagreeable personality — are the same two that Emma Goldman noted in her article "Donald Vose: The Accursed" in the January 1916 issue of *Mother Earth*.

Probably O'Neill was inspired by this same article to formulate his plot of the betrayed mother in *The Iceman Cometh*. Because of her long friendship with Donald's mother, and because of her own horror at having taken in the traitor, Emma Goldman felt deeply the tragedy of Gertie Vose, addressing her as the "unfortunate mother of your ill-begotten son." She urged her to "be brave" like "the heroic figure in Gorky's *Mother*," and making no excuses for him, "save the people from your traitor son."

This heroic mother, conjured by Emma Goldman's article, intrigued O'Neill, and he put into his play such a suffering anarchist woman, "old, worn, bruised, beaten," as Emma described Gertie, yet an indomitable fighter. Something of the mature radical leader Emma Goldman thus became blended into this image of the tragic mother. In her article, Emma Goldman declared that Donald's treachery had been "the most terrible blow in my public life of twenty-five years." She felt "torture, agony, disgust" and would gladly, she said, "give ten years of my life if Donald Vose had never stepped over my threshold." Thus the betrayed mother of the play took on some of the power of the indomitable Emma herself. Although O'Neill had never met her, he knew a great deal about her. When Emma Goldman asked her nephew Saxe if O'Neill knew her, Saxe replied, "If he doesn't know you," and intimately too, it is the "fault of my inability to convey you to him, for often I have told him about you."

The link by which O'Neill's image compounded from Emma Goldman and Gertie Vose became connected to Terry Carlin, for the plot of *The Iceman Cometh* was forged, most probably, by two of Hutchins Hapgood's books on anarchism-syndicalism. Whether O'Neill already had them, or they came among the books that Saxe Commins sent, no one can now say, but O'Neill must have first read at least one of them years before he reread them as inspiration for *The Iceman Cometh*. In the years following that first Cape Cod summer, O'Neill and Hapgood became close friends. After taking the Fall River Line ship from Cape Cod to New York with Hapgood in 1920, O'Neill wrote Agnes: "Hutch and I sat up in a deck stateroom and theorized the universe to sleep until about midnight. I have grown to love Hutch. He's a peach!" Hapgood had written in *The Spirit of Labor* of an anarchist who loved both his wife "and her boy by another man." This anarchist accorded to her a freedom in love that he did not take himself. As a result, she switched her love to another man. "The situation" Hapgood said, tore the anarchist's "heart out," but "he thought it against his sense of justice and freedom to object." Such cases happened frequently in radical society, Hapgood said. Just such a case formed the subject of a second book by Hapgood, *An Anarchist Woman*, published in 1909, and this one would have especially interested O'Neill because it told the story of Terry Carlin's great love affair years earlier with a young woman he recruited to the movement.

To shape the plot of *The Iceman Cometh*, O'Neill had only to make his Terry character, like the man in *The Spirit of Labor*, one who loved both a woman and her child by another man. O'Neill created that son in the image of Donald Vose, one who in adulthood was to betray his mother's trust and her comrades. The betrayal in O'Neill's play is even more unforgivable in that the mother has been arrested with her comrades and sentenced, as was Matthew Schmidt, to life imprisonment. The remainder of the play plot rests fairly closely on Terry's old love for a willfully promiscuous woman as told in Hapgood's *An Anarchist Woman*.

Yet O'Neill's plot came out altogether different from the real story, although faithful in depicting Terry's reactions. The transformation came of the fact that O'Neill did not base his story on the real Marie, seventeen years old when the love affair started and not over twenty-four years old at its finish. Rather, he depicted her as a mature woman from the outset and long-time devoted radical like Gertie Vose, as well as infused with something of the grandeur of leadership and courage of Gertie's friend Emma Goldman. In naming this character "Rosa," O'Neill probably meant to suggest an almost mythical woman such as Rosa Luxemburg, martyred and assassinated in the cause of workers. At any rate, O'Neill's Rosa Parritt (an offstage character) is, like Rosa Luxemburg or Emma Goldman, almost a symbol of the anarchist movement, one who can actually confuse herself with the movement, she is so identified with it.

Terry Carlin's actual love, Marie, was an uneducated girl who had worked as a maidservant and, already promiscuous, was on the brink of prostitution when Terry (then thirty-five) not only converted her to a social philosophy and commitment, but also introduced her to the world's great literature. Beginning with the Greek drama, which Terry read in the original Greek, they continued together through the works of Nietzsche and Schopenhauer to the great novels of their own time. By the time of their break, she had become an educated woman, very literate, as her autobiographical sketches and letters, which Hapgood transcribed in his book, testify, even if they are not in a class with Terry's letters. It had been Terry, not she, who brought a social philosophy and poetry into the affair.

O'Neill was faithful to the real story only in his account of the difficulties in the union of Terry and Marie because of her reckless sexual adventures, which she flaunted as a right and which Terry bore with on principle for many years, but which ultimately aroused in him anger and hatred. After one of Marie's returns from a particularly self-destructive affair, Terry reported to Hapgood, "She is seriously ill, the result of a mad adventure. As I exist for others when they are in pain, I am her trained nurse. She is now recovering from the drugs, the debauching, and the raving madness of sleepless nights." Nevertheless, Terry admitted, "I feel rather worn out with domestic drudgery, cooking, laundering, wrestling with disease without and demons within." In the end, the demons began to win in Terry. His suffering transformed him into the detached philosopher he was when O'Neill came into his life.

Terry's only hope lay in spiritual development. He told Hapgood, "If an oyster can turn its pain into a pearl, then, verily, when we have suffered enough, something must arise out of our torture—else the world has no meaning." More and more he relinquished his dream of an ideal society, and felt rage rather than hope for his fellow anarchists. "If I cannot have the intellectual red that heralds the approach of Dawn," he declared, "then I want the red light of Terror that ushers in the Night."

Finally, Terry lost all faith in constructing a better world. "I once thought that I could help the mob to organize its own freedom. But now I see that we are all mob, that all human beings are alike, and that all I or anyone can do is to save his own soul, to win his own freedom, and perhaps to teach others to do the same, not so much through social propaganda as by digging down to a deeper personal culture."

Disillusion with Marie and disillusion with revolution went hand in hand for him. Of Marie he said, "She loved me intellectually and sensually, but not with the soul. She wanted my ideas, and sex, and more sex, but not the invisible reality, the harmony of our spirits." So he lost faith in her and, he said, "in all things." Incensed at his coldness, "she began cruelly to fling the amours that I had tolerated as long as I hoped for the spiritual best in my face. It was a kind of revenge on her part." Having lost belief in her, he lost faith in "human solidarity," and, so he said, "I quit my fanatical belief in the possibility of a Utopia. So that now I am not even an anarchist. I am ready to pass it all up."

Instead, he became pure hobo. As he wrote Hapgood, "I am very 'crummy,' badly flea-bitten, overrun with bed bugs, somewhat flyblown, but, redemption of it all, I am free and always drunk." Oblivion, not social justice, was what he sought. He told Hapgood that he was in a state where "I am willing to let everything go by default—everything except my last illusion, that I can never let myself out to anyone. To Marie—and to you—and one or two others—I have been sorely tempted to lay myself out—but not even the moon can seduce me to reveal myself. My dead and buried self is my first and last seduction." He wanted, in Buddhist terms, to remove himself totally from life. He declared, "Nirvana is very welcome, if I could be sure of it, but I had rather stay what I am than start life all over again in some other shape, with a possible creeping recollection of my former existence."

This was the Terry Carlin whom O'Neill brought into *The Iceman Cometh* as Larry Slade, satirically called by his companions at Harry Hope's, "Old Cemetery" or the "grandstand philosopher" because of his repeated assertion that he has let everything go and is looking upon life from the grandstand. Recalling Terry Carlin as he was in that summer of 1916, Max Eastman described him as a "thin, dark, handsome hawk-like type with firm chin and austere cheekbones." Just so Eugene O'Neill depicted Larry Slade, with his "gaunt" face, prominent nose, high cheekbones, and lantern jaw. Like Terry in his hobo phases, O'Neill made Larry flea-bitten, slovenly, and perpetually drunk. He gave Larry Terry's view of life at the time he became a mentor for him, endowing him with both the Carlin skepticism of creating an ideal society and his indestructible belief in the principles of freedom and questioning and search for enlightenment.

The only transformation of Terry in *The Iceman Cometh* came from the fact that, while writing it, O'Neill was himself the older man looking back upon his youthful self, as Terry had once looked upon him. So Larry Slade fuses the mature O'Neill with the Terry who had done so much to shape his philosophy, so that the character is impelled more by Eugene O'Neill's own struggle to face and resolve the looming eventuality of death for himself and his fellow men in that year 1939 than by Terry's evasions back in 1916.

At the time O'Neill began *The Iceman Cometh*, he was watching the ultimate consequences of the butchery of World War I as they were shaping into the more frightful disaster of World War II. By way of his participation in the central protagonist of *The Iceman Cometh*, O'Neill could battle once again for understanding — even acceptance — of the human dilemma, of mortality.

CHAPTER FOUR

Ward Heelers, Pimps, and Prostitutes

I ronically, the first real encouragement O'Neill received as an artist came hand-in-hand with a devastating disappointment that plunged him into one of the most prolonged and destructive bouts of alcoholism of his life. Right after the successful performances of his play *Bound East for Cardiff* at Provincetown on July 28 and 29, 1916, Beatrice Ashe broke her engagement to O'Neill, which plummeted him into a despair as appalling as the one that had brought on his suicide attempt at Jimmy the Priest's back in the last days of 1911 and the New Year of 1912. Both that crisis and this second one were precipitated by the collapse of an ideal of romantic love. Both joined forces to impregnate the meaning, shape the plot, and summon up the characters in *The Iceman Cometh*.

In its appearance, its location on Fulton Street, and its double function as bar and cheap rooming house, Harry Hope's saloon is a ringer for Jimmy the Priest's. Its proprietor, however, is not Jimmy, whom O'Neill had already exploited in *Anna Christie*, but Tom Wallace, proprietor of the Hell Hole on the corner of Fourth Street and Sixth Avenue in Greenwich Village that figured powerfully in O'Neill's life from the fall of 1915 to the bar's extinction during Prohibition. Like Wallace, his avatar of the play, Harry Hope has been, in O'Neill's words, a "jitney Tammany politician" — a reference to Tammany Hall, the New York Democratic Party headquarters. He, has, therefore, come out of the same world of corruption, of ties with the criminal underworld, that typified local Democratic Party politics throughout the later part of the nineteenth century and the early part of the twentieth. Indeed, Wallace came out of the same world in which Al Adams with his policy racket and his bribed police protection had flourished.

Thus the criminal underworld patronized the Hell Hole, and the Hudson Dusters gang habitually hung out there. O'Neill erased them from his play, but they were companions in drink for years, and it was their thefts of alcohol that allowed the saloon to survive the couple of years it did after the start of Prohibition. The real bond that brought Joe Smith (who is called "Joe Mott" in the play) frequently into Wallace's saloon was the fact that he, like Wallace, was a petty Tammany boss, a ward heeler, and his territory bordered on Wallace's. Mary Heaton Vorse said she met Joe Smith when O'Neill brought her to him for help in recovering her dog—who disappeared from the Provincetown Playhouse one evening.

Smith was then, she said, "boss of the Ninth Ward," and, although small, had "the conscious dignity of a chieftain," commanding, as he did, in "Cornelia Street and Minetta Lane, better known as Cocaine Alley," where his word — she said — was "law." Certainly Joe Smith had strong ties with the Hudson Dusters, a local gang of thieves. In December 1919, he told O'Neill that they could get whiskey only twice a week and then only by having "some of the gang" steal it from a warehouse and sell it to "Tom Wallace afterward." For the character Joe Mott, O'Neill erased from Joe Smith both his Tammany and his criminal connections except for the one that had fascinated him most, his former proprietorship of a Negro gambling house with the wealth and prestige it brought him.

In the days O'Neill knew him, Joe Smith was certainly a little "shabby," but exalted by memories of his former days of wealth and power. In fact Joe Smith's pipe dream of the past was one of the first in which O'Neill saw the making of a play. As far back as the summer of 1921, O'Neill had already jotted down a note for a "future play": "'Joe' — tragic-comedy of negro gambler (Joe Smith) — 8 scenes — 4 in N. Y. of his heyday — 4 in present N. Y. of Prohibition times, his decline." The titles O'Neill proposed for this play were "White" and "Honest Honey Boy." The second came from the song "Honey Boy" popular in 1907 — the time, perhaps, of Smith's former glory — and has no part in *The Iceman Cometh*. "White," however — with its double meaning at that time when it was used both to indicate a particularly trustworthy person and also a person of light skin pigmentation — does enter the play as a secondary fantasy of Mott, recalling both the praise he received of being called "white" for his honesty in the days of his grandeur, when he paid his graft punctually to Tammany Hall and the New York police, but also suggesting his submerged ambivalence toward his black identity, the wish to blur out that division into white and black.

As for personality, O'Neill's first note for him was "Joe S. — Jovial cynic." In both his first draft and the final play, O'Neill suppressed what was certainly true of his original: that "it would not be wise to look for trouble with him unless one really wished a whole lot of trouble," stressing rather his natural "good humor." In the final play Joe Mott's dangerous qualities are implied more subtly by a scar from a knife "slash" and the fact that his face would be hard were it not for his good nature and humor. The good nature was certainly dominant in Joe Smith. In a letter to Agnes of December 1919, right after the birth of Shane, O'Neill told her that the Hell Hole's bartender Lefty and Joe Smith "seem as delighted with Shane's arrival as if they were godparents. They urged me to send all their blessings to you—'the little girl.'" In the play O'Neill placed Joe at the table of the Boer War combatants Cecil Lewis and Piet Wetjoen and its reporter Jimmy Cameron—apparently to represent by way of Smith's ancestors a token South African population.

As a fellow Tammany boss, the actual Joe Smith would have belonged with the group at Wallace's table. According to Mary Heaton Vorse, Wallace supported "at least a dozen bankrupt and down-and-out saloon keepers and barkeeps." Since he owned the "whole building," he could give them shelter as well as drink, so although it was not actually a rooming house like Jimmy the Priest's, O'Neill did not overstretch the truth when he had the patrons of Harry Hope's bar stay in rooms there. Mary Vorse said that Wallace and his cronies would get "tight" together and fight with one another every night, so that when the uproar became deafening, John Bull, the bartender, would reassure customers in the other back rooms by murmuring "Wallace."

Instead of the crowd around Wallace, O'Neill placed at Harry Hope's table only two cronies, neither of whose originals came from the Golden Swan. One—whom O'Neill turned into Harry Hope's brother-in-law—actually derived from O'Neill's old drunken days before Prohibition at the Garden Hotel. His name was probably Jack Croke, although reporters to whom O'Neill talked of him in interviews invariably misspelled his name as "Jack Croak." He is forever immortalized to O'Neill fans as the man who gave O'Neill the impelling idea for *The Emperor Jones.*

Jack Croke was an "old circus man"— O'Neill explained—who had worked at the "ticket wagon" of "a tent show" touring the West Indies during the incumbency of President Vilbrun Guillaume Sam in Haiti. Sam had taken office on March 4, 1915, and was deposed in less than a year by a revolutionary group under Dr. Bobo. After murdering—in his panic—167 political prisoners he had jailed, President Sam took refuge in the French legation, but it was penetrated by a small party who threw him to the furious crowd below. They literally tore him to pieces and then paraded his head and the "dismembered body" through the streets.

The story Croke told O'Neill was that President Sam boasted his enemies could never get him with a lead bullet; he would get himself first with a silver one. The story came out of old folklore—it appears among the historical novels of Sir Walter Scott—but it struck O'Neill as authentic for Sam, and he made a note of it. About a half year later he got the idea for the effect "of the tropical forest on the human imagination" from the days of his "prospecting for gold in Spanish Honduras," when he had been haunted by his frightful involvement with Kathleen Jenkins back in New York, and the jungle solitude had accentuated his private horrors. That idea did not quite bring the play to life, but a year later he read of the effect of the drum beat in Congo rituals, which began at a normal pulse rate and accelerated to bring the heartbeats of its participants to frenzied rapidity. Those ideas, plus the trauma of his father's death in August 1920, carried the entire play about the fear of death to writing pitch, and O'Neill wrote it early that fall. No wonder the man who first set the play in motion—some time in 1918—became later a character in *The Iceman Cometh*, with its concentration on the meaning of death.

Certainly O'Neill kept in his pocket for years afterward a coin with President Sam's portrait on it that Jack Croke gave him, and Croke's exuberant stories of his colorful past may possibly have inspired his creation of Ed Mosher's hilarious story that concludes the first act, about the "old Doc," seller of snake oil, who hoped his cure-all would end by leaving no grave plot unoccupied in the entire United States. Whether that was actually a story that O'Neill heard from Jack Croke, no one can now say for sure. As O'Neill himself pointed out, "I knew all the circus people" because "I used to meet them all in the bar" of the Garden Hotel. So he might easily have blended stories he heard from other circus friends into Mosher's dialogue. Later, when George M. Cohan came to know O'Neill from the rehearsals of *Ah, Wilderness!*, he kept marveling at the fact that O'Neill, as he said, "knows all the old circus jokes." So Mosher may have touches—over a foundation of Jack Croke—of other circus men out of those "old drunken days."

The other crony who shares a table with Harry Hope and preys upon his generosity is Pat McGloin, a former police lieutenant, cashiered during a reform investigation, when he was caught red-handed taking graft during the flush times of Tammany corruption. By making him a crony of Harry Hope, an old-time Tammany boss, O'Neill suggests he had the same tie-in between criminal activities and party corruption that had protected Al Adams in the days when his friendship with the chief of New York police made him impervious.

The remaining residents of Harry Hope's—that is, the three prostitutes and their two pimps (bartenders)—came out of the events and their emotional tone of O'Neill's plunge into alcoholism and debauchery when his romance with Beatrice Ashe, which dominated more than two years of his life, was smashed irreparably. O'Neill had tried by letter to get his beloved fiancée Beatrice to come to Provincetown to share his triumph of having *Bound East for Cardiff* produced, but she did not go. Therefore, as soon as the productions were over, O'Neill rushed to New London to urge her face to face to marry him at last. Instead—unnerved by the prospect of leaving her family and joining the still penniless, if finally more hopeful, O'Neill, an anarchist as well as a reformed rake who had had one or two relapses in the past year—Beatrice decisively broke their engagement.

For two years, her influence had kept him uncharacteristically chaste, because he did not wish to besmirch the great love of his life with the "grimy smears"—as he designated them—of his former profligacy. Except for the relapses, he had also stayed off liquor all that time for her sake. The crash of his dream sent him plunging into all she had prohibited: frenzied drinking and degrading promiscuity.

Worried, his father, James O'Neill, asked Eugene's friend Art McGinley to get him back to Provincetown, where, his father hoped, the example of all those creative people would reawaken Eugene's creative devotion. During the entire trip to Cape Cod that August, McGinley and O'Neill both stayed blind drunk and remained so for the rest of the summer of 1916 and on into the fall and winter. Only a few vignettes testify to their destructive intensity. One day that summer—so O'Neill recalled years later—he and Terry Carlin sent Art McGinley for more "hootch" (McGinley having the money to buy it). They awaited him eagerly, leaning out of their door at the top of the last flight of stairs as he came up. "He had a quart under each arm and a straw hat on," O'Neill recalled. "To our horror, he wavered and plunged back down the stairs, through the window at the foot of the stairs taking it with him, and wound up on the roof of Francis' store. He pulled himself together, still sound in wind and limb, still with a quart under each arm and his straw hat on, and marched up the stairs to us." Terry Carlin exclaimed devoutly, "Well, thank Christ, the whiskey didn't break its neck!"

That fall in New York O'Neill and McGinley remained "close pals" in debauchery as well as alcoholism. As O'Neill told it, "He and I got in some of the craziest stunts together. Sometimes it was his alcoholic inspiration and sometimes mine, but it was always nuts." As to what they did: O'Neill suggested years later to his son Eugene Jr., who was seeing McGinley in Hartford, "Get Art alone sometime and tell him I release him from any pledge of silence. Then you'll hear something." Out of all that madness, Art McGinley reported to me his recollection of a single moment in a gray dawn after a night's debauch as he and O'Neill stood detaching themselves from the two tarts with whom they had dissipated. The girl O'Neill had been with clung to him affectionately, asking, "Don't you love me any more?" O'Neill replied somberly, "You have a body odor like the market place in Baghdad."

On his part, it was clearly all sex out of hate, not love. As he would later have the protagonist in his play *Welded* say to the prostitute with whom he wishes to revenge himself, "You have the power — and the right — to murder love! You can satisfy hate!" No wonder, then, that O'Neill put into *The Iceman Cometh* three specimen "ladies of the evening" like the tarts of those days, even though they were out of place in the setting of the backroom at Jimmy the Priest's. "You wouldn't find any ladies in Jimmy's," O'Neill said. It was the Hell Hole that accommodated women through its family entrance. Among them were some of the dubious variety of "ladies" that went into *The Iceman Cometh*.

For instance, O'Neill wrote Agnes at the start of Prohibition from the Hell Hole: "Some 'hard' ladies of the oldest profession who seemed to know me, were in the back room along with a drunk. Where this latter got his jag, I don't know. He had a huge roll of money and was blowing the House." The only alcohol to blow — O'Neill explained — was "comparatively harmless" sherry, and added, "Suspected he was being 'framed' for a 'frisk' and kept my eyes to myself." This sideline of streetwalkers enters *The Iceman Cometh* when Cora talks of the drunken sailor with one of those "polite jags" whom she had given a frisk. As for the other two tarts, Margie and Pearl, they have picked up "a coupla all-night guys" — as O'Neill and McGinley had been often — on Sixth Avenue, so clearly O'Neill saw them as working out of Wallace's saloon on the corner of Fourth Street and Sixth Avenue, not out of Jimmy the Priest's downtown on Fulton Street.

The other four women in *The Iceman Cometh* are all very important to the story but never appear on stage. Indeed, two are dead and the third is among the living dead, with lifelong imprisonment ahead of her. The most important for the plot is Hickey's wife Evelyn — she who is, according to the increasingly sinister joke, at home in the arms of the iceman. All four characters — but she in particular — evolved from Eugene's recollections of that period of revenge and self-destruction in 1916–17 that began when he was jilted by Beatrice.

The murder story for Hickey — so O'Neill said — was his own "imaginative creation," and the personality of the man — from two seemingly contradictory statements O'Neill made — came out of both reality and creativity. As O'Neill told George Jean Nathan, there was "a periodical drunk salesman" who "did make that typical drummer crack about the iceman and wept maudlinly over his wife's photograph." The same salesman also kept harping on the cliché that honesty is the best policy. To Kenneth MacGowan, on the other hand, O'Neill declared that he "never knew" a Hickey, but he knew a lot of periodical drunk salesmen, and Hickey is "all of them" and yet "none of them." Apparently the joke about the iceman, as well as Hickey's insistence on truth came from one salesman, while Hickey's other characteristics came from many drunken salesmen.

At any rate, in the first pencil notes for *The Iceman Cometh* there is no reference to a salesman character, and there are unmistakable indications that O'Neill meant to achieve the effects that Hickey brings about by the actions of other characters. For instance, in the notes it is Wallace's bartender John Bull ("Rocky" in the play) who, as O'Neill wrote, "encourages Jimmy Tomorrow and Tom [Harry Hope] to get out of house" — as does Hickey in the final play, to explode their pipe dreams. Also O'Neill noted that the Terry character was to see and express the "real meaning of what is going on" — that is, that they are all reinforcing each other's dreams — and he who regrets "they cannot leave themselves alone — cannot forgive themselves for not being what they are not."

In the finished play the Terry character continues perceptive and articulate but has no wish to tamper with the pipe dreams of his companions. In his place, Hickey enters among the characters and becomes uniquely the dream demolisher of the play in the belief — which is discovered to be false only at the end — that he has achieved contentment by getting rid of his own dream. For this, the story of his wife Evelyn and her indestructible pipe dream is crucial. She has believed, and has made Hickey believe with her, that her love and forgiveness will reform him of his periodical alcoholism and his sexual profligacy. So she is an image of the virtuous small-town girl — like O'Neill's youthful love, Beatrice Ashe — whose love O'Neill had believed could transform and purify him. Like Hickey's Evelyn, Beatrice forgave his early relapses. "Dear Old Big Heart," he had called her after one of them. But perpetual forgiveness was not Beatrice's way. She was too firmly set on practical goals of catching a reliable breadwinner and a husband of prestige to cling to a highly doubtful dream.

By 1939 when O'Neill began *The Iceman Cometh*, he knew she had been right not to. At that point in his life he would never have been able to fulfill that dream of reform. Something of that knowledge went into Hickey's story. Of course, in Hickey, O'Neill was painting no self-portrait, but rather a personality diametrically opposite his own. O'Neill's Hickey is typically a salesman, if one with more shrewd psychological insight than most. He is extroverted, happy-go-lucky, a joker, a flatterer, a dealer, yet genuinely sociable and affectionate. The only ways in which he resembles his creator, O'Neill, are embodied in his insight, in his capacity for remorseful guilt and self-loathing, as well as in the lure for him, when excruciatingly tormented thus, of forgetfulness, oblivion, by way of frenzied drinking.

Hickey also has a story similar to O'Neill's in his love for a small-town girl from a highly respected, socially prominent family who looks upon him as hopelessly disreputable. The difference is that Hickey's story suggested what might have been had O'Neill not suffered that devastating jilting, had become tied at that point in life to a girl who refused to lay down the dream of reforming him, so that her endless forgiveness built into him over the years an intolerable load of guilt and humiliation and self-loathing.

The three other offstage women bear no direct resemblance to Hickey's Evelyn. Nevertheless, their stories reinforce aspects of her story so that ultimately they make one unified commentary on what had been for O'Neill himself, in the years before 1939, one of the most persistent and eternally reborn dreams of all: the dream of ideal romantic love, embodied first in Beatrice Ashe, then in O'Neill's second wife, Agnes Boulton, and finally, at the time of *The Iceman*, in his third wife, Carlotta Monterey.

The first offstage woman to come alive in the dialogue and lead up to the ultimate tragic revelations about Hickey's Evelyn is Harry Hope's wife, Bessie — dead at least twenty years when the play begins. As a nag and a shrew, and a relentlessly ambitious pusher of her husband, she emerges as broad comedy, as does her husband's sentimental revision of these facts in his belief that sorrow for the beloved woman made him give up all pretense of political power, so that he has not gone out since but has spent his time (as he had always really wished to do) in his own back room, drinking with his cronies and dispensing alcoholic charity and shelter to all, including the three streetwalkers whose presence (as he is gleefully aware) would have made Bessie, were she conscious, revolve in her grave with futile outrage.

Also very different from the faithful Evelyn is Jimmy Tomorrow's offstage former wife, Marjorie, who was caught in flagrant adultery when her husband returned unexpectedly to Cape Town. Yet, like O'Neill's own faithless Beatrice she is a singer, and like Hickey's Evelyn and Harry Hope's Bessie she is the subject of a sentimental pipe dream. Just as Harry sees his mourning for Bessie as the cause of his alcoholism, so Jimmy believes he became alcoholic from the shock of Marjorie's faithlessness. Only late in the play does he realize the devastating truth: that his alcoholism caused her faithlessness, rather than the other way around.

The fourth offstage woman, Donald Parritt's mother, Rosa, unlike as she is to Hickey's Evelyn, nevertheless completes by her story the destruction of romantic dreams by tearing their veil from the complexities and ambivalences of realistic romantic love. And those ambivalences hidden under sentimental revisions and alterations of reality are picked up and accentuated in the stories of the three onstage streetwalkers and their two pimps with the dreams that hide the degradation of what they do.

CHAPTER FIVE

The Vital Impulse for *The Iceman Cometh*

⬚ ▣ ⬚

Eugene O'Neill was fed up to his "teeth," he said, with the American theater by the time *Days without End* had been produced. Besides, any new
production would be decimated by (non-tax-deductible) alimony payments to
Agnes. Her minimum alimony was $10,000 a year for her and $5,000 for each
of the two children (later reduced to $2,400). Thus, she was a wealthy woman
in those Depression years. She could not afford to remarry, since that would
make her ineligible for O'Neill's alimony. With the sliding scale of alimony
then in force, any further earnings O'Neill made from future productions
would go largely to her. For instance — so O'Neill confided to Robert Sisk — if
he earned $50,000 in a year, his net after alimony and taxes would be about
$17,000. So he decided he would give himself a holiday from the painful com-
promises of producing for a while: he would live on his income from book
sales and investments, and devote himself entirely to creation.

In fact, from this time on, O'Neill thought, he might allow his plays to appear only as published books. By 1934 he saw no reason for writing other than
that of surpassing himself artistically. He might, for a start, give himself larger
scope. His last plays had been conceived as trilogies to be performed on three
consecutive nights in the theater. *Dynamo* had really been meant as the first
of a trilogy of God plays. *Mourning Becomes Electra* was also a trilogy and
O'Neill at first had meant it to be presented on three separate nights. *Days
without End* was really his second God play, though he kept that fact secret,
and he meant to write a third on money. Inevitably, to surpass himself, he began to think of writing after it a series of four plays to be produced on four
nights in the theater. In it he might extend his technique in *Mourning Becomes Electra* of making the directive power of the past visible and concrete
through recurring emotional situations in several generations of a family. So
it was that O'Neill conceived the cycle, at first calling it A *Touch of the Poet*

and ultimately *A Tale of Possessors Self-Dispossessed.* It would tell the spiritual and psychological story of an American family through five generations as an illustration of the tragedy of the republic that he thought was exemplified in the biblical warning: "What is a man profited if he shall gain the whole world and lose his soul?" But with no monetary aims pushing him to finish and no urgent personal problems directing him, O'Neill became more and more grandiose in his dream of surpassing himself.

Only months after he started work, the cycle of four plays became five. Then it was six, seven, and by June 1936 became a cycle of nine plays. They were outlined and scenarioed, and when he began actual first drafts, he discovered they were all (with the exception of one) developing — against his will — as double-length plays like *Strange Interlude.* He became frustrated and exhausted, and when — after he had taken time out to write *The Iceman Cometh* and *Long Day's Journey into Night* — he returned to the cycle, he found that it immediately exploded into an eleven-play cycle. In May 1941 he declared what he had already realized back in 1939: "Will never live to do it — but what price anything but a dream these days!"

No wonder then that *The Iceman Cometh* took shape as a play about the pipe dreams that make it possible for the human spirit to survive in a painful world. O'Neill himself had held onto that idea as a guiding principle throughout his years. Even in such an early play as *The Straw,* written during the fall of 1918 and the winter of 1919, O'Neill had his tuberculous hero (based on his youthful self) declare that his idea and that of his fellow inmates that they are not "really" sick is the "pipedream that keeps us all going." The entire play rests explicitly on the idea of the saving power of even a "hopeless hope."

In 1922 O'Neill saw the grandeur of tragedy in the fact that the audience could perceive in it "their own hopeless hopes ennobled in art." He thought that life, in itself, was nothing. "It is the dream that keeps us fighting, willing — living!" Man wills "his own defeat" by pursuing the heights. "But his struggle is his success." O'Neill was still living by that principle seventeen years later in 1939, but along the way that vision within himself had become subtly tarnished. While working on *Days without End* in 1932, O'Neill had already expressed, through the character of his skeptical astronomer Hardy, the realization that his belief in striving might be sheer self-delusion.

By creating Hardy, he had come to see his life struggle as so much theatrical posturing before the empty immensity of the universe. Hardy declares that his self — his life — is merely a puppet whom he has made to climb "toy mountains" in a little enclosed garden lit by glow-worm footlights. With the "meaningless nothingness" of death, the puppet hero fades to a ghost, "the walled garden crumbles, and the toy mountains dissolve, and the glow worms go out."

Thus by the time he began working out *The Iceman Cometh*, O'Neill was no longer talking of dreams, but of pipe dreams that have no more substantial reality than the hallucinations of an opium smoker. No longer did he believe, as he had in earlier times, that life attains "spiritual significance" if its dream is only high enough. Yet however little reality O'Neill saw in the pipe dreams, he still believed they were all that kept people "fighting, willing—living!" So the fragile thread of story in *The Iceman Cometh* rests simply on Hickey's belief that he has reached contentment by getting rid of his pipe dreams, and that he therefore can bring contentment to his friends by destroying theirs. The finale demonstrates incontrovertibly that Hickey is wrong about what has happened within himself and about what will bring happiness to humanity. So *The Iceman Cometh* gives no Nietzschean vision of glory in striving for the dream of achieving higher values for living.

George Jean Nathan reported that O'Neill had told him that the play was "a study in the workings of strange friendship." The study had begun for O'Neill years earlier when he wrote the draft of his play *Dynamo* that was performed by the Theater Guild. In a stage direction for their entrance, O'Neill had pointed out that the passionate skeptic Ramsay Fife and the passionate fundamentalist preacher Hutchins Light are "pleasantly engrossed in a violent argument, and it is plain at once that each one's disputatious intolerant religious spirit has found an outlet in the other and, on this basis, they are becoming fast friendly enemies." When O'Neill rewrote *Dynamo* drastically for publication as a book, he cut altogether this subtle alliance between the two combatants, but the idea continued to form.

By the time he came, more than a decade later, to write *The Iceman Cometh*, the idea had grown into the basis for the strong nexus of friendships that unite the varied denizens of Harry Hope's saloon. Each of them has found in another pipe dreamer a reinforcement of the dream by which he lives. In *The Iceman Cometh*, the closest pair to the two friendly enemies of *Dynamo* are the two former combatants of the Boer War, General Wetjoen and Captain Lewis. Through the mock battle they continue in words, they both gain a sense of reality for their vision of themselves as heroic warriors for their country. They also reinforce each other's dream for their future that they can return—altogether against the terrible truth—to their beloved homelands and that they will each receive a hero's welcome.

Some of the other dreamers have combined their pipe dreams to create a myth that lends verisimilitude to both. Thus Willie Oban joins his dream that he will sober up and become the brilliant lawyer he gave promise of becoming to the dream of Pat McGloin that he will be taken back on the police force, out of which they concoct the mutual fantasy that Oban will get him a retrial and victoriously get him acquitted. Others simply exchange acceptances of each other's pipe dreams. Thus the two streetwalkers Margie and Pearl accept Rocky's definition of himself as a bartender, not a pimp so long as he accepts their definition of themselves as merely "tarts" with amateur standing, not actual whores.

All of these pipe dreamers at Harry Hope's have conscious satirical insight into the way their companions have constructed a lie about what their past was like and an impossible hope for their future. At the same time, they remain blind to the fact that they have done exactly the same thing. All of them live in harmony by the unspoken agreement: "I will believe your pipe dream if you will believe mine." One of the most painful events of the play is the snapping of that bond of affection, and its curdling into hatred and cruelty, when Hickey has brought them all to kill their dreams by forcing them to see their falsity by trying to carry them out in actuality.

The variety of dreamers among the fourteen men and three onstage women, plus the four offstage women (Hickey's Evelyn, Harry Hope's Bessie, Jimmy Tomorrow's Marjorie, and Donald Parritt's mother, Rosa) are all needed by O'Neill to present enough examples so they demonstrate the universal compulsion among humans to rewrite the past in memory so as to endure it, and to hold onto an improbable hope for the future. Thus O'Neill knew that his play had "no plot in the ordinary sense; I didn't need plot: the people are enough." Through all those rich people he had known and loved in his youth, O'Neill could arrive at the tragic truth of their lives and his own. *The Iceman Cometh*, he said, was something "I want to make life reveal about itself."

O'Neill added, "I think I'm aware of comedy more than I ever was before; a big kind of comedy that doesn't stay funny very long. I've made some use of it in The Iceman. The first act is hilarious comedy, I think, but then some people may not even laugh. At any rate, the comedy breaks up and the tragedy comes on." In the case of everyone in Hope's bar, the tragedy is death — except that for all but two of them it is not physical death but the death of the dream that allowed them to go on living. So the conclusion of this play without an ordinary plot is a lengthy soliloquy — by Hickey, who has killed their life force — to explain to them and to himself where he has gone wrong in his belief that if they could only accept the truth about themselves, could only give up their impossible dreams, they would find contentment. At the finale of the search, Hickey sees that far from having killed all his own pipe dreams, he has simply replaced them all with a new one. As O'Neill explained at the press conference before the production of *The Iceman Cometh*, "The philosophy is that there is always one dream left, one final dream, no matter how low you have fallen, down there at the bottom of the bottle."

In the midst of telling how he came to kill his beloved wife, Evelyn, Hickey inadvertently comes upon the truth that he has not killed her out of mercy and kindness to liberate her from the perpetual disappointment of her dream of reforming him. Instead, he has killed her out of the suppressed rage that has grown in him during the years of unbearable guilt and self-loathing her endless forgiveness of his periodical alcoholism has made him feel. The instant he sees this devastating reality, Hickey cannot bear it. He grabs the first lie that comes to him so as to mask the anger with which he killed her. Shocked and horrified, he declares he could never have laughed and told her, the moment she lay dead before him, that she knew what she could do with her pipe dream now. He must have gone mad in that moment.

What takes place in the play at that point is virtually a conscious social contract negotiated by Harry Hope on behalf of all the pipe dreamers. They will accept Hickey's newest pipe dream that he had gone crazy in that moment of naked hatred because by doing so they can explain away as humoring a madman their futile attempts to enact their dreams in a real world. Clearly, in writing this play, O'Neill was carrying out his own conscious contract with himself to preserve his pipe dream in the face of his own knowledge of its actual nature. A year before he even began writing this play, O'Neill told Lawrence Langner that the Theater Guild should never have sold out to Hollywood-style moneymaking, but preserved its old ideal. "After all, an ideal is something. Or we ought to lie to ourselves that it is, anyway, for life's sake, because if it isn't, what the hell is anything?"

Only two of the men in Harry Hope's bar end up with a genuine death of their dreams and thus of the will to live — Larry Slade (who is Terry Carlin and also the mature O'Neill looking back at his youthful traumas, including his suicide attempt) and Donald Parritt, the horribly guilty youth who is partly Donald Vose and partly O'Neill's reattaching of the suicide to himself after years of detaching it onto three other companions at Jimmy the Priest's (Christopherson, Driscoll, and Byth). So he had come in *The Iceman Cometh* to accept — free of all delusions — his resort to death in the past and his mature knowledge of the inevitable coming of death in the days to be. So the great theme that compelled O'Neill to lay aside his opus magnus and write *The Iceman Cometh* in 1939 was not merely the conscious relinquishment of belief in his dream of surpassing himself. Far more urgent lay the theme of death, of the meaning of the suicide he had come so close to all those years back, and also of the meaning of the oblivion to come. The pressing question to be answered by this play was not simply how he should take that almost-death long ago, but how he was to take the death looming directly ahead.

That icy approach had become unmistakable in the few years before he came to terms with it by writing *The Iceman Cometh*. With the start of 1936 O'Neill was so engulfed in sensations of mortality that he thought himself "jinxed." It is now clear that the chief malady was appendicitis, but the diagnosis was complicated by the contemporaneous emergence of the devastating neurological disorder — cerebellar degeneration — which would not be diagnosed correctly until after his death, and even then without certainty. The simultaneous appearance of disorders in other organs, particularly the prostate gland, further complicated his condition.

Day after day, O'Neill wrote in his *Work Diary*, "bilious attack," "gastritis," "continual vomiting," "low, depressed." He reported that his doctors told him, "whole person sick but no definite organ to pin it on." So he and Carlotta fled Georgia in October for the shores of Puget Sound on the advice of Sophus Keith Winther, a critic who knew enough of *Thus Spake Zarathustra* to recognize the Nietzschean savior in *Lazarus Laughed*. But the geographical change cured nothing, and as November began, O'Neill was writing in his diary, "sick-stomach," and "nerves bad" just as news that he had been awarded the Nobel Prize broke on November 12, and he found himself surrounded by reporters and "movie news people," and snowed under by letters and telegrams. "Hell of a chance to rest!" he thought. To Theresa Helburn of the Theater Guild he telegraphed, "A little [more] excitement like this and the remains can be condensed into an obituary."

On December 14, 1936, he and Carlotta started for San Francisco from Seattle with Carlotta's daughter Cynthia driving. They went straight to Dr. Dukes, who prescribed medicine for the bladder, but O'Neill still felt, "very sick, weak and woozy," so Dr. Dukes put him in Merritt Hospital at once. On December 29 O'Neill woke there at four in the morning with "terrible cramp, spasms," and with this more conventional symptom Dr. Dukes could at last diagnose appendicitis. O'Neill was operated on that same day at one o'clock p.m.

Then everything else exploded in him, and he suffered all at once with "bad pain kidneys," and "pain prostate." His temperature soared to 103 degrees Fahrenheit; he became delirious; the doctors shot him with "caffeine, adrenaline, codeine, morphine, atropine," and he felt so "ratty" he did not "give a damn whether I croak or not." He remained in the hospital for nearly three months. Even after he was released on March 12, 1937, he was still having "attacks dyspepsia — stomach" as late as May. Not until June 18 did he at last begin to feel "creative mind alive again!" For the next two years he struggled with the pain of what the doctors were calling at that point neuritis, as well as with a diagnosis then popular in California: "sinking spells." No wonder that the "Iceman"—that ubiquitous invader of the homes of housewives when their husbands were at work (that is, up until the coming of the electric refrigerator) took on for O'Neill the significance of that other icy ubiquitous invader of homes, death, and thus sent him back in memory to the years surrounding his own almost death, his attempted suicide at Jimmy the Priest's.

At the end of *The Iceman Cometh* only two of the characters are permanent converts to dreamless truth and therefore to death: Donald Parritt and Larry Slade. Like O'Neill himself, Larry awakens from his pipe dream of detachment and indifference in the "grandstand" of life to his actual compassion for the youth agonized with guilt at having betrayed his freedom-loving mother to a living death in prison. Larry tells the "mad tortured" boy to "Go! Get the hell out of life!"

Thus in this play that O'Neill knew was "a denial of any other experience of faith in my plays," in which he felt he "had locked myself in with my memories," he gave the young man—himself—of his short story "Tomorrow" the death by suicide he had tried, only this time in the manner of his old friend Jimmy Byth by a fall from an upper story (a jump from the fire escape in the play). Although Donald Parritt of the play is totally unlike O'Neill's youthful self, the guilt he endures is the same that drove O'Neill.

At the finale, Larry—that character compounded of both O'Neill's former mentor, Terry Carlin, and O'Neill's mature self looking back upon his youth—ends up cleared of his dream of having passed beyond concern for the world and wanting only release. He realizes that he is filled with pity and compassion and remains in a permanent state of doubt from seeing both sides of every question. Only what was formerly a dream of longing for death has become an actuality. With all his fear and uncertainty, he is left awaiting with acceptance the arrival of oblivion.

The idea for *The Iceman Cometh* had come to O'Neill hand in hand with an idea for a play he described as "New London family one." Both dealt with the crucial year of his youth. Before he could decide which to do, he needed to outline both. He chose to do the "Jimmy the Priest—Hell Hole—Garden" idea first because the rebellious years with the suicide attempt came before the transforming shock of his brief bout with tuberculosis, although ultimately both plays took events from before and after the crucial year of 1912 in which they are set.

As soon as O'Neill had outlined the two plays, finishing on July 3, 1939, he began making notes for the characters and sketches of the sets for *The Iceman*

Cometh. By July 13 he was ready to start the dialogue version of the play. He had forty pages by August 7. The entire first draft was finished on August 25th, when he wrote of it in his work diary, "long but grand!" After completing the second draft on October 12, he followed with three drastic revisions to make a third draft. On December 20, 1939, O'Neill decided *The Iceman* was done, and wrote in his work diary that it was "one of best plays I've ever written."

He was sure that there were "moments in it that hit as deeply and truly into the farce and humor and pity and ironic tragedy of life as anything in modern drama." In some ways, he thought that perhaps of all his plays so far, it was "the best." Indeed, moments in it, he knew, "suddenly strip the secret soul of man stark naked, not in cruelty or moral superiority, but with an understanding compassion which sees him as a victim of the ironies of life and himself. Those moments are for me the depth of tragedy, with nothing more that can possibly be said."

A strange counterpart of his own coming to grips with death in it was the darkening of the world as he wrote under the looming black cloud of World War II. O'Neill recalled his fruitless struggle, along with his fellow anarchists, in 1914 and 1915 to prevent U.S. involvement in all the errors that had culminated in World War I. He recalled even more bitterly the errors after it that had led so inevitably to this Second World War, particularly those of the "swinish British Tories" who had "conspired with Hitler to create Nazi Germany." His despair at the self-destructiveness of humankind joined with the acceptance of death he achieved in *The Iceman Cometh* to make him declare, "Only a blathering nearsighted idiot could desire to live very long in the future."

In writing the finale of *The Iceman Cometh*, O'Neill had put his own self-knowledge into the tragic recognition of his Terry Carlin character, Larry Slade, that his dream of sitting in the grandstand detached from suffering humanity and desiring only death had been self-delusional. Five years after the writing of it, when Lawrence Langner gave him a dictaphone to help him with his writing, O'Neill tried it out by reciting into it a speech of Larry's that, he told Langner, was "a favorite bit of mine." Listening to it, he became fascinated by the "impressive ghostly quality" of his recorded voice. As he told Langner: "When I played the record back and listened to the voice that was my voice and yet not my voice saying: 'I'm afraid to live, am I?—and even more afraid to die! So I sit here, my pride drowned on the bottom of a bottle,'" the eerie intensity of it "sure did something to me. It wasn't Larry, it was my ghost talking to me or I to my ghost." So intimately had he joined his mature self to his old mentor, Terry, that he found his own resolution in the one he found for the character. He admitted of *The Iceman Cometh*, "It is as deeply moving to me as it is ever likely to be to anyone."

All this time he still refused to initiate a production. With the destruction of Pearl Harbor and America's formal entrance into the slaughter, O'Neill became certain that in these times his play's "finest values would be lost or dismissed because the present psychology would not want to face them." In fact, they could not be faced "because now we need an unquestioning faith in all pipe dreams, however irrational, lest we be defeated in spirit and thrown into the sty of final 'realistic' opportunism, where God is a murderous blind hog, and there is no dream, and *The Iceman Cometh* like a thief in the night, and we wearily welcome him."

CHAPTER SIX

Broadway — On and Off

O nly with the end of the war did O'Neill finally allow the Theater Guild to mount a production of *The Iceman Cometh*. Even then, what finally convinced him was the bleak fact that the tremor in his hands had become so severe that on most days he could not control his hand sufficiently to write. Nor could he work with a dictaphone. Somewhere in the intense process of transferring brain to hand lay all his creative strength. The very nature of talk was so obtrusively external as to quench his inner struggle to find the truth.

As early as 1945 George Jean Nathan had brought O'Neill to believe that Eddie Dowling would be the right person to direct the play and also, if he could do both, to act the role of Hickey. When Lawrence Langner sent Alfred Kazan to O'Neill in California as a possible director for *The Iceman Cometh*, O'Neill was unable to see him, being very unwell at the time. He told Langner that, in any event, he did not think a foreign director would do for a first American production of such an idiomatically American play. Besides, he thought they were agreed on Dowling to direct. Only during the rehearsals did O'Neill begin to realize that Nathan's judgment of directors was not as reliable as his evaluations of plays. Dowling as director turned out to be one of a number of errors that would destroy the potential impact of *The Iceman Cometh* during its first run.

The greatest error was the Theater Guild's choice of theater. They had never gotten over the mistake they had made when they first produced *Strange Interlude*. Believing it would have only limited appeal, they had put it into the small John Golden Theater. When it turned out to be an immense box office success, they could not capitalize on it because of the limited seating. Determined not to repeat that mistake, they decided that for Eugene O'Neill's return to Broadway after twelve years they should take the huge Martin Beck Theater on Forty-fifth Street.

As a result, the greater part of the audience at the debut of *The Iceman Cometh* were seated far from the stage and could barely see the faces of the figures on it. For the play, which depends on fine revelations of personality and on delicate interrelationships with almost no large-scale physical action, that separation of audience from play destroyed the audience's emotional involvement.

Not until May 1956, ten years after its first production, did *The Iceman Cometh* come into its own with José Quintero's production in the small, intimate Circle in the Square Theater on Sheridan Square in Greenwich Village. By some quirk of licensing, the seating in that intimate theater was shaped around a central stage, cabaret style, with tiny token tables, so that the audience could feel as if they were companions of the men seated around the tables on stage in the back room of Harry Hope's saloon. With Quintero's brilliant directing (he was by no means handicapped by his Latin American origins), and with the excellent acting of all those rich roles, in particular that of Hickey, performed by Jason Robards, the charm of the comedy and the grandeur of the tragedy were instantly recognized.

One of the earliest difficulties of the 1946 production was the inordinate length of the play. At first, the Guild thought they would need to perform it with an hour's dinner break, as they had done *Strange Interlude*. But O'Neill had not designed *The Iceman Cometh* like the earlier play, which was a two-part drama with a break in the middle that sustained the audience's interest in the part to come. An hour-long intermission of *The Iceman Cometh* for dining would destroy the drama's emotional build. Besides, if the audience were rushed in their eating, they might come back—as O'Neill jokingly declared—"hungry enough" to roast and then "eat the author."

On the other hand, as O'Neill had told Kenneth MacGowan, too many cuts would weaken the vividness of the personalities and destroy the empathy with their life-enjoyment. Both were essential for an audience to perceive the full tragedy of what Hickey does to them. So O'Neill began the grueling job of trying to cut without killing his play. The Theater Guild, of course, was readier to hack speeches than was O'Neill, whose musical repetitions of phrases to sustain the increasing emotional charge of what takes place was probably beyond their knowledge of the play. Theresa Helburn told the press conference photographers, who wanted characteristic pictures of O'Neill, "Take him giving us a definite no." In the end, O'Neill managed to cut enough so that the Guild could ring up the curtain at 8:00 and conclude at 11:30, with only one longish intermission of about a half hour.

Another problem of the first production was the fact that *The Iceman Cometh*—like quite a number of O'Neill's earlier plays—depended on the inclusion of carefully chosen songs to express the atmosphere. Essential to the play are Willie Oban's raffish "Sailor Lad" ballad, Hugo Kalmar's revolutionary "Carmagnole," and Cora's sentimental "Sunshine of Paradise Alley." So it was a considerable disappointment to O'Neill to discover that E. G. Marshall, who played Willie Oban, although a fine actor, was hopeless as a singer. In fact, the entire cast was musically inept. Their deficiency ultimately forced O'Neill to rewrite the ending of the play for this production.

He erased almost all the music from the finale, retaining only Willie Oban's "Sailor Lad" ditty, which could be largely chanted, rather than sung, and on that note, with laughter of the others, the play ended. For the published play, O'Neill restored the original ending in which all the characters except Larry, in the euphoria of a return to their pipe dreams, burst into song: Willie and Hugo returning respectively to their "Sailor Lad" song and the "Carmagnole," Harry Hope taking his birthday song "The Sunshine of Paradise Alley," and each of the others joining in with songs ranging from "Waiting at the Church" to "The Oceana Roll." Thus they present a symbolic image of all humanity, with its cacophony of disparate dreams.

The final ironic summation comes with a solo burst of the "Carmagnole" by Hugo and his comic but ominous quote, "The days grow hot, O Babylon! 'Tis cool beneath thy willow trees!" howled down with roars of laughter by the others, while the only "convert to death," Larry, stares silently out into the darkness, where the boy Donald has—with Larry's pitying consent—wiped out the incurable agony of his guilt in suicide.

James O'Neill as a young actor-manager,
touring the United States with his own
company. From the Theater Collection,
Harvard University Library.

Ella Quinlan O'Neill as a young mother,
accompanying and assisting
her husband all along the way.
From the Beinecke Rare Book and
Manuscript Library, Yale University.

Eugene O'Neill sitting on the rock in front of his father's farmhouse, drawing the boats on the Thames River. Collection of Nickolas Muray.

James O'Neill with his sons Eugene (circa age eight) and Jamie (circa age eighteen) on the front porch of the house that became 325 Pequot Avenue. Beinecke Rare Book and Manuscript Library, Yale University.

Eugene O'Neill in his American Line jersey.
Beinecke Rare Book and Manuscript Library,
Yale University, by permission of
Carlotta Monterey O'Neill.

Eugene O'Neill preparing the scenery for his first New York production of
the play *Bound East for Cardiff* in the fall of 1916. At right, in the foreground,
is Jig (George Cram) Cook, his director. In the middle, seated, Hippolyte Havel.
At left, on the ladder, O'Neill. Photo from European.

Hazel Tharsing (before she became Carlotta Monterey) in her coming-out dress.
Eugene O'Neill used this photograph, and Carlotta's description, in his details
for Mary Tyrone's wedding gown in *Long Day's Journey into Night*.
Beinecke Rare Book and Manuscript Library, Yale University.

Long Day's Journey into Night

CHAPTER SEVEN

The "One-Day Play"

O'Neill confessed that both his plays "outside" the cycle—that is, *The Iceman Cometh* and *Long Day's Journey into Night*—had been on his "mind for years." In fact, some of the ideas for plays that came to him before he thought of his New London family play were, it seems, early approximations of that future play. For instance, O'Neill certainly took his idea on July 17, 1931, for a play about a "house-with-the-masked-dead and two living intruding strangers" from his and Carlotta's trip to New London on July 1—so he said—to "revisit Pequot Ave. old time haunts." On June 18, 1937, he got a "New Idea for Play—1 day—symbolical idea—work on notes for it." Clearly, the day was to be symbolical of a lifetime, for O'Neill declared that the afternoon, for his hero, would show his "attempt to go on free of past," so that it is clearly the afternoon of his life, not merely the afternoon of a day. Also, O'Neill thought of the setting for this one-day play as the protagonist's family home with "the dead (his mother, father, his old nurse)." The protagonist was to have scenes with "his brother (dead), his sister (alive but married, away, dead to him), his 1st real love (alive, married, away, dead to him.)" All of these projected characters paralleled O'Neill's own haunting dead except for the sister, and even she may have been a recollection of his sisterly friend, Jessica Rippin, two years his senior, who told him back in 1914 that he was "very, very young."

Even the first "real love" of the protagonist, who is married and dead to him, may have been a recall of his old love, Beatrice Ashe. Within two years of jilting O'Neill, Beatrice had married a naval officer who would rise to the rank of rear admiral. (Certainly O'Neill must have felt the contrast of this dazzling position to his own youthful pride, when he loved Beatrice, in having been made an able seaman.)

When O'Neill finally came to think about his New London family play in 1939, he saw it, like the earlier idea, as taking place, in one day symbolic of the life story of its characters. His first titles for his family play made on June 25, 1939, all suggest the one-day idea. O'Neill tried "A Long Day's Insurrection," "A Long Day's Retirement," "Long Day's Retreat," and then moved to "Diary of a Day's Journey" before settling on "A Long Day's Journey."

The ultimate form of that title came to him only after he had reached an acceptance of death by way of writing *The Iceman Cometh*. On February 22, 1940, he declared, "Get better title, '*Long Day's Journey Into Night*.'" Of course, the night is obviously death. After his and Carlotta's beloved dog Blemie died on December 17, 1940, O'Neill wrote a supposed last will and testament for the dog expressing the feelings about life and death that he had reached by writing *The Iceman Cometh*. He had Blemie say, "Dogs do not fear death as men do. We accept it as part of life, not as something alien and terrible that destroys life." So in the title for his New London family play, O'Neill had his symbolic day move as naturally into night as life closes in death. As for any hope of a life after death, O'Neill had Blemie decide that was "too much" to expect. Instead, the dog wants only "long rest," and "eternal sleep in the earth I have loved so well." O'Neill, concludes, "Perhaps, after all, this is best."

The first three acts of *Long Day's Journey into Night* take place at the three meals that unite the family: the first at 8:30 a.m. right after breakfast, the second before and after one o'clock lunch, and the third at dinner time, 6:30 p.m. The final act comes with the return of all four to the house at midnight. The day falls in August 1912, the same crucial year and season as *The Iceman Cometh*, which O'Neill had given as "summer, 1912." Also, the conscious theme of the family play, like that of *The Iceman*, comes out of O'Neill's life-long belief in the need for an ideal, a dream, to keep one fighting, willing, living. In the family play, however, this belief is carried to O'Neill's conclusion that therefore life is a struggle, and almost always an unsuccessful struggle because we all — so O'Neill said — "have something within us which prevents us from accomplishing what we dream and desire." He had declared in August 1923, "I see life as a gorgeously ironical, beautifully indifferent, splendidly suffering bit of chaos, the tragedy of which gives Man a tremendous significance, while without his losing fight with fate he would be a tepid silly animal." It is their fight for the dream, doomed to failure by the "something within" that gives the tremendous significance and exaltation of O'Neill's family play, and by way of re-creating that struggle, O'Neill was able to face and resolve the pain of his own life.

The weather in that symbolic day makes the fate of the characters visible and tangible. It moves from a sunny beginning to a hazy overcast noon, becoming heavy fog by evening and impenetrable obscurity by midnight. Inevitably it suggests the way the four tragic Tyrones have lost their way, have strayed from all they had hoped to achieve until it is lost beyond recall. The warning voice of the foghorn is futile and the obscurity welcome for hiding the failure as they journey into the ultimate night.

CHAPTER EIGHT

The False in the True

O'Neill knew that *Long Day's Journey into Night* would have to be "written in blood," out of absolute, even emotionally painful truth. Yet for a number of reasons, however agonizingly honest O'Neill meant to be, this autobiographical play could not be perfectly true as history. For one thing, O'Neill simply did not have access to most of the facts for events that had taken place in the lives of his mother and father in the years before he was born. For his father, James O'Neill, a popular and famous actor, Eugene had scrapbooks and newspaper clippings of interviews and also contemporary accounts of events in his life. But for a re-creation of his mother's life before his birth, he had only a very confused chronology and very few facts. He could only imagine what might have taken place.

O'Neill had the mother character in the play, Mary Tyrone, recall how just before her wedding to James Tyrone her father urged her to buy the "best" wedding gown she could and "never mind what it cost." Nothing of the sort could possibly have taken place in reality. Mary Ellen Quinlan was sixteen years old and in her second year of studies at St. Mary's Academy at South Bend, Indiana, when her father, Thomas Joseph Quinlan, died suddenly just three months shy of his forty-second birthday, on May 25, 1874. A full three years after his death, Ella Quinlan married James O'Neill on June 14, 1877. Thomas Joseph Quinlan never even knew that this marriage would come about, much less took a hand in planning it.

Not only was her father not alive at the time of Mary Ellen Quinlan's wedding to tell her to spare no expense on her wedding gown, but there could have been no formal wedding gown of veil and orange blossoms like the one in *Long Day's Journey into Night*. Mary Quinlan's wedding took place in a private ceremony in the rectory of the American National Shrine of St. Ann at 110 East Twelfth Street in New York City. Four people attended beside the bride and groom and Father Thomas F. Lynch, who officiated: the two witnesses, Mary Ellen's mother, Bridget Quinlan, and her uncle, Thomas Brennan, and Mary Ellen's aunt, Elizabeth Brennan (Bridget Quinlan's older sister), and Mary's brother, William Joseph Quinlan. For such a private ceremony, Mary Ellen Quinlan would have worn a simple afternoon dress and hat, rather than the expensive satin and lace display piece of the play.

The elaborate wedding gown in O'Neill's play provides a visible symbol of the innocence and romantic dream at the start of his mother's marriage to demonstrate how far she has strayed from that ideal in the long day of her life. O'Neill also wanted the grandfather he had never known to offer a contrast to the parsimony Mary Tyrone would discover in her husband.

Also imaginary was the highly romantic story of how his parents met, as offered in the play. Mary Tyrone recalls that during her Easter vacation from her convent school, her father took her to see James Tyrone, resplendent in the role of an eighteenth-century French nobleman, and afterward brought her to meet the handsome young actor in his dressing room. The result—as O'Neill designed it—is love at first sight between the two idealistic and beautiful young people. James O'Neill had been remarkably handsome, yet simple and unpretentious. Ella Quinlan had been very pretty, well educated, and clearly equipped with unusual musical ability. Although there was never any question for Eugene O'Neill of the love between his parents, the romantic story he created for them in James and Mary Tyrone was very different from the historical reality for James and Ella O'Neill.

For one thing, when James O'Neill first came to Cleveland in September 1870 as leading man at Ellsler's Academy of Music and quickly made friends with Thomas Joseph Quinlan, Ella Quinlan was only thirteen years old, and she did not begin her studies at St. Mary's Academy near South Bend, Indiana, for another two years. How she came to meet James O'Neill at first has not been recorded, but she probably saw her father's friend often on Sundays after mass at St. Bridget's Church.

Also, James O'Neill apparently became a regular visitor at the Quinlan family home at 208 Woodland Avenue and made welcome by Ella's mother, Bridget Quinlan, and her brother, William Joseph, as well as her father. If Ella Quinlan did see James perform at Ellsler's Academy, she would have been chaperoned by her mother rather than her father, and most likely at one of the Saturday matinees that James O'Neill soon persuaded Ellsler to initiate, and which became very popular.

By the time Ella Quinlan went off to school at the conservatory of music at St. Mary's Academy in Indiana in the fall of 1872, James O'Neill also left

Cleveland to become leading man at McVicker's theater in Chicago. Nevertheless, he kept up his friendship with the Quinlan family, and he returned to Cleveland in the summer of 1873 with a company he himself had organized for summer performances there. But Ella saw very little of James in the years he was building his career in Chicago, supporting the great stars Edwin Booth, Charlotte Cushman, and Adelaide Neilson as leading man for two years at McVicker's and another year as leading man at Uncle Dick Hooley's Parlor Home of Comedy. By the time Ella graduated from St. Mary's in the late spring of 1875, James was far away in California performing with Hooley's Company in San Francisco. He most probably became engaged to Ella after he returned to Hooley's theater in Chicago in August 1876 and then went on to Cleveland for a month before he was due to open in *The Two Orphans* as leading man at the Union Square Theater in New York on October 2, 1876.

By the time James O'Neill married Ella Quinlan two months before her twentieth birthday, he had seen her grow up from a thirteen-year-old child. There is no evidence to suggest that he had come to love her in a flash at first sight as in his son Eugene's play: rather, the love developed over seven years of ever-growing affection and admiration. Back in his first year at Cleveland, at some time in August 1871, James had become entangled with a very different kind of girl. What we know of her comes from Alfred Hamilton Seaman, who played a role in the story. Eugene O'Neill knew very little about the scandal. He used the trouble that came of it later in *Long Day's Journey into Night* as one of the first disillusionments to Mary Tyrone's romantic dream of love. Right after their marriage, Mary recalls, there came the "scandal of that woman who had been your mistress suing you."

At the time of the scandal, September 1877, Alfred Hamilton Seaman contributed to the publicity, telling a reporter of the *Chicago Tribune* about the woman in question. "Nettie was a very nice young girl—just as good as any you could find in Cleveland. Her mother kept a candy-store, and she used to go around a good deal when she was old enough. She 'got mashed' on Jim. Jim was always a 'masher.' That's really the whole secret of the business, you know. There was a fellow by the name of Zucker—a sheeny—he 'got mashed' on Nettie, and once I remember Zucker came around blazing mad with a pistol in his hand to shoot Jim. Jim, you see, had stolen his girl from him. If Zucker had found Jim that night he'd have let him have it, I tell you."

This account of Nettie's mother is correct, for she appears in the Cleveland city directories starting with 1872–73 as Ann Walsh, widow of James, with a "confectionary and news depot" at 310 Erie Street, where she remains through 1880. From 1881 Ann Walsh has her "news depot" during the first year at 105 and then at 108 Woodland Avenue well into the 1890s. It was very possibly a case of hard-working mother and wayward daughter. Later, Nettie was ready to beg money from almost anyone but her mother. Apparently Nettie opted out of assisting her mother in the store, or of doing any remunerative work at all then or thereafter. Seaman's assertion that as soon as she was old enough she went "around a good deal" suggests she took up with men directly as she entered adolescence, and indeed she was only fifteen when she jilted Zucker for James O'Neill.

Alfred Hamilton Seaman was probably correct in seeing the "whole secret of the business" in James O'Neill's extraordinary attraction for women. Even in James's youthful days as "walking gentleman" supporting the stars at the National Theater in Cincinnati, while playing Hendrick Vedder to Joseph Jefferson's Rip in *Rip Van Winkle,* the *New York Clipper* reported in January 1869 that he received the most applause next to the star and that "some enthusiastic fair ones even went so far as to favor him with bouquets."

He was always recalled in Cleveland (see the *Cleveland Plain Dealer* of February 25, 1910) as having been, during his days as leading man there, a "handsome, dashing young blood with whom half the girls in town were smitten." William E. Sage recalled in his column The Passing Show in the *Cleveland Leader* of August 23, 1907, that when James O'Neill was leading man at "the old Academy of Music," "the whole town was stirred up over Mr. O'Neill. Maids and matrons fell in love with him. . . . Every bit of muslin you encountered sighed to play Juliet to his Romeo." No wonder if he succumbed to the flattery of one of them.

Alfred Hamilton Seaman, "Pop," as he was familiarly called, was very close to James O'Neill in those years. As an older actor, Seaman liked to brag about O'Neill that he had "brought him out" at the old National Theater in Cincinnati. Apparently Seaman had helped O'Neill in his first small parts with advice and instructions. With his usual generosity to anyone who helped him get his start as an actor, O'Neill took Seaman with him when he was offered the position of leading man at Ellsler's Academy, and the directories of Cleveland show that they were both living there at 19 Johnson Street from the fall of 1870 until the spring of 1872. Although Seaman is listed in the municipal directory as an "actor," James was actually employing him as his "dresser"—he who assisted an actor to make the many rapid changes of costume and make-up required by the drama then.

When James O'Neill left for Chicago in September 1872 to become leading man at McVicker's, he took Seaman with him—again as dresser. Nettie visited him there for at least two lengthy visits, but by that time James was struggling to extricate himself from the relationship. He knew that Nettie had been intimate with several other men in Cleveland after he left. When she was discovered to be pregnant in 1873, no one could be sure of who had fathered the child. Meanwhile, James tried to set Seaman up in business so that he would be self-sufficient. In the Lakeside Directory for 1874–75, James is listed as actor at Hooley's Parlor Home of Comedy, residing at 43 Third Avenue, and Alfred Hamilton Seaman appears as the proprietor of Theatrical Costumes, premises at 45 and 47 Third Avenue.

After James O'Neill broke with Nettie, she took up with Seaman. In fact, she named the child "Alfred Hamilton" after Seaman. When James O'Neill left for California with Hooley's company in 1875 for a year in San Francisco, Nettie was living with Seaman as his wife. James must have thought he had provided for both of them. But 1875 was a period of severe economic depression in the United States. Indeed, Uncle Dick Hooley was staving off bankruptcy by sending his company to California and placing the Chicago theater under a partnership with Simon Quinlan (no relation of James's friends in Cleveland). As for Pop Seaman, he survived in business into 1876, for he was in the 1875–76 Chicago directory as "costumes" at 185 Ohio Street, but the business must have collapsed sometime in 1876, for it disappears from the directories thereafter.

Thus by the time of James O'Neill's marriage to Ella Quinlan in June 1877, the two he had left back in Chicago were once again in need. James must have had alarming messages from friends in Chicago, for Nettie was trying to cage money from them and complaining that James should have been supporting her. The scandal did not come—as it does in the play—as a sudden and painful disillusionment to Eugene O'Neill's mother, as it does to Mary Tyrone.

Even without the problem of Nettie, with his modesty James O'Neill might have opted for a quiet private wedding like the one he and Ella actually undertook on July 14, 1877, in the parish house of St. Ann's in New York, for he always avoided conspicuous displays in private life. But there is every reason to believe that he and Ella had Nettie in mind when they chose to keep the wedding entirely secret from all but Ella's close family.

Nevertheless the news leaked, and a few wildly inaccurate announcements of it appeared within two weeks of the ceremony. On June 30, 1877, the *San Francisco Evening Post*, declaring that "Mr. O'Neill had not let even his most intimate friends know of the event," went on to announce erroneously that the actor had married a daughter of Hooley's partner Simon Quinlan, and that the officiating clergyman was the "Rev. Preston" (instead of Lynch). This was probably the name of the priest at St. Ann's who confirmed that such a wedding had taken place. *The Spirit of the Times* on June 23 also gave the officiating priest as Preston and called the bride "Miss Helen Quinlan of Cincinnati."

Learning of the marriage thus and fearing the loss of their gold mine, Nettie and Pop decided on desperate measures to assault the newlyweds when James came to Chicago with the Union Square Company, as had been already announced. Although Nettie knew perfectly well there had been no marriage, she filed suit for divorce, declaring that James had wed her in Cleveland in August 1871 and then deserted her and their child. To make the story as ugly as possible so that James O'Neill would be disposed to settle out of court rather than prolong the bad publicity, Nettie also accused him of adultery with a famous actress who had since died. This was a reference to James's leading lady at Hooley's Parlor Home of Comedy, Louise Hawthorne; rumors spread in Chicago while they performed together that she and James were passionate lovers not merely on stage but also behind the scenes. Actually, what the scandal mongers had not known then, but Nettie certainly did know, was that the character actor George Morton in the company was Louise Hawthorne's husband and her constant companion offstage.

Certainly James O'Neill understood that it was all a ruse to extract money from him. He declared at once, "I think the whole thing is a matter of blackmail on the part of this woman, or her friends, or her lawyer." To the *Chicago Tribune* reporter he found in his dressing room that night, he added, "Her statements are untrue from beginning to end. She was not my wife. There is only one woman in the world that I ever asked to become a wife to me—." Here he broke off and his eyes filled with tears. To further questions, he replied, "Well, sir, I don't see why I should be required to tell you my private history. Not that I would object, perhaps, to see it in type, because I conceive that I have in the matter endeavored to act squarely and honorably from beginning to end. But I fancy the public have no interest in me beyond what I can do for them in the way of furnishing amusement, and I don't see why anybody should pry into my personal affairs."

When James and Ella left Chicago, their lawyer, Charles H. Reed, took over negotiations with Nettie. Before the suit was scheduled for trial in December, she had settled out of court, and the case was dismissed for lack of evidence of a marriage. There is no evidence of what Nettie did in the following years until 1882, when a window was opened on her by way of the letters and diary of a young actress in James O'Neill's company then, Elizabeth Robins. Apparently Nettie Walsh once again was haunting James O'Neill for money when he returned in July 1882 to Chicago. She took to stalking him through the streets with the eight-year-old Alfie in tow whenever he emerged from the theater.

Painful as all this was to Ella O'Neill, she was far from the passive victim that her as-yet-unborn son Eugene would portray her to be in Mary Tyrone. Instead, Ella and James O'Neill faced the problem of Nettie together. They met with her at the stage door of Hooley's Theater, conferred with her and, united, decided what to do. Nettie was demanding support and education for Alfred, who, at this point, was old enough to resemble James O'Neill sufficiently to convince him that he (despite the other men she had) was indeed the boy's father. James and Ella agreed to adopt and educate the child as their own if she would grant them custody. They planned to place him in a good Catholic boarding school in Detroit on their way back to New York. Sympathizing with their trouble through Ella's confidences, Elizabeth Robins declared herself filled with admiration of Ella "for standing by her husband."

At the last minute, Nettie demanded cash and refused to give up custody of the boy. One would like to think that she could not bear to be parted from him, but it seems more likely that she could not bear to be parted from her hold on James O'Neill's purse by way of the boy. However "wretched" and "sleepless" the whole affair made Ella — so Elizabeth Robins reported — it gave equal pain to James. For both of them the trouble was rendered more bearable by their firm unity in facing it and their agreement throughout on what to do about it.

In the tragic vision of *Long Day's Journey into Night*, the appearance of the former mistress causes Mary Tyrone to feel disillusionment in and alienation from her husband. The scandal, plus the outrage of her family and friends at her marrying an actor, leaves Mary shattered in her dreams as well as isolated from her earlier friends for the remainder of her life. In historical actuality, Eugene's mother suffered no such exile from the respectable world of her girlhood.

For one thing, the rejection of theater and acting as snares of the devil in the United States was entirely limited to certain Protestant circles. Ella Quinlan had not met with any of it among her friends at St. Mary's Academy. As a matter of fact, in the school of music, many of the girls with her were training to sing in the comic operas (what today would be called musical comedies) which were then very popular throughout the country. Ella's seatmate there, Lillian West, who graduated a year before she did, became "a clever comic opera singer," and she married "that excellent comedian Harry Brown."

She and Ella remained in touch, and they happened to be together in Chicago right after Ella's marriage when the scandal over Nettie Walsh had just broken in September 1877. Years afterward when Lillie had become the theater reporter of the *Chicago News* under the pen name Amy Leslie, she recalled that time. "Ella Quinlan never seemed to know what it was all about or worth. She had been my seatmate in college for a year and was almost a child when she married O'Neill, but when, kidlike, I blurted out one day: 'Oh, Ella, what on earth can you do about this woman?' Ella looked a little blank and said sweetly: 'What woman, honey?' and I had to explain to bring it to her mind. She did not care a rap, and, having myself fallen at the feet of James regularly I was allowed a matinee." Young as she was then, Ella had known exactly how to handle Lillian. Nor did she feel anything but pride in her actor husband before her or any of her other school friends.

She kept up a particularly close lifelong friendship with two other classmates from St. Mary's. One of them, Daisy Green, took the veil to become Sister Mary Evarista at St. Mary's. Whenever James O'Neill performed at South Bend, Indiana, Ella would preside in an evening over as many as four theater boxes full of friends from among the nuns and priests of St. Mary's and Notre Dame.

Ella also kept in touch with her closest friend from St. Mary's, Loretto Ritchie — later Loretto Ritchie Emerson — right up until Mrs. Emerson's death in 1916. During February 1893 when James O'Neill was touring in *Fontenelle* through the southwest and Texas, he rented a house in El Paso for Ella so that she could avoid the stress of travel and enjoy the companionship of Loretto Emerson, who lived there with her husband and two daughters. Helen Emerson, one of them, recalled being sent as a little girl with a message to Mrs. O'Neill and seeing the four-year-old Eugene "playing in the front yard, rolling down the little incline and banging into an iron fence." The desolating desertion by her convent friends that Eugene O'Neill created for Mary Tyrone as a result of her marrying an actor never took place in his mother's life. But it is needed in the play to convey the tragedy of what life has done to the mother.

Lack of knowledge of family events that took place too early for him to know of them also allowed Eugene O'Neill to draw a tragic picture of where Mary Tyrone has ended up. In the play it appears that she has landed in a broken-down summer home in a town she hates because of her husband's fear of spending and his thoughtlessness of her welfare. The story of the O'Neills had been very different.

Mary Ellen Quinlan's family had first settled in Connecticut, where she had been born on August 13, 1857, in New Haven. Her father, Thomas Joseph Quinlan, kept a candy store there (that is, a store that sold confectionaries, candies, and cakes as well as tobacco, newspapers, and magazines). When he decided he would do better in a new city of the Midwest and transferred to Cleveland in 1858, he left his wife Bridget's close family behind. Bridget's sister Elizabeth was almost a mother to her, as she had been born eighteen years before Bridget. Elizabeth had married Thomas Brennan, from New London, and was living in that whaling port. Thomas Joseph also left relatives in the East.

After the death of her husband, Thomas Joseph, in the spring of 1874, Bridget Quinlan is listed in Cleveland directories up through the year 1875–76 as the widow of T. J. Quinlan in the house at 208 Woodland Avenue with her son, William Joseph, who was a bookkeeper. In the directories for 1876–77, neither Bridget nor William Joseph appear. Most likely once the engagement was contracted between Ella and James O'Neill (sometime in late summer of 1876) Bridget moved with her son and daughter to join her elder sister in New London, where (with James O'Neill acting at the Union Square Theater in New York) they would be close enough for the engaged couple to see each other from time to time. After the wedding and honeymoon, the bridal couple made a visit back to Cleveland (on their way to California). Her brother William was still there for he is listed in the 1878 directory as "flour and feed" in the Quinlan home on Woodland Avenue. He apparently sold the house that year, for he is not in the 1880 directory, but reappears as "grocer" at a new address on 465 Detroit Street in 1881.

From Cleveland James O'Neill and Ella went on to Chicago and then San Francisco, where he was rooted for the next three years as leading man in stock. After that he formed his own touring company, and from then on needed to take his summer vacations near New York City, the theatrical headquarters of the country. The first few years, James O'Neill took his family to Orient, Long Island. Afterward, when he began making big money through *Monte Cristo,* he began to think of establishing a permanent summer residence — particularly with his wife's yearning for a real home. The little fishing village of New London, still very rural at the time, was a natural for this, since Ella would have both her mother and her Aunt Elizabeth nearby.

All this was extinct history for Eugene O'Neill, who never knew his grandmother. She died in New London at the end of July 1887, more than a year before he was born. Also, he was just two—with most of his infancy spent touring the country—when his Great-Aunt Elizabeth died in New London on December 29, 1890. Thus, although he grew up knowing his Brennan and Sheridan cousins in New London summers, he had no memory of his mother's close relations who had first made New London an excellent choice for her permanent summer home.

In at least one case, O'Neill's lack of facts about his mother's past actually worked against the expression of his basic ideas in *Long Day's Journey into Night.* The truth, in this case, would have served his symbolism much better than the story he created. Telling his son Edmund that his grandfather was not the great noble gentleman his mother recalls, although "good company," Eugene O'Neill's James Tyrone adds, "He was prosperous enough too, in his wholesale grocery business." But he became at forty an addicted champagne drinker and it killed him quickly—"that and the consumption."

O'Neill scrambled the facts here. The wholesale grocer in Ella O'Neill's family was her brother William Joseph Quinlan, not her father, as the directories of Cleveland have shown, with his listings first as "flour and feed" in 1878, and then as "grocer." What became of him is not clear. By 1884 he had vanished from the Cleveland directories. Perhaps he moved to another city at this point. He does not figure in O'Neill's play, and it appears that Eugene knew little about him. Perhaps he, like Ella's mother, Bridget Quinlan, had died before Eugene O'Neill's birth in 1888.

At any rate, Thomas Joseph Quinlan, Ella's father, was never a grocer. He had been city circulator for the *Cleveland Plain Dealer* in the years before James O'Neill arrived in Cleveland. Had Eugene only known it, in his father's first year at Ellsler's Academy of Music in 1870–71, the directories show that Thomas Joseph Quinlan had gone into business with Ambrose Spirnaugle (listed as "bartender" for the year before) to form in 1870–71 "Quinlan and Spirnaugle retail dealers in wines, liquors, cigars, tobacco, and smokers' goods" at 204 Superior Street, an enterprise that continued until Quinlan's death in May 1874. The following year, A. Spirnaugle is listed as "saloon" at 154 Seneca Street.

From this it becomes clear that the truth, had he only known it, would have given Eugene O'Neill all the fated connection of drinking from her father to her husband to her sons for Mary Tyrone in the play. In fact, Quinlan and Spirnaugle sold liquor probably by the glass as well as by the bottle from a bar serviced by the bartender Ambrose Spirnaugle. That would have brought James O'Neill very quickly into sociable contact with the other proprietor, Quinlan. The play story of the sudden champagne drinking on the part of Mary's father is both less vivid and less convincing than the real story that Eugene never knew.

Naturally O'Neill could not be historically accurate with so much of his family history a blank to him. But it was not lack of information alone that brought certain of the facts contrary to reality into his play. The pressure within him of other crucial memories shaped and took over his story. For instance, in *Long Day's Journey into Night*, part of Mary Tyrone's terror at the possibility that her son is tuberculous comes from the fact that her beloved father died of that disease. Ella Quinlan's father, Thomas J. Quinlan, did not die of consumption if the notice of his death in the *Cleveland Plain Dealer* of May 26, 1874, is correct, for it declares, "Mr. Thomas J. Quinlan died at his residence no. 208 Woodland Avenue at three o'clock this morning after a short illness." Even a galloping consumption that was galloping very fast would never have been described as a "short illness."

Eugene O'Neill's wife Agnes had suffered from her father's death by tuberculosis. Toward Agnes, O'Neill felt something of the guilt he had felt all his life toward his mother, believing himself, as he did, somehow responsible for her addiction to drugs. In November and December of 1926, Agnes found that her father, Teddy Boulton, an impecunious artist who had been down on his luck for many years, had become dangerously ill of tuberculosis. As O'Neill wrote Boulton at the sanatorium in Shelton, Connecticut, where he lay, "It pained me like hell to realize that T.B., my old enemy, had taken a fall out of you. Also I know from my own experience what you must be going through now. The first weeks at a San. or a hospital are the devil's own for getting one at the bottom of depression." Eugene O'Neill had seen to it that his father-in-law had the expert opinion of his own tuberculosis specialist at Gaylord Farm back in 1913, Dr. Lyman, so that he could write, "Doctor Lyman's reports to me have been most encouraging." Nevertheless it became evident soon after that Agnes's father was hopelessly sick; he was dead by the spring of 1927.

Those days were painful for both Agnes and Eugene O'Neill, for their marriage was also dying. Eugene O'Neill found himself torn by the love of two women, his new love, Carlotta Monterey, and his old love and marriage partner for nine years, Agnes. No wonder he felt undermined by guilt. The memory of that guilt, and the strong link he perceived between his own fears of that old enemy tuberculosis and those for Agnes's father gave him the elements for the story he created years later for his family play. Not his grandfather's death but that of his father-in-law gave him the boy's guilt feelings toward his mother and her overwhelming fears for him.

Whatever memories of Agnes entered this play, it was Carlotta, Eugene O'Neill's wife as he wrote, who came into it so pervasively as to transform the character of Mary Tyrone, in part, into herself. Carlotta, not Agnes, like his mother was concerned with beauty in clothes and house and always looked "fashionable" and elegant. Mary Tyrone's entirely fictional wedding dress was never based on Ella Quinlan's, but O'Neill did find an actual model for the dress of the play in Carlotta's magnificent yellow satin gown for her "coming out in London" when she was about seventeen years old. Her marriage to her first husband, John Moffat, came soon after. He was, she told me, a "Britisher of very good family." (They were married on March 31, 1911, in New York, and Carlotta filed for a divorce from him on August 21, 1914, in the Superior Court of California, County of Alameda.)

This very costly coming-out dress had all the elements that O'Neill selected for Mary Tyrone to recall of her wedding dress, although Carlotta's gown, which was designed for evening wear, had a décolleté neckline and was bright yellow — details inappropriate for a wedding. O'Neill's account of the fine features of Mary's gown came from Carlotta's explanation to him as they examined a formal sepia photograph of Carlotta modeling it in the photographer's pose of fingering a long pearl necklace. Like Carlotta's, Mary's gown was made of "shimmering" satin, trimmed, like hers, with duchesse lace on the boned basque; ruffles of duchesse lace formed the short sleeves. Finally, like Carlotta's coming-out dress, Mary Tyrone's wedding gown was elaborately draped in folds at the back to create a "bustle effect," making for a short train twisted into full view for the photograph. So the mythical wedding dress that O'Neill attributed to the mother in *Long Day's Journey* came from a romantic image of his own wife Carlotta in her youth and from her own detailed description of that sumptuous costume of her girlhood.

Carlotta also contributed to Mary Tyrone the afflictions she was suffering as an aging woman in 1940, while O'Neill was creating the play. There is no hint in the biographical record that O'Neill's mother ever suffered as does Mary Tyrone from "rheumatism" in her hands. Although O'Neill used the 1912 term, he was certainly thinking of the arthritis that stiffened Carlotta's fingers and swelled her knuckles. His mother had never been impeded in her piano playing by rheumatism. But Carlotta's hands pained her dreadfully as she typed her husband's manuscripts. In those days O'Neill kept noting in his *Work Diary* "Carlotta's arthritis bad again" or Carlotta "in bed — arthritis bad." He attributed Carlotta's arthritis to Mary Tyrone because it symbolized perfectly the way that life and forces within us prevent us from achieving our dreams. Mary's loss of her hope of becoming a concert pianist is movingly visible in the ruin of her hands.

Similarly, O'Neill was thinking of Carlotta when he gave Mary Tyrone eye trouble. This lifelong problem for Carlotta became particularly acute while O'Neill was writing this play. In January 1939 his *Work Diary* records that he and Carlotta went to San Francisco for an eye examination by Dr. Barkan because she "has been having trouble — probably brought on by typing my handwriting!" No wonder the guilt he felt toward Carlotta — whom he always thought of as being not only his wife and mistress, but also his "Mother" — resurrected his feelings of guilt toward his mother as he was dramatizing the way in which all four Tyrones are guilty, yet innocent, of frustrating each other's most impelling dreams.

By February 19, 1939, Carlotta was in Stanford University Hospital for an eye operation, and O'Neill was tormented by "sleepless" nights worrying about her. Even after Carlotta returned home and was able, by March 4, to dispense with the care of a trained nurse, O'Neill felt—as he noted in his *Work Diary*— "still too upset to work." From that time on, Carlotta had unrelenting difficulties with her eyes. As late as May 1962, long after O'Neill's death, Carlotta was still reporting, "I have not been very well—my eyes have been very bad." So attributing this trouble of Carlotta to the play mother vividly illustrated her battering by a long journey through life.

In fact, Carlotta became so powerfully part of the mother character that O'Neill ascribes to Mary Tyrone Carlotta's youthful hopes, since he really could not have known his mother's. Like his mother, Carlotta had been educated by nuns. For several years she boarded and studied at St. Gertrude's Academy in the Rio Vista Convent of California. After a lonely childhood, Hazel Tharsing—her name before she adopted the flamboyant "Carlotta Monterey"—had attached herself to the nuns with a desperate need to win their love and approval. In fact, as her mother Nellie Tharsing later revealed, Hazel would get up at four o'clock in the morning to be sure she had gotten her lessons letter-perfect. In fact, she was under so much stress to appear perfect that she suffered a nervous breakdown at the age of fourteen.

Mary Tyrone's admission that she wanted to become a nun also derives from Carlotta, not Ella Quinlan. The nuns advised Carlotta, because of her Protestant background, to give herself time to be sure that she wished to convert and that she truly had a vocation. All of this Carlotta later confided to her husband, Eugene. She told me (many years later) that she did not know he had used her own girlhood dream of wanting to become a nun until she was typing his handwritten manuscript of *Long Day's Journey into Night*. Carlotta was humorously indignant at this cavalier theft of her own life story.

As for Mary's other dream of becoming a concert pianist, O'Neill was using the fact that his mother had majored in piano at St. Mary's Academy and certainly had graduated with honors as an accomplished pianist. But Mary Ellen Quinlan never had Mary's exalted goal of becoming a concert pianist. In those days—before Edison's invention of the phonograph and the development of radio brought recorded music into every home—any competent pianist had many, less demanding, opportunities for remunerative employment. Besides, musical ability added to a young woman's attractions as a marriage partner. In the two years between her graduation from St. Mary's Academy and her marriage to James O'Neill, there is no evidence that Mary Ellen Quinlan made the slightest effort to initiate any kind of professional career as a pianist.

Nor did she take those years to study abroad, as Mary Tyrone tells us she had wanted to do.

A very different convent girl — Carlotta — had in mind a professional career in music and not only wanted to but did go abroad to cultivate her promising contralto and to study dance and pantomime at Sir Beerbohm Tree's Academy of Dramatic Arts in London. She was bent on a professional career in musical comedy. Carlotta later liked to talk of being educated in Europe, for she had also studied, after London, at a finishing school in Paris, but her daughter Cynthia believed she went there because John Moffat's sister had studied there, and he wanted her to take on an aristocratic manner for meeting his wealthy family. Certainly Carlotta gave up her professional dreams to marry Moffat. Months before her divorce was finalized in 1915, Carlotta had already gone back to the stage in musical comedy. She toured with Lou Tellegen in *Taking Chances*, and her high point came in 1915 when she became leading lady in *The Bird of Paradise*, playing the role of a Hawaiian beauty, singing and dancing hulas.

Of course, Carlotta's dream of starring in musical comedy would have been all wrong for the image O'Neill was creating of Mary Tyrone. He probably made Mary's dream that of becoming a concert pianist because it fit his mother's degree in piano and because he knew something of the idealism and unremitting work that went into such an objective from his close friend Saxe Commins's wife, Dorothy, who as a concert pianist knew from experience its competitive difficulties — particularly with the loss of opportunities during the world economic depression of the 1930s. So for Mary Tyrone's lost hopes, O'Neill blended Carlotta's dreams with Ella O'Neill's piety and her musical history, raised to a more exalted level by the example of Dorothy Commins.

From Carlotta, too, Eugene took the peculiar loathing of theatrical touring that embitters Mary Tyrone. Ella O'Neill had indeed always wanted a beautiful permanent home and regretted having only a transient summer house with most of the year spent moving from city to city and hotel to hotel. But the sordid image of a succession of "dirty" rooms in cheap hotels conjured by Mary Tyrone's complaints does not really come from his mother's experience. For one thing, James O'Neill played in only the larger cities, not in the "hick" towns where hotel accommodations were minimal. When he had a series of one-night stands in different cities, in later years he usually sent his wife ahead with his advance man to the next big city, where she would be comfortable in a good hotel. Also, we know from Eugene's references to how his parents lived in New York hotels that they took not a room but a suite with living room, bedroom (two when one of the children was with them), kitchen, and bath, all well and even luxuriously furnished.

On the other hand, Carlotta's experience of touring on the road had filled her with disgust. In part, some of her bitterness came from the fact that, though beautiful, she lacked the magic for greatness in acting. The shows she toured with were not prestigious enough to play exclusively in larger cities. After her tour in *The Bird of Paradise*, she declared in 1916 that she would rather "not work at all" than "go on the road." She found it horribly distasteful: "the middle-of-the-night 'jump'; the stuffy, dirty hotel rooms; the stomach-racking meals; the loneliness." In fact, she left the theater for a second time that year of 1916 for a second disastrous and short-lived marriage, this time to Melvin C. Chapman Jr.

Later, Carlotta's loathing for the road spread to the entire profession, and as late as 1961 she was declaring emphatically that she hated acting, hated the theater. When O'Neill wrote *Long Day's Journey into Night* in 1940, Carlotta's very vocal disgust with touring and an actor's life echoed in his mind for Mary Tyrone, rather than any complaints his mother might have made back in 1912. So in some ways Mary Tyrone came to be as much a portrait of his third wife as of his mother.

An invasion of his characters as powerful as Carlotta's was that of Eugene himself — and not at all restricted to the character of Edmund Tyrone, who represents his youthful self. Of course, as dramatist, he had to enter all his characters and fight out their fight with them. Accordingly, he had maximum temptation to attribute to them — that is, to his father, mother, and brother — some of his own pressing emotions as he wrote.

Eugene was able to infuse a bit of himself into the character of Mary Tyrone, thereby merging his mother's convent years with his own, for, like his mother, Eugene had been taught by nuns. At the age of seven Eugene had begun boarding at a convent-school, Mount St. Vincent on the Hudson, which was primarily a school for girls but also took a few little boys, often the younger brothers of the girls. In *Long Day's Journey into Night*, he looks back to his own time, as well as his mother's, among the nuns, when he had had an absolute belief in a kindly universe run for the benefit of humanity by loving heavenly powers.

Most of O'Neill's memories of religious piety are from his boyhood at Mount St. Vincent. The crucifixion that is really a resurrection in the final scene of *Days without End*, for instance, was really a remembrance of Brumidi's altarpiece in the chapel of St. Vincent, with its crucified Christ seemingly already bounding up to eternal life in heaven. No wonder, then, that he placed Mary Tyrone's vision of being blessed by the Virgin in her wish to become a nun at the shrine where he himself had worshipped the Holy Mother as a boy.

Mary Tyrone recalls that she had seen the Virgin smiling in blessing when she prayed for guidance in her wish to become a nun at the shrine of Our Lady of Lourdes on a little island in the lake at her convent school. Carlotta had had no such vision, nor had O'Neill's mother. If Ella Quinlan had any vision of the Virgin at St. Mary's Academy, it would likely have taken place in the Holy House of Loreto, the shrine there, in replica of The House of Mary, or the Santa Casa, in Loreto, Italy. As a boy at St. Vincent, Eugene himself had often crossed the little bridge to the tiny island on Lourdes Lake, where Our Lady's Grotto stood. He was bringing his own childhood piety into substantiating Carlotta's dream attributed to his mother in the character of Mary Tyrone.

The only authentic memory of his mother's schooldays that Mary Tyrone echoes is her admiration for Mother Elizabeth. Mother Elizabeth would certainly have been prominent in whatever recollections Ella O'Neill might have shared with her son of her schooldays. Mother Elizabeth founded the music department at St. Mary's Academy and directed it when Ella was a student there.

The only other nun Mary Tyrone recalls in detail came, as did the vision of the Virgin, not out of recollections by O'Neill's mother, but out of Eugene's own memories of St. Vincent on the Hudson. Mary Tyrone recalls lovingly Sister Martha, who was old and a "little cranky," but somehow a reassuring presence who could cure her of any ills. Recalling his own schooldays, Eugene asked Joseph McCarthy, who had been one of the boys with him in the stone foreman's cottage at St. Vincent, "Do you ever think of Sister Martha who used to knuckle us on the bean? And Sister Gonzaga? They often come back to me." So he has Sister Martha come back to his mother via Mary Tyrone, his mother's stand-in, in this intimate family play.

As powerfully as O'Neill put Carlotta and his childhood self into the mother character, he put his adult self of 1940 into his representation of his father as James Tyrone in the play. At the time Eugene was writing it, he had reached a crisis of exasperation with his son by Agnes, Shane O'Neill. All his own pain and disillusionment as the father of a bitterly disappointing child went into his representation of James Tyrone's frustration of hopes for his son Jamie. Something of Eugene's curdled feelings over long years toward Agnes, as well as his anger at what she was making of his children, entered into and rendered far more resentful the criticisms of the play father than those of his own father had been.

Yet Shane's history and that of O'Neill's brother Jamie were totally dissimilar. Jamie had been a brilliant student at the high school at Notre Dame until his discovery that his mother, whom he had idolized, had become addicted to drugs. As James O'Neill wrote to the president of Notre Dame, the Reverend Andrew Morrissey, CSC, on August 27, 1894, Jamie had then "lost heart" for his studies and suddenly became "devoid of ambition." So James decided the boy might be stimulated by a total change: in September he transferred Jamie to Georgetown University and then to the New York area to finish his high school credits at St. John's Preparatory School, from which he would enter Fordham University in 1896.

The change apparently worked, and Jamie received top grades at Fordham until he smashed his academic career in 1899 by a gross breach of the rules, presaging Eugene's suspension from Princeton eight years later. Whatever Jamie did, it certainly had nothing to do with his academic record, for up until the end he was receiving prizes and distinction in English composition, Greek, Latin, and elocution, and even in chemistry and mathematics.

Eugene O'Neill's son Shane left no such eminent record at any of the expensive private schools to which Agnes sent him. When Shane did badly at one place, Agnes would (without consulting Eugene) simply transfer him to another. All of Eugene's letters to Shane in these years before the writing of Long Day's Journey into Night urge him to "dig down and get to work." But work was the last thing Shane wanted to do. Instead, he wrote his father in the depths of the Great Depression of the 1930s asking for $400 to buy an outboard motorboat.

Eugene O'Neill replied that he could not afford such a sum at this time. Moreover, to deserve such gifts, Shane had to prove he was not "lazily expecting something for nothing," but was "willing to work for it." During the period when newspapers were full of stories of O'Neill's closeness to death right after being awarded the Nobel Prize, he had no word of either congratulations or later concern from his teenage son. Afterward, he told Shane that if he wanted to be a son in more than name, "you will have to learn to act with a little more decent consideration and gratitude," because "you can't expect something for nothing even from fathers."

When Shane's disasters at schools led to his unexpected return to Lawrenceville Academy, where he had already failed and dropped out, O'Neill told him that instead of feeling sorry for himself he should get to work. "Don't you know you are being given a better break than nine out of ten boys in this country get?" The sudden shift back there after Shane had been all for the ranch school he had been attending in Colorado led his father to remark: "It is nonsense for you to expect me to believe you suddenly decided it was no good. When you were here, you said it was a fine school. So what is the truth? Were you fired or what?" Shane decided that what he would really like was for his father to buy him a farm so he could raise horses. O'Neill told him: "How the devil can you ever expect to learn how to raise horses unless you start at the bottom? Do you think you know enough on the basis of having gone for a few months to a ranch prep school in Colorado?" If he really loved horses as much as he thought he did, O'Neill suggested, "you would rather start working in a stable on a breeding farm than do anything else in the world." And O'Neill added, the trouble was that Shane expected to "start at the top" without taking the trouble to learn how to do it.

To his old friend and lawyer, Harry Weinberger, Eugene O'Neill exploded that Shane had been to too many schools already. What he needed was to take a job. "The whole point is that Shane is a Boulton [that is, like his mother's family] and just naturally dumb and shiftless like all the rest of them where education and books are concerned. Not one of them ever got through any school." He felt that he had done more for Shane than he deserved "without ever receiving the slightest sign of gratitude or appreciation. I am through — until such time as he proves himself not to be a parasitic slob of a Boulton."

With all his exasperation at Shane's "lazy weakness," O'Neill could not help releasing some of it in the play father's disappointment in his son Jamie, where he speaks of Jamie as if, instead of a long record of brilliant academic achievement, the boy had been a hopelessly lazy failure like Shane. James Tyrone tells his son, "All you did was get fired in disgrace from every college you went to." In reality, however, James O'Neill Jr. had done brilliantly everywhere up until his deliberate act of rebellion near the end of his career at Fordham University.

After that, Jamie O'Neill had himself opted to follow his father's career. He had not been guilty of expecting — as James Tyrone accuses his son of expecting, and as Shane appeared to have expected — "to sit back like a lazy lunk and sponge on me for the rest of your life." Certainly, James Tyrone was repeating Eugene's own complaint of Shane when he declared, "I wouldn't give a damn if you ever displayed the slightest sign of gratitude." It was Eugene O'Neill — not his father — who realized that his son had always taken the easy way out and was — so he said — "never willing to start at the bottom." Certainly Eugene O'Neill ended by making the play father more acrimonious than ever James O'Neill, with his poise and equilibrium, had been.

Another of the ways in which Eugene O'Neill took over the character of James Tyrone is in the representation of his drinking. In the play, the drinking of the three male characters is identical, both a cause and a result of Mary Tyrone's drug addiction. Historically, however, there was a great difference in the drinking of the three O'Neill men. James O'Neill was primarily a social drinker and, being Irish, a cultural drinker. He never was controlled by a desire to drink and never allowed alcohol to interfere with his responsibilities.

On the other hand, both his sons were alcoholics. Jamie was a continual alcoholic; Eugene was a periodical alcoholic, with long stretches of abstinence broken by bouts of compulsive drinking for a few weeks at a time several times each year, rising to a crescendo when he was under stress, such as in the months after Beatrice jilted him or the year when his marriage to Agnes began to break up.

Except for three or four brief relapses after his first year of reform from drinking in 1926, O'Neill remained teetotal thereafter. By 1940 both his own drinking and his father's were altogether past tense. Thus he came to mix memories of his own conquered compulsion to drink with his father's hefty but never compulsive consumption of alcohol in his depiction of James Tyrone. One of the bitterest blows to Mary Tyrone's romantic dream of marriage comes from O'Neill's own remembrances of guilt rather than from anything his father ever did.

In the third act, Mary Tyrone recalls that during their honeymoon her husband drank so much that his barroom friends had to dump him, comatose, outside his hotel room. She tells of how she waited fearfully for hours in that "ugly" hotel room, as she would wait during the years that followed for the return of her drunken husband. James Tyrone tells her — as James O'Neill often asserted — that he never in his life missed a performance from drink.

Certainly no such degrading episode happened to Eugene O'Neill's mother on her honeymoon in the mountains. From all reports, James never drank beyond his control. Thomas Dorsey Jr. reported to me that he often acted as bartender for the weekly talk sessions that Thomas Dorsey Sr., James O'Neill, and Supreme Court Justice Edward White held during the New London summers. At those times, Dorsey added, "I've seen him pretty well loaded, but never that he couldn't handle himself."

On the other hand, during his drunken days, Eugene O'Neill often deliberately sought oblivion. Hutchins Hapgood recalled a time during the early days in Provincetown when he, Eugene, and Terry Carlin were suddenly joined during a genial drinking session by two horrible degenerates in the town whom Terry had taken up with in accord with his belief in the hidden poetry of lost souls. As Hapgood reported, "Gene took one look at them and began to drink with great rapidity. Certainly within the hour he had drunk himself into a state of complete insensibility." While "Terry and I put Gene to bed" — so Hapgood continued — they "compared notes," and both decided that Gene had acted in "self-preservation." He had "sympathy" for even such specimens as these, but he "couldn't endure them."

Neither the comatose drunken husband nor the lonely young woman awaiting him in a cheap hotel room came out of Ella O'Neill's experience. Far from
a bewildered neophyte in an alien world, Eugene's mother—with her convent
experience of friends training for the stage—had entered fully into her husband's profession, devoting all her energies to supporting and assisting his career, so that the theater was as much her home as his. From the beginning of
their marriage, she was always with him there, helping him to learn his roles,
attending and commenting on rehearsals, even working as his dresser for important performances. And in her youth and good health during the early
years of their touring, she accepted his more grueling train journeys from city
to city as staunchly and calmly as he did.

When they were in a city with friends or family, she would entertain them
in a box at his performances. Otherwise she was backstage throughout. Once
her children were born, she always engaged a nurse for them so that she was
free to devote herself to assisting her husband. The only times James O'Neill
left her by herself was when a men's club—Elks or Knights of Columbus, usually—invited him and some of his company for a celebration after the performance. Since these occasions were very important for building the reputation
and drawing power of an actor, Ella O'Neill took them for granted and would
not have waited up for her husband. Any waiting she did was always in the best
hotel the town offered.

Mary Tyrone's loneliness and her experiences of desertion so necessary for
the tragic meaning of O'Neill's play were very different from the actual story of
his parents' marriage. It was Carlotta—as she said—who suffered from the
"loneliness" and the "dirty hotel rooms" when she toured as an actress; and the
alcoholic who drank himself into "complete insensibility" was O'Neill himself
during his drinking years. It was he who had guilty memories of giving pain to
women he loved through his alcoholism, as when his relapses into intoxication
led Beatrice to break their engagement in 1916 and almost lost him
Carlotta during their trip to China in 1928. The tragic destiny of the Tyrones essential for the meaning of O'Neill's play was not a factual history of his parents'
union. O'Neill took materials from his own old sins to depict the play father.

Another reason the play could not confine itself to historical accuracy lay in
the fact that O'Neill had to compress events from many years and an entire
lifetime—that is, the long day's journey—into one day of play time and a few
hours of acting time in a theater. Chronology inevitably underwent drastic
distortion. As a result, part of the play's action includes events that could not
and did not take place in the summer of 1912 but a good seven years after
in a very different context. The effect of that deformed chronology makes

James Tyrone appear strangely contradictory. It also accentuates his supposedly miserly attributes to the point of virtual lunacy.

In *Long Day's Journey*, James Tyrone is presented as having the highest opinion of bonded bourbon as tonic and aperitif so that a tray of drinks is habitually served before meals in his home, and both his sons are sure that their penchant for drink comes from him. His toast to his sons as they imbibe is "Drink hearty!" so he clearly is encouraging their drinking. Nevertheless, when Jamie and Edmund "sneak" an extra drink before the ones their father gave them as aperitifs, they try to hide their depredations by adding water to the bottle so the level does not go down.

Later in the play we learn that James Tyrone keeps a padlock on the door to the cellar where the whiskey is stored. Jamie has already picked an earlier lock to get at the alcohol, and the father has had to put on a burglarproof lock to foil Jamie's thefts. As far as historical reality goes, these events set in 1912 appear both contradictory (in that the father both encourages and prohibits drinking) and extreme. They make the play father seem to be ludicrously parsimonious.

But the padlock and the restraints acquire a totally different significance in the actual history of the O'Neills, for they took place after Prohibition had been in force for some time. Thomas Dorsey Jr. told me that when James O'Neill saw that Prohibition was inevitable — and no one could tell for how many years it would last — he bought a great deal of excellent whiskey to give himself a comfortable supply in the dry times to come. But, as Thomas Dorsey Jr. reported: "It went sooner than he expected because Jimmy would tap it on the sly."

Jamie O'Neill was also more desperately alcoholic in 1919 and 1920 than in 1912 because his acting career had lasted only as long as his father could stipulate Jamie's employment as part of his own contract in the supporting roles he played for Liebler and Company after dissolving his own company. By the time of his father's partial retirement, James Jr. was already too well known for going on stage muddled with alcohol to get jobs on his own. After James O'Neill retired thereafter, Jamie fell into hopeless unemployment and began drinking even more destructively than before. Thomas Dorsey Jr. recounted that in the last year of his life, James tried to employ Jamie as rent collector for his New London properties. By then James's stockpile of whiskey had been fully depleted, so Jamie spent all the rent money he collected for the ruinously expensive and dangerous bootleg whiskey that would ultimately blind and then kill him in 1923.

Eugene O'Neill's autobiographical play is not autobiographical in the sense of presenting an accurate family history. Even the characters — although rich in traits of his mother, father, brother, and himself — are invaded by emotions and actions foreign to their originals. Mary Tyrone dreams Carlotta's dreams, is afflicted by her physical ailments, and also takes from Carlotta her intense bitterness toward a touring actor's life. James Tyrone is invaded by Eugene O'Neill's disillusionment with his son Shane and in his drinking takes on guilts that in reality belonged to Eugene, not his father. Events that never took place in the O'Neill family shape the destiny of the Tyrones.

In fact, had O'Neill restricted himself to an accurate retelling of his family's story, the play would never have developed into a meaningful work of art. It would never have transcended a few lives to epitomize the moving tragedy implicit in human destiny. Only bits and pieces of what makes for tragedy are integral to a factually accurate history of the O'Neills. The profound tragedy, the autobiographical drama written, as Eugene O'Neill declared it was, "in tears and blood" grew out of truths that lie beyond a literal fidelity to outer events.

CHAPTER NINE

James Tyrone

Eugene O'Neill had no wish for readers to take *Long Day's Journey into Night* as autobiography. He wanted them to see it as an exemplar of the tragedy pervasive in human existence, in the very nature of human life. Naturally, he took for his characters fictional names (partly or completely changed from those of his family). Nevertheless, the names chosen by O'Neill were faithful to the spirit and even the actual significance of the real names. He called the fated family "Tyrone," a name virtually synonymous in Irish history with "O'Neill."

When close Boston friends suggested to James O'Neill that he adopt a stage name less typically Irish than his actual one, which was likely to "militate against his success," he replied, "If the name 'O'Neill' was good enough for the Kings of Ireland in the days when the harp resounded through Tara's halls, it is good enough for me." When Eugene was five years old, his father opened on March 5, 1894, in San Francisco in an Irish historical play, written especially for him in blank verse by the California playwright William Greer Harrison, called *The O'Neill or The Prince of Ulster*. The story was set in 1562 and the protagonist was "Shane O'Neill, Earl of Tyrone and King of Ireland." The first scene opened on a wild glen in County Tyrone, and the concluding scene showed Shane O'Neill in the English court, triumphantly extracting a promise of home rule for Ireland from Queen Elizabeth.

Even at five years old, Eugene O'Neill probably saw some rehearsals and even a performance or two of this play. As soon as Eugene became a proficient reader, he became avid for Irish history, poring over the various accounts in his father's library. This passion enters into the setting for *Long Day's Journey into Night*, where O'Neill specified that the volumes had all been "read and reread." No wonder then that years later Eugene named his son by Agnes "Shane," after the heroic Shane O'Neill who had been Earl of Tyrone and

King of Ireland. No wonder either that he substituted "Tyrone" for "O'Neill" in this intimate family play.

The only alterations O'Neill made in the first names appeared in those for the character representing his mother and the one representing his youthful self. His mother's full name at birth was Mary Ellen Quinlan, but she was always called "Ella." By naming the mother character "Mary," Eugene O'Neill simply employed his mother's unused first name. The name "Mary" must have sounded particularly right to Eugene because his mother in her indestructibly girlish charm and her profound piety always bore for him strong associations with the Virgin Mother Mary of his own childhood piety.

As for the name he gave himself in the play, nothing could have been more in line with all of the acceptances of his early suicide attempt and his approaching destiny of dying that he had worked out in *The Iceman Cometh*. Eugene O'Neill simply swapped names in *Long Day's Journey into Night* with his long-dead brother Edmund. Having exchanged names, he also exchanged destinies with the baby who had died three years before his own birth in 1888. Thus in the play he became his mother's beloved lost baby and also became united—in the person of Edmund—with his entire family who were all together—Edmund O'Neill, James O'Neill, Mary Ellen O'Neill, and James O'Neill Jr.—in St. Mary's cemetery at New London, while he, Eugene, stood apart from them as he wrote, isolated in the world of 1940 from which they had all, one by one, vanished years ago.

Although O'Neill put some of his own failings and feelings into James Tyrone in the play, he meant, nevertheless, very consciously, to re-create his father in the character. Curiously enough, his account of his father's early years in Buffalo—the time most distant from him—is quite accurate historically. In *Long Day's Journey into Night*, Mary Tyrone tells us that James's father deserted wife and children "a year or so after they came to America" to return to Ireland. Later in the play, James Tyrone speaks bitterly of his father's dying in Ireland from mistaking rat poison for "flour or sugar or something." Of course Eugene O'Neill would not have known the dates for these events. His best information came of stories his father James O'Neill told of his childhood. The notes on James O'Neill's family left by the grandson (Manley Mallett— Eugene's second cousin) of James's sister Anastasia place the immigration of the O'Neills from Ireland to Buffalo, New York, in 1851. But James O'Neill's father, Edward O'Neill, first appears in the Buffalo city directory for 1854, where he was living at 74 Fifth Street. He and his family (wife, Mary, along with three boys and six girls) probably arrived in Buffalo sometime in 1853 to be included in the 1854 directory. In 1855 he is listed as "Edward O'Neill,

Mechanic, near boatyard," and in 1856 he is a "laborer" at West Side Terrace. Then he vanishes from the Buffalo directories, so his desertion of the family and return to Ireland probably took place in 1856. The flight came unquestionably because Edward O'Neill was elderly (sixty-five years old according to the Buffalo census of 1855), and by 1856 he was apparently too weak and sickly to do the heavy work as a "laborer" — such as unloading ships at the docks — which was all he could try for.

In 1856 Edward's son Richard had just died, and his son James, as James himself told his son Eugene, was apprenticed "at ten years old!" in "a machine shop." The Buffalo directory lists James O'Neill as "with Israel C. Ely, pump and block maker" on Water Street. So James Tyrone's recollections of working twelve hours a day for fifty cents a week echo what Eugene remembered of his father's stories of his youth, as does the account of a cruel eviction of the family left destitute by the flight of their only adult male and breadwinner. To pay his fare back to Ireland, Edward O'Neill seems to have decamped with the family's last pennies. His wife Mary was so shocked and shamed by his flight that she announced herself in the 1857 Buffalo directory as "Mary Ann O'Neill, widow of Edward." Even though her husband was still alive, she was as alone and helpless as if he had died. In fact, he lived with a sister and her family in Tinneranny, Kilkenny, until July 18, 1862, and might well have lived longer had one of the women not accidentally used poison in the cookery, as roughly alluded to in the play. The coroner's inquest reported that the entire family had been made deathly ill from arsenic — perhaps mistaken for baking soda — baked into the soda bread. Edward's was the only fatality because, the inquest concluded, he was both old and "sickly."

Luckily, at the time of Edward's flight, Mary and her children were not without friends. When they had arrived in Buffalo, there were other O'Neills in the city, though there is no evidence that any were family. The 1854 directory listed William O'Neill, a machinist, working for J. A. Pitts, a threshing machine maker. He was still with Pitts through 1856, when he was joined there by John O'Neill, an "iron finisher," perhaps a brother. Despite their lack of family connection, they came to the rescue of Mary O'Neill when she and her children were thrown onto the street after the flight of Edward: in the 1857 Buffalo directory, the widow Mary Ann O'Neill is listed as living at Carolina Street near Sixth Street, and William O'Neill, machinist, is listed as living and working at this same address.

Whether or not John and William O'Neill were helpful in getting Mary and her children from Buffalo to Cincinnati, the fatherless family had in any case moved there before the end of 1857. She is listed in the 1858 Cincinnati directory as "Mrs. M. O'Neill," and she appears to have set up as a rooming house keeper at 359 Broadway there, a position that would bring her enough money to pay the rent and feed her children. A William J. O'Neill, clerk—not William O'Neill, machinist, from Buffalo—is listed as living with her at 359 Broadway and working at 43 Main Street.

John O'Neill remained in Buffalo for part of 1858, for he is listed in that city directory as a machinist at 100 Sixth Street, but he must have moved to Cincinnati before the end of that year, for he is in its directory for 1859 as a "pipe fitter" at the Eagle Iron Works, with no home address listed. Probably he was already rooming with Mary O'Neill at 359 Broadway, for he is listed as having that home address in 1860, with a shop at 25 West Fourth Street. William J. O'Neill was still rooming at 359 Broadway that year listed as a salesman. John disappears from the Cincinnati directory in 1861—probably recruited for the Civil War—but at this point William O'Neill, machinist, suddenly appears in the Cincinnati directory with a shop at 92 West Fourth Street and his home address with Mary O'Neill at 359 Broadway. William J. O'Neill was also still living there, and, apparently to distinguish himself from William the machinist, called himself in the directory for that year "W. J. J. O'Neill, clerk."

By the outbreak of the Civil War in 1861, Mary had lightened her load by relegating her younger children to the homes of her older daughters, who by that time were married. In the 1860 Cincinnati census, Anastasia O'Neill is living with her older sister Anne, who was married to James Jones, a file maker. At the beginning of the Civil War, Mary's son Edward was in the Union army, and her son James—as he himself told it long afterward (in 1917)—"exchanged the trade of machinist for the profession of clothier," going to work in a store one of his brothers-in-law had just set up at Norfolk, Virginia, selling cloth and military uniforms in what was a marshaling point for the Union army during much of the war.

The brother-in-law was not likely to have been the husband of James O'Neill's older sister Josephine, for he was a "saloon keeper" and would not have had the know-how to enter the clothier's trade. Nor would he have been Anne's husband, the file maker. Unfortunately, there is no way to trace the brother-in-law or James O'Neill in Virginia because Norfolk discontinued publishing its city directory during the Civil War, and no family records or letters are known to have survived.

What happened to the clothier brother-in-law is not known, but the young James O'Neill returned to Cincinnati immediately with the ending of the war in the spring of 1865. His soldier brother Edward had died as a result of his war injuries, and his mother and younger sister Margaret, listed as "Maggie," no longer had the rooming house, and both appeared in the 1865 directory as "servants." James O'Neill took a job in Cincinnati with his brother-in-law James Jones, the file maker, since, as Pop Seaman would tell it much later, James O'Neill was "only a file cutter" when he first went on stage in Cincinnati. The file cutting very brief, for by the time the 1866 directory came out, James O'Neill was already listed as "actor," living at 238 East Pearl Street with "Maggie" and "Mary, widow."

So Eugene O'Neill was fusing two of his father's reminiscences when he had James Tyrone in his play recall his ten-year-old self as "learning to make files" in a dirty cold barn of a place. As a ten-year-old in Buffalo, James O'Neill was apprenticed to a "pump and block maker," and would not have been making files. It was fully ten years later that he had to learn to make files in his brother-in-law James Jones's shop in Cincinnati. It was after work in that city that, "as an established gallery god," James O'Neill happened to be playing billiards before the play in the National Saloon next door to the entrance to the National Theater when the stage manager rushed in looking for supers, and James went on stage to find his true profession at the age of twenty.

In the following years when he worked to overcome his heavy brogue to become famous for the beauty of his diction, James O'Neill maintained his connection with the two machinist O'Neills, William and John, who had come to his family's rescue when his father left them destitute. What happened to them is not known, but when the scandal of Nettie Walsh erupted right after James O'Neill's marriage to Ella in 1877, he submitted a sworn affidavit from John O'Neill, as a close witness to his life, denying the marriage Nettie claimed. In fact, John O'Neill was still close to James O'Neill at the time of his son Eugene's birth on October 16, 1888, in New York City. Thirty years later, in May 1918, the flattering reviews of O'Neill's play *Ile* brought to the young playwright a letter from Mrs. Elizabeth Murray, his nurse in the first weeks of his life. She recalled, "I carried you in my arms to the church the day you were christened, a beautiful baby." She reminded him that his godmother was Miss Anne Connors and "your godfather was Mr. John O'Neill." Whether or not Eugene knew what John O'Neill's role had been in rescuing his father from a destitute boyhood, he certainly knew that the trauma of desertion and destitution had shaped his father's life. When O'Neill came to write his family play in 1940, he made the early poverty a major force in deflecting James Tyrone and his family from fulfilling their highest ideals. Again and again, as his characters move deeper into the long day of their lives, they reveal how compulsive economies practiced by James Tyrone have brought on major tragedies in their lives.

In O'Neill's play, all four Tyrones are both guilty and yet innocent because their actions have been determined — against their wishes — by forces from their family past and accidents that befell them along the way. In fact, beyond all the conscious purposes of his play, Eugene O'Neill was wrestling in *Long Day's Journey into Night* with the entire question of guilt and innocence, trying to determine the extent to which any human being is responsible for the tragic failures in his life struggle. This question of guilt and responsibility and suffering had already been a theme in *The Iceman Cometh*, where an insupportable sense of guilt had both precipitated Hickey's tragic act and made the truth of it too agonizing for him to look upon it unprotected by a pipe dream. Moreover, the agony of guilt in the boy Donald Parritt had forced Larry to get off the grandstand, come to terms with death, and direct the boy out of pity to take release in oblivion. Similarly, in *Long Day's Journey into Night*, guilt is a major question, the innocent guilt of James Tyrone whose boyhood poverty has caused him — against all his conscious desires — to bring about, by way of a cheap doctor, Mary Tyrone's drug addiction with its destructive effect on himself and his sons.

As Eugene O'Neill saw it in his play, the traumas of his father's youth had left him with a permanent fear of spending money. Actually, this was not an accurate diagnosis. It was not lack or loss of money that precipitated James O'Neill's sudden bouts of panicky austerity. Only when an experience recalled his terrifying helplessness as a ten-year-old, powerless to save his deserted and destitute family, did James O'Neill begin wildly considering how he might cut back expenses — just as he must have tried to do in that terrible time of his childhood.

The old feelings of helplessness returned when Nettie Walsh refused, at the last minute, to give James O'Neill custody of the boy Alfie so he and Ella could adopt him and raise him as their son, along with Jamie. The expense of that, a lifetime commitment, would have been much, much more than that of paying off Nettie's blackmailing assaults on his purse whenever his tours brought him to Chicago. So it was not the expense, but the frustration of his efforts to set things straight that put James O'Neill in a panic. And it took the form — as in his boyhood — of searching out a way to save money.

As Elizabeth Robins noted, the panic took the shape this time of telling Ella that for his next tour he would not pay the "terrible expense" of a nurse for Jamie. The nurse was expensive, what with her salary, travel expenses equal to their own, and charges for sharing their first-class hotel suites. Of course, firing the nurse was hardly feasible if he wished — as he certainly did — the full support and assistance of his wife in his work. So this demand lasted only as long as the feeling of helplessness, and the nurse stayed. If Eugene experienced many of these resorts to economy on the part of his father, he did so because in his wild years he brought that feeling of helplessness to the fore as he destroyed, one after the other, all his father's efforts to render him independent and self-sufficient—first the university education, then the position in business, and finally, after his disastrous marriage, the hopeful openings abroad in Honduras and then in Argentina.

Nevertheless, Eugene O'Neill certainly knew in reality—although it would have undermined his tragedy had he put it into his play—that the uniform picture of parsimony he presented in James Tyrone was refuted by all the generous traits in the complex person of his father. Asked by a research group for anecdotes of his father, Eugene told them he would need to write a book "because he had many extraordinary contradictory sides to his character. I can't think of any one or two anecdotes that would give you a true picture."

By attributing his wife Carlotta's loathing of the dirty small town hotels she stayed at on her tours to Mary Tyrone, forced into them by her husband's parsimony, O'Neill was conveying a picture entirely unlike the way his parents lived while on tour. When Elizabeth Robins accompanied them on tour in 1881–82, James O'Neill talked her into spending the money so she could stay at the best hotels and eat at the best restaurants, as the O'Neills did. She noted, "Mr. O'Neill argues you have only one life, the world owes you a living, get the best you can. Go to the first class hotels, the best is none too good for you, besides it is false economy to eat bad food and sleep in poor rooms." There were many areas in which James believed in spending freely so as to get the best of everything. Certainly Eugene must have been aware that the literal truth about his family was far more complicated than—indeed very different from—the story he told about his characters to convey the tragedy of unrealized dreams. The only contradiction to parsimony in *Long Day's Journey* is James Tyrone's confession that when "full of whiskey" he has "thrown money" over bar counters to buy drinks for everyone and has lent money to sponges who would never pay it back. The facts of James O'Neill's life give a very different picture. Reports by his contemporaries testify again and again to an ideal of charity and generosity that actuated James throughout his life.

Fred Wren, his fellow actor, declared that James was "liberal, giving according to his means, which is ten times more than Rockefeller and Carnegie give. He does not teach a Sunday school class and never lets the world know of his charities." Tom Dorsey, James O'Neill's great crony in New London, described him as "a soft hearted man, always good for a touch." James's own philosophy was that "life is really worth living" if for no other reason than "the fortunate circumstances which enable one to come to the assistance of a fellow-being."

As one of James's Chicago friends, a drama critic, put it, "He never forgets a face or a name," for he had "a man's size heart of the warmest sort." Another summed up his portrait of James O'Neill by saying that he "gave freely to those less fortunate and to many charitable ends."

When he died, James O'Neill was mourned by the whole town of New London. The *New London Day* recalled that he first came to New London because he had relatives here, but he stayed out of love for the "Harbour town." "Mr. O'Neill was very democratic and sociable. He was easy of approach to anybody; he was affable, kind and courteous; he was kind-hearted and generous to a fault and it is an open secret that his acts of charity were many, while many of his acts of philanthropy will never be known. Among those of his own profession he was known as 'The man with a heart.'" He had always "a handshake and a smile for everyone."

The testimony from James's life record is a complete contradiction of the picture in *Long Day's Journey into Night* of James Tyrone as a compulsive miser except for flings of drunkenly sentimental profligacy in barrooms. Although, as Fred Wren had said, James O'Neill never let "the world know of his charities," some of them, by their very nature, could not remain secret. For instance, in October 1892 at Woonsocket, Rhode Island, James learned that the horses transporting his scenery had run away, throwing the driver to the ground and breaking his right arm and leg. Instantly, as the *New York Dramatic Mirror* reported, James "started a subscription for the teamster, heading it with $50." Also James did much to organize the Actors' Fund to assist theater people in financial difficulties.

When the fund was incorporated in June 1882, the elder O'Neill was one of the original members, paying his dues and making a donation of fifty dollars. From that time on he always added a "personal contribution" of at least twenty-five dollars (at that time a considerable sum). He was very active in the 1892 Fund Fair to raise money for the organization, and suggested required membership to all in the profession, as a form of insurance. Milton Nobles, one of his fellow managers, declared in a letter to the *New York Dramatic Mirror* of April 9, 1892, "I want to approve Mr. O'Neill's proposition that managers require members of their companies to join the Fund. I will go now a little farther, and state positively that hereafter a paid-up membership in the Fund will be a condition precedent to an engagement in my company."

When the Actors' Fund acquired a communal cemetery plot in 1886 (where Eugene's dear friend Jimmy Byth—destitute at his death—was buried long afterward), James O'Neill donated twenty-five dollars for a monument to be placed there. (Most donations ranged from one to three dollars.)

James O'Neill was also generous in donating his work through the many charity benefit performances he participated in throughout his life. As early as 1876 he was performing in New York City as Romeo to Sara Jewitt's Juliet for the annual Benefit of the Catholic Asylum. Other benefits he performed for ranged from one for the theater ushers (on May 31, 1894, in Canton, Ohio) to the Benefit for Madame Modjeska at the Metropolitan Opera House in New York on May 2, 1905, in which James O'Neill played Macbeth to Madame Modjeska's Lady Macbeth, in two scenes, and to Louis James's Macduff and John Malone's Banquo in another.

Certainly Eugene knew that about his father as well as anyone in New London. He was not writing accurate autobiography in Long Day's Journey into Night, much less any kind of record of the real reasons he had pride in his father. He was writing a universal tragedy of the ways he had observed, particularly in himself and his nearest and dearest, in which the family past and the accidents of life inevitably come between and frustrate the human struggle to live true to the highest ideals.

So his picture of James Tyrone as deflected from his loving kindness by a compulsive drive to get bargains and do everything in the cheapest way possible came much more out of the needs of his play and his tragic vision than out of family recollections. Eugene himself knew — and even prided himself in — the entirely opposite and contradictory side of his father's character in the question of whether to buy cheap or buy for lasting value.

Like James Tyrone in his play, O'Neill himself liked to feel he was getting a bargain. On his return to the United States from France in 1931, he gloated to the drama critic Brooks Atkinson that he had "snared" a slightly used second-hand Cadillac with over a thousand dollars off the price. No one, he declared, could have resisted such a "gift" from the worldwide depression. "Not I who have always been an A-One snob when it came to cars and boats, which must have speed, line, and class or 'we are not amused.' This snootiness dates back to early boyhood days. My father, the Count of Monte Cristo, always got me the classiest rowboats to be had, and we sported the first Packard car in our section of Connecticut, way back in the duster-goggles era." Certainly Eugene knew that his father, when it came to many things, bought not the cheapest but the "classiest" item "to be had." Before boats and automobiles, James O'Neill had chosen only the "classiest" in horses.

Of course he was always glad — as his son Eugene would be later in the question of the Cadillac — to get a bargain. But he aimed primarily at finding excellence. In "Mademoiselle Mephisto's Anecdotes" for the New York Clipper, September 29, 1900, there is an account of one such bargain. When

James O'Neill returned to New York City in May 1900 at the end of his theatrical tour, having "cash and to spare," he decided "to treat himself to the very best" in horses. "During his wanderings in and about theatrical territory, he came across a beauty of a team which he bought and settled for there and then, the price being quite a bit over a thousand dollars. The bargain was an exceptional one, for the pair was worth more than double the money. Giving the dealer his New London address, and being assured that the horses would be shipped that day, he hastened around to the Liebler offices, to acquaint the boys of his luck."

Instead of congratulating him, Tyler and Connor told him about recent newspaper stories of "how certain smart teams had been sold by sharpers at absurdly low figures, spot cash, and never delivered." Worried, James O'Neill "didn't wait for the elevator but tore down four flights, thence four blocks away to the little stable where he had paid out his money. The solitary hostler informed him that the proprietor had just driven away with the team which he was going to ship, though from what point he knew not, and that he would not return till next day.

"O'Neill asked around, got no answers, and returned full of misgivings to the Knickerbocker Building." Whereupon "George Tyler offered to bet his next month's income against a roasted peanut that he would never again behold horses or price. Bet not taken.

"Late in the evening he telegraphed to his place in New London, but no horses had been delivered." James was then sure he had been "buncoed," sent another telegram in the morning, "dashed around to interview the stable boy, and inquired at a neighboring livery only to learn that his stable had just recently been occupied by new tenants of whom nothing was known." On returning to the office, he found a New London telegram and read it aloud in a "husky voice." "Team just received in good order."

"Say, Tyler, I wish I'd risked that peanut," was James's only comment. The whole episode was typical of both James's often seeking the very best, bargain or no, and also of the conviction of his closest friends — later repeated by friends of his son Eugene — that, with his trust in and affection for his fellow men, he was very likely to be cheated.

Although he was never ostentatious, James did often succeed in getting the best. A case in point is the old New London farmhouse he bought for a summer home, with all its land, along the Thames River where it widens into Long Island Sound. According to the *Boston Times* of September 11, 1887, it had cost James $40,000. Long afterward (in 1948) when Eugene and Carlotta bought what Eugene called a "grand little place" on the ocean in Marblehead,

Massachusetts, which he "loved," he commented, "Reminds me of the first home my father bought in New London, also on the waterfront" where he had spent his summers when he was "a kid." He thought the Marblehead house might give him back "some roots — of seaweed" in the New England sea he had loved. "It is like coming home," he said, and made him "feel happier than in many years."

That first little farmhouse — bought with the original land and outbuildings, including a large barn in which James O'Neill kept his carriage and horses — was already being spoken of as James O'Neill's "home in New London, Connecticut," in the July 18, 1885, *New York Dramatic Mirror*, which announced that he had named the house Monte Cristo Cottage for the play that brought him the money to buy it. This first eighteenth-century cottage — a small, two-story white building without verandas, pointed out to me by Thomas Dorsey Jr. and others — was the only one ever to be called Monte Cristo by James and his family, contrary to later claims.

This modest house with trees around it overlooks the Thames River. There is a picture of Eugene O'Neill shortly before his third birthday seated on a rock in front of the house, drawing the boats moving in and out of Long Island Sound where the river pours into it.

In the summer of 1892 James O'Neill brought the artists doing the scenery of his new play *Fontenelle* to work in New London at the Lyceum Theater so he could supervise them. When dress rehearsals began at the end of August, Will Connor announced that "half of the week will be spent rehearsing in Boston and the remaining half at New London," it being easier to bring the actors to the scenery than vice versa. That gave James O'Neill the realization that he could always rehearse in New London, renting (and thus subsidizing) the Lyceum Theater for morning rehearsals, and building a more commodious house for the family so he could put up his company free in the old farmhouse. Certainly he used New London the following summer, for the September 9, 1893, issue of the *New York Dramatic Mirror* reported that he and his company had been rehearsing a repertory of four plays at the Lyceum Theater in New London, "where Mr. O'Neill spends his summers."

Whether the larger family home was built in 1893 or 1894 is not known, but it was built and the family comfortably established in it by the summer of 1895, for on August 22, 1895, James O'Neill tried out a Harvard student, Owen Davis, to act in his company. Davis recalled it long afterward in 1931 when he published his recollections, *I'd Like to Do it Again*. He had been given a room in the farmhouse for the night and was established on the rock in front of it looking at the river, as he testified, most likely the one Eugene O'Neill had posed on a few years before, and so had a ringside seat for the sensational event of the evening. What Davis did not recall in his book, the *New London Day* of August 23, 1895, published in full.

The evening of the twenty-second, James O'Neill, his son Jamie, and Will Connor, who was staying in a guest room at the new house with them, were all walking into the town center to see, from O'Neill's box at the Lyceum Theater, the great prize fighter Gentleman Jim Corbett demonstrate his sparring technique in a melodrama that circumvented the legal prohibition of public boxing. They were taking the shortcut over the railroad trestle at the Howard Street bridge when a freight train came along. Stepping back to let it pass, James O'Neill missed his footing in the dark and fell sixteen feet to the stone paving of the street below.

As Davis recalled it James O'Neill fell right at his feet, but the house was in a "secluded spot," and what he really saw was the commotion of getting the carriage and horses to rescue the actor lying under the bridge with a severely damaged kneecap. Will Connor exclaimed, "God is certainly good to the Irish! Nine hundred and ninety-nine men out of a thousand would have been killed by the fall." In the end James O'Neill had to cancel his opening performance of the season scheduled for the Lyceum on August 27, 1895. But the event left a record for the year the O'Neills were certainly living in the new house.

The new, substantial house (later numbered in 1900 as 325 Pequot Avenue) had never been the jerry-built "dump" that appears in *Long Day's Journey into Night*. I saw the house in 1955 when the owners were Lawrence and Dorothy White. Mrs. White showed me around the house as it was at that time. She pointed out with considerable pride the fireplace in the front parlor, with its imported tiles and the solid walnut doors and woodwork. She told me that when the back wing of the house with dining room and kitchen had been demolished, the construction company had not charged for the work on condition that they might keep the beautiful hand-wrought nails and the valuable wood. In 1955 the view from the three long windows in the parlor and from the veranda was unobstructed down to the waters of Long Island Sound.

Of course, James O'Neill had never designed the house as a "conspicuous consumption" display piece meant to impress others with his wealth and importance, such as the newly rich in New London and indeed all over America were building in those years. If there was one trait everyone associated with James O'Neill it was "modesty." As he declared of his New London home in March of 1904, when he had brought the company of the all-star revival of *The Two Orphans* there for rehearsals, "No, I haven't got a pig, or a horse, or a cow, nor three acres either. I've a simple little place, where I can dally with the fish round about." (The interviewer, in this case, described James O'Neill as "a bluff and genial fisherman of New London" who would "rather be casting a line than playing a part.")

One of the many guests James O'Neill entertained in the new house spoke later of O'Neill's "beautiful home in New London, Connecticut overlooking the Sound." He described his host as a "family man" and "hospitality personified." How then was Eugene able to see this home of his youth as a "dump" that never would be right because, as Mary Tyrone says, "your father would never spend the money to make it right"? What appears to have happened in the play, where most of the criticisms of the house come from Mary Tyrone, is that Eugene took and accentuated a real trait of his mother so as to express — as he needed to do for his tragic vision — her suffering over the disillusioning reality of her romantically embarked-upon marriage.

What was certainly true of Ella O'Neill was her perfectionism in dress and surroundings as the many people have testified who spoke of her as "fashionable" and "elegant." After the death of James O'Neill in August 1920, when Ella O'Neill broke up and sold their home on Pequot Avenue, she gave all the household linens to Eugene and Agnes for their home at Peaked Hill Bar, Provincetown. Agnes, who came from a careless, Bohemian background, was no housekeeper. The wife of Eugene's cousin Philip Sheridan told me that, after a visit to Eugene and Agnes at Peaked Hill Bar, Ella complained bitterly over the way they treated like rags the beautiful hand-embroidered sheets and towels she had given them. Ella O'Neill liked beautiful things, and Mary Tyrone's distress over anything in her home that fell short of her high standards had its source in Ella O'Neill's elegance.

When he and Carlotta returned to the United States and New York City in 1931 from France, O'Neill found himself haunted by memories of his boyhood New England home beside the sea. He had just finished his play *Mourning Becomes Electra*, a work charged with memories of his lost family. In writing it, he had discovered the insight so crucial to *Long Day's Journey* that a family's past may take on a terrible power to shape and determine its present and future. As soon as he was free to do so — on June 30 and July 1 — he and Carlotta set out for his boyhood summer home on Pequot Avenue, which he had not seen in many years. Those years, it turned out, had brought about shocking changes. The first trauma came when they became hopelessly lost trying to direct the chauffeur from the town center to his old neighborhood. Instead of the meadows full of daisies and country greenery that had separated 325 Pequot Avenue from the city when it was sold in 1920, there were endless blocks of identical bungalows. When they finally came to Pequot Avenue, O'Neill was even more severely shocked by what had happened to his beloved home.

It was shorn of almost all its surrounding trees, bushes, and lawns. Baldly set on this desert stood the much-battered remains of the house. Disrepair had deformed it beyond recognition. The upstairs front porch, already hopelessly weakened, had been finally swept away in a storm, leaving a great blank in the facade between the two upstairs windows. Also, the kitchen and dining room wing (to and from which the four Tyrones of the play move by way of the back parlor) had been demolished altogether. As Carlotta O'Neill told me, Eugene was so shocked to see this travesty ("a bird cage of a house," she called it) that he took her advice to leave at once, and they drove on and away from the sight of it.

Something of that episode with its shattering disillusionment entered into his depiction of the Tyrone home. By way of it, O'Neill was able to portray 325 Pequot Avenue in 1912 as if it were already tottering under the disrepair and deformity that was to overtake it. For O'Neill it represented the shattering truth of what time and life can do to beautiful, fragile things, a truth that permeated his tragedy. Only as an autobiographical picture of the O'Neill home in 1912, the year of the play, it is, of course, darkened beyond recognition and far from the simple charming home set amidst greenery beside the sea that it had then been.

Another aspect of the father in *Long Day's Journey into Night* that is far from historically accurate is the picture of James Tyrone as a perpetually foolish investor, endlessly victimized by his wily friend McGuire. The name O'Neill chose for the character "McGuire" is certainly redolent of Thomas Dorsey.

James O'Neill's law firm in New London was Hull, McGuire, and Hull, and the prominent partner of the firm was James O'Neill's friend Dorsey. New Londoners were familiar with the sight of Tom Dorsey in those years, with his great shock of white hair and a stuffed briefcase under his arm, dashing about the city in a lather over his business affairs. Judge Thomas E. Troland, in the old days just a fledgling lawyer, recalled that during the summer months Dorsey was often with James O'Neill, who — as Judge Troland recalled — had a reputation for doing "well for his friends in town," and — so the judge concluded — "maybe he was doing well for Dorsey." In fact, Judge Troland explained, "Dorsey got a commission on all the property James O'Neill bought and sold."

Dorsey's son, Tom Jr., told me that his father handled all James O'Neill's real estate, and that they had made "a lot of money selling property to the railroads." He also remembered James's penchant for buying "bargains" in real estate, odd lots, "secondary properties," rather than "good commercial properties."

According to him, James also owned some very good lots on Bank and Ocean Avenues. As the New London postmaster declared at James's funeral, "He believed in the future greatness of our city and proved this by investing heavily in real estate."

Certainly, James O'Neill usually invested any surplus money. He was also alert to the dangers in those days of trusting the stocks and bonds of the robber barons then fleecing the public. His investments were usually in land, mines, or occasionally in various business enterprises. Long before James came into the money from *Monte Cristo*, he was using whatever surplus cash he had to secure his family's future, rather than dissipating it in conspicuous consumption.

There is no complete record of his holdings, but some were noticed occasionally in theatrical journals. For instance, on April 2, 1881, the *New York Clipper* announced that the Cumberland, known as the Actor's Mine, in Arizona had "busted" and that James O'Neill, George M. Ciprico, and Louis Morrison had lost heavily by it. During a morning interview in New York City, James told a reporter from the *New York Dramatic News* (April 9), "The mine is all right yet." But they had had to close the San Francisco office when investors had asked for their money back because, after expenses for machinery, there was "not enough money to carry on the work." O'Neill thought they only needed "working capital." "Why, it is one of the best properties in Arizona. The ore realized $100 to the ton, and there is a vein seven hundred and fifty feet long and eight feet deep, which only awaits development. The Vulture Mine, right by it, is one of the very best paying properties out there, and I don't see why the Cumberland shouldn't be likewise."

Altogether, James O'Neill declared, "I don't consider that I have sustained a loss. I am certain that both Mr. Owens and myself will get all our money back and more, too. I haven't lost faith in the Cumberland by any means. But even if nothing should ever be realized from the Cumberland, I have six other claims out there which will bring me in all the money I have expended. They are undeveloped yet, and have never been worked, but the properties about them are being worked, and are panning out splendidly."

James also denied rumors "that we were swindled out of all our investments, and that Ciprico was at the bottom of it. Now, that is likewise untrue." Typically, O'Neill exonerated Ciprico as "the poorest of the lot; he is one of those men who are always under a cloud, always in debt. There was no swindle at all. You will yet see us get our money back."

But within the year it was clear that they never would. In Cleveland when he was touring through the Midwest in *The American King*, his first starring venture, the *Cleveland Herald* reported him "sitting at supper with a crowd of companions" and recalling "affectionately" his old days as leading man in Ellsler's Academy of Music. Speaking of the varied fortunes of an actor, O'Neill remarked: "I once got a quarter of a million together in California, in stock deals, but it went again, partly in the same currency and partly in other risks. Now Jim O'Neill is but a poor actor, and I have about made up my mind that acting is all that I am good for."

But as soon as acting in the "bonanza" of *Monte Cristo* came to him, James O'Neill was once again hopefully investing his money. His then manager Edward Zimmerman declared in June 1886 that James's "season" in *Monte Cristo* was one of "the most successful" he ever had, and that the actor would spend the summer in his home in New London: "One of the results of Mr. O'Neill's last season was his investment of $20,000 in the Millner cattle ranch at Fort Benton, Montana, while he was in Chicago. This ranch is the largest in the Territory, with a capital stock of a million and a half dollars, and is the same one in which Nate Salsbury (impresario of the Buffalo Bill shows and a particular friend of James O'Neill), Frank Maeder, and a number of the boys are interested."

What returns James O'Neill had on his shares in the cattle ranch over the years is not known, but Eugene inherited the ranch as one of James's investments, and he had reason to be thankful for it. A half century after, Eugene was able to rush to the assistance of Eugene Jr. when the young man's bank failed and he lost all his savings in January 1932 during the Great Depression. O'Neill told Eugene Jr. that he was endorsing over to him the dividend check. "A grand surprise to me, this one was! It represents a small share in a cattle ranch in Montana your romantically-investing Grandfather left me. I thought those cows had all perished of hoof-and-mouth disease long ago!"

The year after this purchase, in February 1887, James O'Neill was caught — according to the *New York Clipper* — in Tennessee, while performing to standing room only, by the "Chattanooga craze for 'dirt,' and has concluded to drop a few dollars in Chattanooga real estate." Six years after that (July 1893), a report in the *New York Dramatic Mirror* declared, "James O'Neill is a firm believer in life insurance, not only for family protection but for purposes of investment. He carries a number of heavy policies in the leading companies. One tontine policy matured a few days ago and he received a cheque in settlement for $10,000." Three years later, in June 1896 he was reported by the *New York Dramatic Mirror* as having just "bought a valuable piece of improved property, on Columbus Avenue in this city. Mr. O'Neill has valuable realty in several states."

The following year (on March 6, 1897), the *Chicago Evening Post* reported specifically that "Monte Cristo has proved a gold mine for James O'Neill.

If the story told is true, his investments from money he has made from *Monte Cristo* include a mine in Colorado, a farm in Jersey, three houses in Kansas City, an orange grove in California, and five houses in New London, Connecticut, where he makes his home." This list was by no means complete. On that same day the *New York Dramatic Mirror* pointed out that James "is one of the most level-headed stars in the profession. Years ago he took to endowment insurance, and last year the company paid him $25,000 in cash. He has but one more payment to make before he will get $10,000 in cash, and last week he started in on $10,000 more."

Quietly, James O'Neill continued investing in New London. On May 3, 1908, came the announcement in the *New York Telegraph* that in "New London where he maintains his residence, Mr. O'Neill has built a garage at an expense of $10,000 which he has thrown open to the public." Joking, the Telegraph added, "He has named the garage 'Monte Cristo' after the new play which is being written for him." Later Eugene O'Neill recalled that the garage had been "the local agency for the Buick car," which was then a prestigious machine and thus carried out his father's delight in dealing with the best in transportation: elegant rowboats, magnificent horses, and when they came in, the finest automobiles.

Certainly, James O'Neill's investments played an important part in his son Eugene's early life. In fact, when Eugene opted, after just one year at Princeton University, to withdraw after his punitive suspension, he found immediate employment in Henry Brittain's New York–Chicago Supply Company because his father was a major investor in it. Even the glamorous adventures that later were to cast a romantic glow upon his youth — after he had become America's leading playwright — were impelled by his father's influence as an investor, rather than his own bent for exploration.

This was surely true in the case of his gold-prospecting in Honduras. Eugene himself never realized fully that he was not asked to accompany Earl Stevens on this adventure because Stevens needed him. The trip was really his father's tactful way of rescuing him from his despair over having had to marry the pregnant Kathleen Jenkins. James O'Neill was clearly behind Stevens's venture, for later that year in an interview with a Philadelphia reporter, he declared that his older son, James Jr., was playing an "important role" in the touring company of *The Traveling Salesman*. As for his younger son, "Six weeks ago Eugene was sent to Yucatan, Central America, to take charge of some mining properties owned by his father." So little did Eugene realize his position, that he wrote his father miserably only a few months after his arrival in Honduras, "I don't know if I am getting any salary or not as Stevens has said nothing about it. It would sure be some shock to find out I was enduring all this for love. Better find out for me."

Most of the staff at Liebler and Company knew perfectly well that James repeatedly rescued Eugene from the mess he had made of his life. John Peter Toohey, who wrote publicity for George Tyler at that time, tried long afterward to peddle an anecdote about Eugene (become famous) to Alexander Woolcott at the Algonquin Hotel's restaurant. Toohey had difficulty getting a word in edgeways of Woolcott's usual monologue. As reported later, Toohey's story was that Eugene "had once been shanghaied to sea by his father to get him out of the way until a scrape could be resolved." (Toohey appears to have got this idea from James's second rescue of Eugene by paying his passage on the *Charles Racine* to Argentina.)

The second rescue was necessary because malaria brought Eugene O'Neill back from Central America after less than six months to throw himself once again on his father—whom he found opening on March 14, 1910, at St. Louis in *The White Sister*. By the time the company reached Boston, James O'Neill had lined up a job for Eugene as a draftsman at Western Electric in Buenos Aires, and added to its romance by booking the young man's passage on a sailing vessel. Perhaps James got the Argentine job for Eugene, as he had gotten the others, through his influence as an investor. In later interviews, although Eugene never spoke of his father's role in arranging his early adventures, he would recall the two investments of his father that failed. Brittain's company went bankrupt during the depression of 1909, and no gold ever came of the prospecting in Honduras. The only conclusion Eugene appears to have drawn from his father's many rescues was an unshakable conviction that his father's investments were frequently foolish and futile.

After his father's death, Eugene told George Tyler that the money his father had made from *Monte Cristo* had been "thrown away, squandered in wild speculations, or lost." His mother—so he said—had been left "with the barest sufficiency," and she was having great difficulty "getting his messed-up estate into a sane condition where it can maintain her with a fair degree of comfort. The treasures of Monte Cristo are buried deep again—in prairie dog gold mines, in unlubricated oil wells, in fuelless coal lands—the modern Castles in Spain of pure romance."

At the same time he was confident of his mother's capacity to deal with it, although she had never done anything like that before. He assured Tyler that his mother was "developing into a keenly interested business woman," and that "under her hand, I honestly have a hunch that some dividends may finally accrue from the junk buried on the island of M. C." Tyler agreed, telling Eugene,

"Your dear daddy's queer investments were a continual source of worry to both Will Connor and myself. When we protested, he pooh-poohed. But there was a pathetically humorous side to it all. He was nearly always 'done' by an Irishman! Such a lover of his own people was he that any plausible swindler had simply to possess an Irish name in order to get his ear, and if he happened to have an O' in front of it, all the king's men couldn't hold the dear fellow back. And yet, he was really cautious when Will Connor advised—and Will loved him more than he loved anyone in the world. Strange, wasn't it?"

No wonder, then, if in *Long Day's Journey into Night* Eugene depicted his father in James Tyrone as a perpetually foolish dupe. No wonder either that he placed most of the criticisms of Tyrone's deals in the mouth of his wife, Mary Tyrone. As for McGuire's treacherous role in these deals, Eugene certainly knew that Tom Dorsey always profited greatly from his business with James O'Neill. When Ella O'Neill took charge of the property after James's death, and sold the three houses on Pequot Avenue James then owned, she saw no reason to give Dorsey a cut of the profits. Within the year, Dorsey was suing the estate for $35,000 in unpaid commissions. Ultimately the case was judicially dismissed. Its chief effect besides troubling the widow was to leave Eugene with the conception he distilled years later in *Long Day's Journey:* Dorsey (McGuire) as the fleecer, his father as the sheep, and his mother as the astute critic of it all.

Yet that impression is not really just. In all his business dealings, James O'Neill liked to share the benefits with both his personal friends and with his fellow refugees from Ireland's poverty and oppression by the "cursed Sassenach." If on occasion he was swindled, and by one of his fellow Irishmen, he apparently thought that a price worth paying to keep his kindness and humanity ever fresh and unstinting.

Nor was as much of James O'Neill's money "squandered," as Eugene thought. With his mother's death in February 1922 and his brother James's in November 1923, he became the sole heir to all his father left. Even as late as August 19, 1924, the estate—as Eugene reported—was "more balled up" and unavailable to him than ever. But when it seems to have been settled soon after, it was certainly not a negligible sum. Exactly how much the estate came to is not clear now, but Eugene certainly knew how much came to him. It is very possible, given how rarely O'Neill quotes numbers in his plays—and the fact that they usually correspond to real numbers—that he actually cites the correct sum in *Long Day's Journey into Night* when he has Edmund, the character representing himself, declare emphatically that his father owns property "valued at a quarter of a million." In the days when $3,000 was considered a

comfortable yearly income for a middle-class family, $250,000 was a sub-
stantial inheritance. Transferred into conservative stocks and bonds, it gave
O'Neill underlying security for life, through all of the ups and downs in
income of even as successful a playwright as he became.

Whatever his inheritance, Eugene was convinced that—as he told George
Tyler—his father had died "broken, unhappy, intensely bitter." He was sure
that the play *Monte Cristo* had "wrecked my father's chance to become one of
our greatest actors. Since he did not mince this matter himself but confessed
it to me during our very close 'palship' last winter, I feel free to state it. Monte
Cristo, he often said with great bitterness as he lived over his past out loud to
me, had been his curse. He had fallen for the lure of easy popularity and easy
money—and he suffered as a retribution in his old age the humiliation of supporting such actor-yokels (by comparison) as [Brandon] Tynan, [Viola] Allen,
[Pauline] Fredericks."

According to Eugene, James O'Neill came to realize that he had "made a
bad bargain." His words, as he lay dying, had been, Eugene said, "seared on my
brain—a warning from Beyond to remain true to the best that is in me though
the heavens fall." This resolution became steadily more powerful over the
years. A quarter of a century afterward, Eugene was telling Hamilton Basso that
his father "had thrown away his chance for a distinguished career," and Eugene
himself had therefore resolved indelibly "that I would never sell out."

Tyler agreed. He told Eugene, "Your dear father's point of view I was quite
familiar with. But wasn't it the point of view of every other man or woman" who
had spent "their lives in quest of the 'ideal?'" All of them had been at least "dis-
appointed" and most of them "mentally wretched." After a lifetime in "intimate
acquaintanceship with genius," with playwrights, poets, and actors, Tyler knew
from experience that is "how nearly all of them feel at the finish."

Thus all those years before O'Neill came to write his intimate family play
Long Day's Journey into Night, he had already stated its central theme to Tyler,
and Tyler had generalized that perception into a conclusion about the tragic
destiny of all who wish to fulfill an ideal. From that time on, Eugene held that
tragic vision—altogether consciously—as the inspiration behind his plays. He
told Mary B. Mullett in the fall of 1922 that tragedy brought "exaltation,"
showed audiences "their own hopeless hopes ennobled in art." The hopes
were hopeless, O'Neill explained, "because any victory we may win is never
the one we dreamed of winning. The point is that life in itself is nothing. It is
the dream that keeps us fighting—willing—living!" For O'Neill at that time,
"A man wills his own defeat when he pursues the unattainable. But his struggle
is his success: He is an example of the spiritual significance which life attains

when it aims high enough, when the individual fights all the hostile forces within and without himself to achieve a future of nobler values." Certainly at that time Eugene thought that his father had not remained true to the unattainable, but had, as he implied in his letter to Tyler, sold out.

Yet by the very writing of *Long Day's Journey into Night*, O'Neill was bringing himself to a less Nietzschean, more compassionate view of the failure to achieve one's dream. Underneath his conscious theme for the play, O'Neill was trying to answer just that question of how to judge the innocence or guilt of what one has done, of how to decide whether defeat came about because the struggle had not been fought hard enough and long enough to bring one closer to the ideal. Throughout the deepening of the fog, the intensifying of the pain in the long life journey of the four tragic Tyrones, the question of whether they are innocent or guilty of what has happened to them arises throughout. The paradoxical answer — that they are both innocent and guilty at the same time — gives the play its profound meaning and, as O'Neill himself wrote in the dedication to the play, "its deep pity and understanding and forgiveness for all the four haunted Tyrones." So he had arrived at a resolution for even his own guilt, being the last of the four, had arrived at an acceptance of his own past and of the entire human past by way of writing *Long Day's Journey into Night*.

No play could have emerged more closely from O'Neill's intimate experience, or arrived more honestly and painfully out of a reliving of reality. Nevertheless, for all its truth for human destiny and its fidelity to "old sorrow," its compassionate acceptance of the defeat implicit in the very nature of human life, Eugene O'Neill certainly was not creating — or even meant to be creating — an accurate biography of his family with all the contradictions and complexities of their lives and characters.

The story of James Tyrone is not the story of James O'Neill. Even though Eugene's father himself told him that *Monte Cristo* had been his "curse," Eugene's conclusion that he had "fallen for the lure of easy popularity and easy money" is not by any means a necessary judgment of his life. As far as the history of James's career goes, the facts add up to a different picture. For one thing, the number of other plays he performed in for long periods between the inception of *Monte Cristo* in 1883 and his retirement from the stage at the end of 1917 is impressively long. Only the fact that he was playing in repertory most of the time with *Monte Cristo* as one of the plays makes it appear to be the one play of his mature career.

James O'Neill accepted from John Stetson in February 1883 the part of Edmund Dantes in *Monte Cristo*, the Charles Fechter version of Alexandre Dumas's novel. It went so miraculously well in New York and on tour that

James asked for and received a percentage of the box-office take, as well as a salary in the continued tour from September 1883 to the end of May 1884. For the tour of September 1884 to June 1885, James settled for the largest cut of the box-office receipts. That summer he was able to buy the rights to the Fechter version from Stetson, who had thought it was "a lemon that had been squeezed dry." From the fall of 1885 to the fall of 1890 James O'Neill managed his own company and toured the country starring in the play. In those five years, the only other play he performed in was Shakespeare's *Hamlet*, for a series of performances starting in January of 1887 in Mobile and Birmingham, Alabama.

From 1890 *Monte Cristo* persisted, but James O'Neill performed other plays, as well.

September 1890 to May 1891. Repertory of *The Dead Heart* (a London success played by Henry Irving the year before) and *Monte Cristo*.

September 1891 to June 1892. *Monte Cristo*.

September 1892 to June 1893. *Fontenelle* by Minnie Maddern Fiske and Harrison Grey Fiske.

September 1893 to June 1894. Repertory of *Fontenelle, Monte Cristo*, Sheridan Knowles' *Virginius* and Bulwer-Lytton's *Richelieu*.

September 1894 to June 1895. Repertory of *Virginius, Monte Cristo*, *Hamlet*, and *Richeleiu*.

September 1895 to June 1897. Repertory of *Virginius, The Courier of Lyons* (a revamping of Bulwer-Lytton's *The Lady of Lyons*), *Hamlet*, *Richeleiu, Monte Cristo*, and *The Dream of Matthew Wayne* (adapted by Minnie Maddern Fiske from the French by Auguste Vacquerie).

September 1897 to 1898. The same repertory as 1895 to 1897, with the addition of *The Dead Heart*.

September 1898 to March 1899. Repertory of Joseph Hatton's *When Greek Meets Greek*, and *Monte Cristo*.

March 14, 1899, to January 1900. A spectacular production (with very impressive scenery and costumes) of Sydney Grundy's *The Musketeers* from the novel of Alexandre Dumas.

January 1900 to June 1900. Introduced a spectacular *Monte Cristo* to alternate with the spectacular *Musketeers*.

September 1900 to June 1902. The spectacular *Monte Cristo* alone.

September 1902 through December 1902. *The Honor of the Humble* (an adaptation by Harriet Ford of Pierre Newsky's *Les Danicheffs*).

December 21, 1902, to May 9, 1903. *The Manxman* by Hall Caine, dramatized from his novel.

June 4, 1903, one week. James O'Neill took the role of Mercutio in place of Eben Plympton for the last week of Shakespeare's *Romeo and Juliet* starring Eleanor Robson.

September 1903 to March 1904. *The Adventures of Gerard* dramatized by Conan Doyle from his novel.

December 1903 to March 1904. James O'Neill added the one-act curtain raiser, *The Sacrament of Judah* by Louis Tiercelin, to *The Adventures of Gerard*.

March 1904 to June 1905. The all-star revival of *The Two Orphans* (as adapted by Hart Jackson).

September 1905 to June 1907. The "hope-to-die farewell tour" of *Monte Cristo* (with some performances of James Slevin's *The Voice of the Mighty*).

September 1907 to May 1908. Repertory of *Virginius*, Shakespeare's *Julius Caesar*, and *Monte Cristo*.

September 1908 to May 1909. *The Abbé Bonaparte*.

September 1909 to May 1911. James O'Neill touring as Monseigneur Saracinesca in support of Viola Allen in *The White Sister* based on Marion Crawford's novel).

September 1911 to mid-March 1912. *The Orpheum Vaudeville*, two-a-day, forty-minute version of *Monte Cristo*.

January 1913 to January 1915. James O'Neill touring, playing both Jacob and Pharaoh in support of Brandon Tynan and Pauline Frederick in Louis Parker's *Joseph and His Brethren*.

January 23, 1917, to January 1918. James O'Neill touring as the father of the prodigal son in Maurice V. Samuel's *The Wanderer, a Biblical Extravaganza* based on William Schmidtbonn's *Der Verlorener Sohn*.

James O'Neill had always wanted to encourage American playwrights. On May 9, 1891, he produced in New York what he thought a "sterling" play, *The Envoy* by a Philadelphia author, Edward J. Swartz. Although he "did all he could to save the play" by the "intensity" of his acting, *The Envoy* failed dismally with audience and critics. James O'Neill thought perhaps "the financial state of the country" was to blame, but his tour in *The Dead Heart* and *Monte Cristo* that year during the depression had, he admitted, made "money hand over fist." Undismayed by this failure, James had already purchased yet another American play, *The New South*, by Francis Reinan and Louis Ludovisi in July 1891, but despite a part for O'Neill "full of fine opportunities," it did no better.

Not until May of 1892 was he able to announce that "a new romantic drama"—*Fontenelle* by Minnie Maddern Fiske and Harrison Grey Fiske set in the court of Louis XV—would be his "trump card next season." In this play James O'Neill achieved once again "Standing Room Only" signs in crowded theaters all along the way. *Fontenelle* was every bit as dazzling a success as *Monte Cristo* had been in money and applause. Nevertheless, in truth, James O'Neill had never succumbed—as his son Eugene came to believe—to the "lure of easy popularity and easy money." As early in the tour as November 4, 1892, James O'Neill's manager William F. Connor was asking William Seymour, on O'Neill's behalf, about the scenery and wardrobes from the Barrett estate coming up for auction, as the actor was bent—so Connor said—"upon taking up the 'legitimate' next season." Although the O'Neill company was "doing remarkable business with the new piece, giving satisfaction every-where,"—so Connor explained—"still Mr. O'Neill thinks the part not good enough for him and that he is wasting time."

Whatever might be said of *Monte Cristo*, it did offer endless opportunity for great acting; indeed it depended on great acting for its effect. In it Edmund Dantes goes from exultant happiness, full of youthful trust and love, to near madness of despair and anguish through his betrayal by almost everyone he knows. Completely innocent of any crime, he finds himself walled up in a dark dungeon of the Chateau d'If without hope of release. From that nadir, Dantes moves—by the error in calculations that brings the Abbé Faria tunneling into his cell—to a transforming education in languages, literature, and life, and then later to a miraculous escape into freedom and untold wealth.

Besides, the character is not resurrected to freedom as just one person in the story, but as several, disguised as whom he can reward the few who tried to save him and punish the ones guilty of sending him into a living death. Thus an actor in the role must convey both the varied personalities Dantes takes on in his disguises and at the same time convince an audience that he is the same person throughout his transformations as he goes from felicity to despair to res-urrection as the gentle, unworldly Abbé Busoni and the drastically opposite and powerful Count of Monte Cristo.

No matter how many times James O'Neill performed this demanding role, he never ceased to throw himself altogether into bringing it freshly to life for his audience. As one critic declared after O'Neill had been doing so more than twenty years, "In the many times the writer has seen him in this role, there has never been a time that he has not surprised and delighted with some new turn to the emotional scenes, with some fresh indication of an undying interest in a part practically limitless in its opportunities." In the small city of Augusta, Georgia, during many years of playing there, he was still drawing crowded houses, with every seat "from upper gallery to the boxes" sold out "long before the doors opened" and the audience wildly enthusiastic with applause and curtain calls. In fact, the critic was sure that this play had become a "masterpiece," not because of the name of Dumas, but "because of the genius of O'Neill."

It was James O'Neill who raised the play to its extraordinary popularity in the American theater, and his son Eugene would ultimately come to know so. When, thoroughly sick of having played the part so many times, James thought to free himself permanently of the role without losing altogether the money it brought, he decided for the tour starting September 1902 to lease the rights and scenery to Mark Ellsworth and Claude Gilbert — former members of his company — to star Edmund Breese, a fine young actor he himself had developed into a first-rate leading man, as Dantes. The dismal result of that tour of *Monte Cristo* showed that without James O'Neill's magic, the play lost its drawing power.

As Eugene declared to a prospective producer of *Monte Cristo* in 1940, the very year in which he was writing *Long Day's Journey into Night*, it might seem odd to a modern audience that *Monte Cristo* had been "the most successful romantic melodrama of its time, and one of the most successful plays of all time in America." To Eugene, so he said, "The answer, of course, was my father. He had a genuine romantic Irish personality — looks, voice, stage presence — and he loved the part. It was the picturesque vitality of his acting which carried the play. Audiences came to see James O'Neill in *Monte Cristo*, not *Monte Cristo*. The proof is, *Monte Cristo* has never had much success as a play at any time, either here or abroad, except for the one dramatization done in this country by him." *Monte Cristo* "without a James O'Neill," Eugene declared, would turn out to be just "another old melodrama."

So even as he was creating the tragic disillusionment of James Tyrone, Eugene O'Neill knew that in reality, James O'Neill's undiminished drawing power in that role might be interpreted as a triumph of acting rather than the betrayal of an ideal. Sick of the role as his father certainly became, he continued to make it a great experience for his audience.

In fact, when he returned to *Monte Cristo* in September 1905, James O'Neill announced — with undertones of restrained bitterness — "Yes, I am going back to the old piece, and why shouldn't I? The managers and the public want me in it, and when you come right down to facts, where is there a better melodrama to be had for love or money? The more I see of other pieces, the better I like *Monte Cristo*, and when I produce it this time, if I meet with the success I anticipate, I'll keep on playing it until I retire for good from the stage.

"[Joseph] Jefferson played Rip van Winkle for forty years, and while he sandwiched in *The Rivals* and one or two other little pieces, it was Rip made big money, and things have got so now that all there is in acting is money. If animated by a love for art, a man wants to produce a legitimate play it takes a small fortune to do it; it must be a production which means big expense for scenery, lights, properties, and costumes, to say nothing of the company and other incidental expenses; and after all this risk and trouble, you are likely to make a failure."

Everything Eugene O'Neill said about his father's regret and bitterness was true — just as true as was its opposite, the fact that his father had "loved the part" and that only the power of his acting had transformed it into "one of the most successful plays of all time in the American theater." True to his father, too, was the scorn, as Eugene told Tyler, that his father felt for the slovenly acting of the so-called "stars" he supported in his old age. Even before he took his first nonstarring role, he was saying, "There's many a star who ought to be shovelling coal and many a staress who ought to be over a wash tub." He wondered "where the good young actors" were to come from, for "the younger players are too lazy to study," unlike the actors of his youth, who "believed there was something more in acting than the mere drawing of a salary." James O'Neill was also declaring in these days his contempt for the actor who does not "look" and "live" the part he is portraying, but "allows his own personality to override that of the character." James could only wonder that "this sort of a slip-shod performance" was not "hissed from the stage."

Yet when the *New York Morning Telegraph* sent him congratulations on his sixtieth birthday in October of 1907 when he was acting in repertory at Boston, he replied with thanks, declaring that life still had for him the "same charms" in seat sixty as he knew at fifteen in the gallery. "Must say that all my years on the stage form one grand poem of happiness to myself," he said, and he was delighted at being "so graciously recalled" in the belief "that I must have afforded in turn some pleasure to playgoers."

"From seat sixty I can see life's stage without the aid of glasses, and the air is filled with roses and sunshine. I love life fully as well as ever, and my friends a whole lot better. It has been the best sixty years I have ever experienced, and I feel today as if I were going to live sixty more."

James O'Neill certainly had a buoyancy and joy in living in sharp contrast to the poignant regret of James Tyrone in Eugene O'Neill's play. And yet no one would have been prouder of that mighty tragic vision of the nature of life than James O'Neill himself. He declared (in the days when he was alternating *Hamlet* and *Virginius* with *Monte Cristo*), "Tragedy deals with the passions in their highest and grandest moods; it carries the actor completely out of himself, transports him as it were to scenes beyond the ken of ordinary minds."

In the days when he was still hopeful about finding a good tragedy by an American playwright, James O'Neill responded to a critic's comment (in January 1895) on his return to tragedy, "Yes, and I ought to have done so immediately after Edwin Booth's retirement. The field was open, and I had met with considerable success at one time in many of the characters with which Mr. Booth was identified. It is nonsense to say that the public no longer care for the legitimate drama. The public will always go to see tragedy if the production is up to the requisite standard of merit."

At the same time James O'Neill pointed out the difficulty of finding excellent new tragedies by American authors. He confided: "I suppose you know that I produced a play in Boston about two months ago. It was called *Don Carlos de Seville* and was written by Eugene Fellner. I regret to say that it wasn't much of a success. My experience in reading plays has convinced me that American authors would be greatly benefited by collaborating with some practical stage manager. I am very far from underrating the value of bright dialogue, but the story and strong situations are paramount — in the other words, 'the play's the thing.' I have always been willing to encourage the American drama, but dramas of native authorship of sufficient strength and merit to suit my purpose are few and far between. I am not referring to comedies or comedy-dramas. Bronson Howard, Henry Guy Carleton, Augustus Thomas, and others are very clever playwrights in that line. But take tragedies like *Francesca da Rimini* and *The Gladiator*, both written by American authors of a former generation. They may write plays of equal strength to-day, but I must confess they have not been submitted to me."

Asked if he thought we needed schools to teach "the technique of play-writing," James O'Neill replied, "I certainly do! Now and then a genius may write a play without any degree of technical knowledge in regard to the requirements of a stage production. The average writer for the stage, however, has to serve a dramatic apprenticeship of some sort before he is qualified to write a play of any practical value. It seems to me that a series of lectures on the art of constructing plays would greatly benefit some of the people who have submitted plays to me in recent years."

One of the entirely happy endings that did not belong in *Long Day's Journey into Night*, that had to be excluded of necessity, was the fate of the youngest son in the family. During Eugene O'Neill's childhood, adolescence, and young manhood, James O'Neill had given him the steady training in practical stagecraft that would allow him to become the first truly great American playwright, known, produced, and read the world over.

Certainly, Eugene himself never underrated the brilliant theatrical training he began to absorb in earliest childhood from listening in on his father's talk with theatrical people, from witnessing myriad rehearsals, and from seeing a perpetual stream of theatrical productions. Asked in 1946 how one set about becoming a playwright, Eugene replied, "Take some wood and canvas and nails and things. Build yourself a theater, a stage; light it, learn about it. When you've done that you will probably know how to write a play . . . if you can." First and foremost, for him, came knowledge of the theater.

At the funeral of James O'Neill, William F. Connor said that he had been universally considered the "most popular actor" of the American theater. "Everyone loved him. From the boys in the theater up to the managers he was highly admired. It must have been a great satisfaction to him to have lived to see his son Eugene reach the position he now occupies as the foremost playwright in America." So Connor said on August 12, 1920, many years before the whole dazzling plenitude of Eugene O'Neill's plays, culminating in *The Iceman Cometh* and *Long Day's Journey into Night,* had been conceived and written. To console Eugene's grief at his father's dying, his wife Agnes told him, "You can certainly boast that you've given your father a real happiness — a tremendous gift — in your success, and in that feeling that has grown between you the last year or so — that you love one another — that you are his son, of whom he can be as proud as any father in the whole world."

The tragedy of James Tyrone in *Long Day's Journey into Night* is profoundly true of human life, but is by no means a correct summation of the lives of James O'Neill or his son Eugene. The real story contains contradictory opposites that cancel one another out. Historical biography is quite unlike the meaningful revelation of life encapsulated in a work of art. James Tyrone is not James O'Neill. Eugene O'Neill applied extraneous facts that invaded the character, including guilt that belonged to him, not his father. Also, Tyrone's story erases, of necessity, the "roses and sunshine" that illuminated the life and career of James O'Neill. Only by these changes could Eugene O'Neill dramatize the poignant truth of how noble ideals become tarnished and lost in the passage of years.

CHAPTER TEN

Mary Tyrone

I f the historical James O'Neill was very different from James Tyrone in *Long Day's Journey into Night*, the historical Ella O'Neill differed even more sharply from Mary Tyrone. Eugene O'Neill's mother became mixed with the character of his wife Carlotta, being afflicted with her arthritis and her eye trouble as well as taking on Carlotta's youthful dreams and Eugene's own as a boy at Mount St. Vincent on the Hudson. She also departed from her original by being given a father who died of tuberculosis, as did Teddy Boulton, the father of Eugene's second wife, Agnes, and endowed with fictional prodigies of generosity that never took place in reality.

Besides, the most important attribute of Mary Tyrone—her need to hide from life by taking morphine—is one that cannot be satisfactorily checked against any actuality in Ella O'Neill's life. No records of Ella's addiction or cures have come to light. Whatever facts have emerged demand considerable interpreting and hypothesizing. Yet there are clues enough to suggest that the intense feeling of an overwhelming fatality and compulsion in the play were achieved by Eugene's tragic vision of the past, not by a recording of actual events.

The uncertainty lies in the fact that, for the sake of his drama, O'Neill was likely to attribute to his characters unhistorical destructive actions, even ones that calumniated the original as he did when he gave James Tyrone, as his father, his own former sins against the women he loved, of drinking himself comatose. On the other hand, he could, at times, be historically accurate, as in part of his account of his father's experiences in childhood as an apprentice ironworker.

From what he said, Eugene O'Neill certainly believed that the onset of his mother's trouble, like Mary Tyrone's, came from a doctor's prescription for the pain she suffered from his birth on October 16, 1888. In O'Neill's first draft for the fourth act of the play, he had Edmund accuse his father, as he does in the final play, of causing his mother's addiction by choosing a cheap doctor who prescribed morphine. In this first draft, Edmund then accuses his father of neglecting to have her cured. In reply, Tyrone cries, "Why didn't I send her to a Cure? you say. Are you a fool? You know this last one she went to was the fourth."

If, in the years between 1888 and 1912, Ella had only four episodes of addiction and four corresponding cures, she would have been free of drugs for long periods. This passage was cancelled for the final play, not, perhaps, because it was untrue of Ella, but because it weakened the impression of a fatal compulsion out of the past that has progressively destroyed the life of Mary Tyrone. Newspaper interviews of the day referring to the charm and elegance of James O'Neill's wife during the times she and her husband were always together on his tours, do make it clear that during almost all that time over many years she appeared fine, certainly very unlike Mary Tyrone under the drug: confused, unreachable, disheveled. The drama critic of the *Chicago Chronicle* who saw them whenever James O'Neill played in that city reported on February 28, 1897, of the actor: "He never forgets a face or name. He has a most peculiar memory, not unconnected, I imagine, with a man's size heart of the warmest sort. His domestic affairs have been very happy and serene. Almost always his wife, a handsome woman of charming personality, is with him, and one of his two sons also travels with him. The other son, young James, is at college [at Notre Dame's elementary and high schools]. In the summertime you will find the family far from the garish glare and the plaudits of the theater in a villa near New London, Connecticut."

Whenever James O'Neill performed in St. Louis, he and Ella spent time with his sister Maggie Platz. Her son, Paul Alwyn Platz, who became a journalist, wrote in the *Cleveland Leader* of February 22, 1914, that James O'Neill's wife "was born and raised in this city. She was Miss Ella Quinlan. To that union two sons were born—James, Jr. and Eugene—and they have made the ideal couple, their home life being very congenial and happy." Others, too, such as the actor Fred Wren, wrote of the happiness of James O'Neill's marriage, calling him "a family man, who forgets the world and his many artistic triumphs in the bosom of his family." Wren also described him as having "all those lovable qualities which go to make up the father, husband, and friend." It is not likely that observers over the years would have characterized James O'Neill's home life thus had Ella ever been seen by then wandering around stupefied and disheveled from drugs, as Mary Tyrone does in the play.

One of the crucial clues to how short the periods of addiction and cures were compared to the whole of her married life appears in the fact that any suspicion of addiction was virtually unknown in New London until after the

publication of *Long Day's Journey into Night*, when biographers asking leading questions muddied the record. When I interviewed a number of New Londoners in 1955, only Tom Dorsey Jr., whose father had been James O'Neill's
closest companion over all those years, was able and ready to recall that sometime around 1916 or 1917 Ella O'Neill had a breast removed because of cancer
and afterward, he had heard, she "became used to drugs." If her immediate
family—Brennans, Sheridans, and Morans—believed this, they could never
have seen her muddled and unreal from the effects of morphine at any previous time.

Shortly after *Long Day's Journey into Night* was published, I had an indignant telephone call from Mrs. Philip Sheridan telling me that the family was
very upset by the portrayal of Ella in the character of Mary Tyrone. They were
sure that Ella had never become addicted to drugs until she underwent a mastectomy around 1917. So their story matched Tom Dorsey Jr.'s. Assuming, then,
that Eugene, in this case, was also correct that the addiction started sometime
around his birth, it appears that whatever relapses and cures for morphine addiction took place in those years, they were few and successfully hidden from
both family and friends until after Ella's 1917 relapse, when James O'Neill was
retired and no longer away from New London most of the year touring or staying, as they did during O'Neill's active career, at a New York City hotel during
theatrical season. To stay in New London during Ella's recuperation from the
operation, he would have had to confide something of her problem to her relatives there. So apparently he led them to believe this was a unique instance
of addiction brought about by the operation. And this was also the story told to
Thomas Dorsey Sr.

Ella's relapses probably didn't occur in New London before the 1917 incident. Perhaps the summers the O'Neills did not come to New London in May
or June as usual were periods that Ella was under the influence of drugs or in
treatment, and therefore in no condition to be seen by her relatives. That
would not be true, of course, for the trips to Europe in the summers of 1887
and 1906, when she was likely in good health. But there are several other
absences that seem likely to have come about because of relapses she suffered
between 1888 and 1912.

According to the announcement in the *New York Clipper* of June 28, 1884,
right after James O'Neill's very successful appearance at the California Theater in *Monte Cristo*, "James O'Neill is to summer in 'Frisco, where he thinks
he may bring out his play *The American King*, which has been remodeled and
rechristened *The Millionaire*." If he actually did spend the summer of 1884 in
California, the first summer he spent in New London would have been that of

1885, when James bought the Monte Cristo cottage and its tract of farmland at 134 Pequot Avenue. From then on, notices in the journals through 1892 announced that "Mr. O'Neill and his family will go to New London, Connecticut where they will spend the summer at his country place."

The first absence noticed in the journals comes in the *New York Dramatic Mirror* of June 17, 1893. It declared, "James O'Neill will spend the Summer at his farm near Bound Brook, New Jersey." The only notice besides came later that summer in the August 19, 1893, issue report that "James O'Neill will begin rehearsing his company at the Lyceum Theatre, New London, on August 21." In the September 9 issue, the *Mirror* reported, "His company has been rehearsing in New London, Connecticut, where Mr. O'Neill spends his Summers."

It is therefore possible (although by no means sure) that the summer of 1893 really was spent largely at Bound Brook and therefore can be taken as a clue to a relapse into addiction by Ella. If so, there is still no way to determine exactly when it began and when it ended. Nevertheless, it appears to coincide roughly with the first indications of disturbance on the part of Jamie.

Of course by 1893 Jamie (born in 1878) was moving into adolescence, a disturbing period under almost any circumstances. James O'Neill's letter to the Reverend Thomas E. Walsh of Notre Dame on January 9, 1893 (after Jamie had spent Christmas vacation with his family in Chicago), worries over his beginning to smoke and also over his loss of innocence with his loss of childhood. In it James wrote, "He has some very old ideas of life and not the best by any means." He needed to be watched, and James O'Neill planned to "write him often, doing all I can to keep him at his work and in the right path."

Certainly during the school year 1893–94 Jamie, previously a really brilliant student, slipped off the honor role, and for the first time at Notre Dame took no awards. By the following summer they did go to New London, for the *New York Dramatic Mirror* of June 30, 1894, reports that James O'Neill had come to New York that Friday to meet his son (Jamie) returning from school in the middle west and that he then "went to New London on Saturday." Whether Ella was cured, but still in bad health from the destructive effects of the drug, is not clear from a second, significant letter James O'Neill sent on August 27, 1894, to President Morrissey of Notre Dame. The letter tells of James and Ella's hope that they could galvanize Jamie into renewed effort by sending him to a new school nearer to his mother. As to his mother, James explained, "Mrs. O'Neill's health may not permit her to go west with me." (He would be touring California and the Northwest that fall.) "She will likely spend most of the winter in New York. Under these circumstances we have decided to send

James to Georgetown where his mother can run over to see him frequently doing all in her power to keep him on his metal."

Apparently Ella was well by the summer of 1895, when again they went to New London, but the August 1, 1896, *New York Dramatic Mirror* announced, "James O'Neill and family are spending the summer at Twilight Park, Catskill mountains." If this meant a relapse for Ella into addiction, it may well have been one of the most intractable, for a full year later on May 1, 1897, the *Dramatic Mirror* quoted James O'Neill as declaring, "I shall spend the summer in the mountains with my family. I like my place at New London, but the sea air does not agree with Mrs. O'Neill."

But her problem certainly wasn't the sea air, for they never went to the mountains. The *Mirror* for July 24, 1897, told the anecdote that "James O'Neill was standing near the Staten Island shores where he has a cottage one day last week during the bathing hour. A lot of young women were diving from a raft. One of them climbed on after a struggle, struck an attitude, raised her hand to heaven and cried, 'The world is mine!' And she never guessed that the original of the pose was the man who smiled at her from the shore."

As Eugene O'Neill confided to Eugene Jr. long afterward, whatever went wrong within their immediate family, the O'Neills presented to the world "an indomitably united front and lied and lied for each other." Whether Ella was with James and her sons in the cottage on Staten Island or being treated nearby is a matter of pure speculation. Nor is it clear whether the week or two in the second half of August when the family returned to New London for rehearsals of O'Neill's company, Ella was there with them. Certainly James's New London friends showed they were especially glad to have him back that August. When he opened his season at nearby Norwich, Connecticut, on August 31, 1897—so the *Dramatic Mirror* reported—"A large delegation of Elks from New London where Mr. O'Neill spends his summers attended the performance of *The Dead Heart* and afterward tendered the actor and a few of his company a supper. A magnificent basket of flowers was also presented to Mr. O'Neill by members of the order."

The trouble for Ella must have seemed resolved for the time being, for the following year the *Dramatic Mirror* of May 28, 1898, reported, "Mr. and Mrs. O'Neill will go to New London, Connecticut this week for the summer." Also, the June 25 issue announced, "James O'Neill spent Thursday in New York, and returned to New London with his youngest son, who has just finished his term at Mount St. Vincent convent school. Mr. O'Neill is enjoying his vacation, amusing himself with gardening and aquatic pastimes." Finally, the September 3 issue reported that Minnie Radcliffe had been engaged for his new play

When Greek Meets Greek. "Miss Radcliffe left town Wednesday to join Mr. O'Neill's company at New London, Connecticut."

All that time up through James O'Neill's opening on March 13, 1899, in a spectacular production of *The Musketeers* at the Broadway Theater in New York, Ella was well and with her husband. Supporting James O'Neill in *The Musketeers* as leading lady was Margaret Anglin. She recalled in 1943 that she had then met Eugene backstage. "His mother brought him to see me, a little dark-eyed boy in a sailor suit. He was diffident until I said, 'Don't be afraid, I'm not going to kiss you. I have little brothers of my own and know they don't like it.'"

Nevertheless, Ella was again in trouble several months later. The June 10, 1899, *Dramatic Mirror* reported, "James O'Neill is spending a few days in town. He ran down to his cottage in New London after finishing his tour in *The Musketeers*, but it is not likely that he will spend the summer there, as the salt air does not agree with Mrs. O'Neill, and her physician recommends a sojourn in the mountains."

Whether or not they went there, James O'Neill was certainly in New London later that summer. The August 19, 1899, *Dramatic Mirror* announced that he would "begin rehearsals of the company which will support him this season in *The Musketeers*, August 21, in his private theater at his summer home, New London, Connecticut." It was thought that his would be "one of the largest companies on the road this coming season. Mr. O'Neill will be accompanied by seventy people."

This last uncertainty in the summer of 1899 about Ella's health appears to be the final episode in this siege of addictions, with "cures" and relapses stretching through the seven years from 1893 to the summer of 1899. They did go to New London thereafter (until her breast cancer diagnosis and mastectomy in 1916–17), so if the family's not going to New London for the summer is the salient clue as to Ella's drug state, she must have been free from trouble in those years. By 1900 she was once again in charge of her household.

Mount St. Vincent did not take boys after their twelfth birthday. In the fall of 1900 the O'Neills were transferring Eugene to De La Salle Institute at Central Park South (the present site of the Barbizon-Plaza Hotel). On September 18, 1900, James O'Neill would open in Boston for a month of the spectacular Liebler production of *Monte Cristo.* (The spectacle included a full-rigged ship coming into harbor onstage in the first act, a candelabra in the ball room scene nine feet high with over one thousand incandescent lights in imitation of candles; two hundred magnificent costumes; and thunder generated by rolling cannon balls around the stage on elevated runways.) After Boston the play would go to New York City to run from late October through the New Year of 1901. So Ella and James decided to take a furnished apartment there for the fall.

It was Ella—fully restored to her usual competence—who found them just what they wanted a few doors from Fifth Avenue on Sixty-eighth Street, ten blocks from De La Salle Institute. It happened that James O'Neill was the first of the family to arrive in New York, and he went, "lease in pocket," to take possession of the apartment. The woman of the house declared in dismay that she had no intention of giving it up.

"This is number 8, first floor, is it not?" James O'Neill asked, handing her the lease. She broke into smiles and replied, "This paper reads 68th Street. You are four blocks off on 64th." So James O'Neill was the erring member of the family, with a laughable story to tell as a joke on him perpetrated by a careless car conductor who let him off on the wrong street.

Not only was Ella fully recovered by 1900 and never absent, except for a trip to Europe, from New London thereafter (or at least there is no evidence that she was), she also seems to have been perfectly all right throughout the summer of 1912 (and the following winter as well)—and the summer of 1912 was the one in which Eugene O'Neill set the disastrous relapse of Mary Tyrone in *Long Day's Journey into Night*. Mary's relapse is as unhistorical for Ella as is her father's death from tuberculosis and her son's innocent guilt of driving her—through worry over his illness—into a relapse.

The only worry Ella O'Neill had at the end of the summer of 1912 was for her husband, not for Eugene. James O'Neill had planned to retire from the stage that summer of 1912. As he later confessed, "I spent the summer at my home in New London and got through the warm months without any trouble, but my first visit to New York made me restless. I felt like an old war horse that had been put aside, and it was uncomfortable, for since I first went into stock in minor parts in 1868, the stage has been my home. I had too much leisure. I didn't know what to do with myself. I tired of reading and would spend hours pacing up and down. This made my wife nervous, for she didn't understand what was the matter." Her worry over her husband was resolved when Tyler came to his rescue with the offer of the role of Jacob in his coming production of *Joseph and His Brethren*, which would open in New York that January of 1913.

Whatever worry she felt over Eugene when he became ill with pleurisy late in November 1912, it did not drive her to drugs. She was with James, Jamie, and Eugene when, as the *New London Day* announced on December 10, "James O'Neill, the actor, closed his home on Pequot Avenue and went to New York," and, they added, his son Eugene hoped "a change from this city's climate" would "better his recent illness of pleurisy."

Eugene was to be examined in the great city by two noted lung specialists there, Dr. Livingston Farrand and Dr. James Alexander Miller. Dr. Miller diagnosed "signs at the right apex and a few at the left base in addition to the thickened pleura at the right base," and recommended Eugene on December 17, 1912, to Dr. David Lyman at Gaylord Farm, Wallingford, Connecticut, as a "good case for your sanitarium." Certainly both James and Ella O'Neill knew Dr. Miller's opinion that Eugene "is in excellent general condition and is, I believe, a very favorable case." So with James and Jamie rehearsing *Joseph and His Brethren* and Eugene entering Gaylord Farm with a reassuring prognosis on Christmas Eve 1912, things would have been good for Ella.

Surely Eugene O'Neill was recalling other memories of being inadvertently guilty of precipitating his mother's relapse into addiction. Most likely he had in mind the final relapse of her life in 1917 when at last James O'Neill let out an admission of it to the Dorseys and the New London relatives. It was then probably that, while in New London for the first time when addicted, she had pleaded in vain for the drug, as Mary Tyrone recalls in the play. During 1916–17 when she was burdened with the anxiety of the diagnosis of malignancy and then the mastectomy, Eugene was in the midst of the frightful descent into drunken promiscuity that he indulged when Beatrice Ashe broke their engagement. Worry over him as well as suffering from her operation certainly brought on that last relapse of hers.

As for the characterization of Mary Tyrone under the watchful eye of her worried loved ones, Eugene O'Neill had his own memories of being in such a position. In the last years of his parents' lives, they were very worried about and watchful of him. He could stay sober for months in the safety of Provincetown, entirely focused on writing the plays that were beginning to make him famous. But when he came to New York for rehearsals, he was almost always led by his alcoholic friends in Greenwich Village into weeks of irresponsible and self-destructive intoxication.

With all their pride in his growing fame, both his parents tried, when he came to New York, to keep him sober enough to help in the production of his plays. Early in 1920 when he came to New York to see about prospective Broadway productions of two of his full-length plays, he wrote back from the Prince George Hotel to Agnes in Provincetown, "Most of the P. M. has been spent in the P. G. chatting with the old Governor and Mama who both appear extremely glad to see me—especially after the detective work at the greeting failed to discover my breath guilty." He assured Agnes that he intended to "spend most of my time right under their wing. So don't worry about me! I'm a good, good boy!" In fact, as Ella O'Neill had told Agnes after an earlier visit of Eugene's just before Christmas of 1919, "He was a very good boy while here the last time."

At the same time, Eugene was quick to resent any direct attempts to keep him from excessive drinking by his loved ones. When Agnes wrote warning him against his Greenwich Village friends who would try to drag him into drink, he replied that her "lecture" letter was both "unkind and unreasonable." "I've never in my life stood for that stuff, even from my mother." So however little he had seen of his mother on the brink of a relapse, he could portray Mary Tyrone's resentment of her family's suspicion and watchfulness out of his own reactions during his own relapses in his old drinking days.

What was true of Ella O'Neill's addiction was the genuine pain and guilt it produced in her family. But the sense of overwhelming fatality conveyed by the play and necessary to its tragic vision by no means represented the many years Ella spent free of that pall. Neither is the play's picture of Mary Tyrone's unrelenting, heartbreaking loneliness in accord with Ella's life. For one thing, although Eugene O'Neill believed that his mother shrank from theater people and was isolated while traveling with her husband on tour, these are belied by the records.

Actually, Ella O'Neill had warm relationships with many of the women in her husband's company, particularly the young, unmarried ones. Both she and James would include them in their excursions and dining out so they would not feel lonely. In fact, Ella became friends with several of these young actresses. One of the first we know about is Elizabeth Robins. From her first days with the company, both James and especially Ella O'Neill enveloped the young actress in kindness. As Elizabeth confided in a letter to her father on January 2, 1882, Ella often "prompts his kindness." Soon the O'Neills were including Elizabeth in their habitual exploratory outings of the area before they were due at the theater. The *New York Dramatic Mirror* reported that on January 12, 1883, Ella and Claire Raymond—Elizabeth's stage name—met with an accident in Rochester, New York. "While enjoying a sleigh-ride, the horse ran away, and the cutter tipped over; Mrs. O'Neill was quite seriously injured, cutter destroyed, and the horse crippled by jumping into an open area." But the whole matter was, the *Mirror* declared, "satisfactorily adjusted by Mr. O'Neill," who had been driving, by paying the owner fifty dollars.

This happened just weeks before James O'Neill disbanded his company to take up John Stetson's offer at the beginning of February 1883 of the role of Edmund Dantes in *Monte Cristo* at Booth's Theater in New York City. Thereafter, Elizabeth Robins and Ella O'Neill corresponded and met when they could. As late as January 29, 1887, Ella was writing Elizabeth from Montgomery,

Alabama, to tell her that James had finally done a performance of *Hamlet*, and she had acted as his dresser for it at Mobile a few evenings earlier.

Another friendship of which we have a record is that of Ella O'Neill with the actress Grace Raven. Grace made her debut as Mercedes in *Monte Cristo* when James O'Neill opened in that play to standing room only on September 9, 1886, at Springfield, Massachusetts. The *New York Spirit of the Times* described her as "very pretty and clever, but too tall for an ingenue." By May 1887 she was close enough to join them, when they reached South Bend, Indiana, in a morning visit to see their young son Jamie in the Minim department of the college of Notre Dame, where the boys recited for James O'Neill and he responded by giving them a very funny comic recital to their "deafening applause."

Also a friend of Elizabeth Robins, Grace Raven had heard much of Elizabeth's admiration for Ella O'Neill and gratitude for her kindness. Grace wrote Elizabeth about her own feeling for Ella. "If angels are on the earth, she certainly is one." Grace thought that Ella had "the most lovely, refined, patient disposition I have ever met."

After the New York opening trial run of *The Envoy* in May 1891, James O'Neill declared in answer to a question of who would be in his company for the fall 1891 tour, "Grace Raven, who has made an unquestionable hit in *The Envoy*, will remain with me as leading lady." Although Grace Raven retired from the stage altogether at the end of 1891, she, James, and Ella remained lifetime friends. Six years after her retirement from the company, the *New York Dramatic Mirror* reported from Dayton, Ohio, on January 17, 1897: "Mr. and Mrs. James O'Neill were the guests of Grace Raven. Miss Raven was leading lady of Mr. O'Neill's company several years ago, but forsook the stage and is now making this city her home."

Some time after this, Grace Raven became a nun, and Eugene O'Neill learned about her from his parents. To Sister Mary Leo Tierney, who had written to him of a "pupil" who had joined his father's company and later became a nun, Eugene O'Neill replied on February 6, 1925, "I remember that one of my father's leading ladies in Monte Cristo—Grace Raven—left the stage to enter a convent of the Good Shepherd (I think) and later became the Mother Superior there. But I have not heard of her in years and perhaps she may be dead by this. She could hardly be the pupil to whom you refer, I judge." Grace Raven's piety must have made her especially congenial to Ella O'Neill.

The circle of close family friends grew over the years. During his days as leading man in Uncle Dick Hooley's Parlor Home of Comedy, James O'Neill began a great friendship with the company's "heavy man," Nate Salsbury. They were both ambitious to succeed financially, Nate having made his own way in the world by the time he was nine years old, even as James had been apprenticed at ten. A year before James O'Neill left Hooley's for New York, Nate had organized Salsbury's Troubadours, had written a musical variety show for it, and was soon touring the world with it and making bushels of money so that by 1885 he could bring his friend James into investing in his million-dollar Millner cattle ranch at Fort Benton, Montana. Later Salsbury was managing both Barnum and Bailey's Circus and the Buffalo Bill Wild West Show.

From 1887 when Nate Salsbury married Rachel Samuels of Newburg, New York, and established a home on Sheridan Avenue in Chicago, both James and Ella became their close family friends, visiting with the Salsburys whenever James O'Neill's tours brought him to Chicago, or off-season in New York. On April 8, 1893, for instance, the *New York Dramatic Mirror* reported from Chicago of Salsbury, "O'Neill dropped out to see him last Friday and found him at table with his brood — four healthy youngsters, two of each sex, including a pair of twins. Sweeping the juvenile horizon with a proud hand he said to O'Neill: 'Jim, did you ever expect this when I used to growl out heavy man's speeches at you at Hooley's and when you were doing the handsome heroes?' James shook his head."

Even long after Nate Salsbury's death on December 24, 1902, both James and Ella O'Neill kept a friendship with his widow and her children. So when Ella died in 1922, Will Connor, who had rushed to Eugene's assistance, made every effort to get in touch with Rachel Salsbury and her family for Ella's funeral. Eugene wrote apologetically to Nate's son Milton Salsbury on May 17, 1922, that Will Connor and he "tried to locate your family via the phone book but with no success. I wished very much to have your Mother — all of you — present at the services which were held in New York." Also, because there was a confusion about the train connections from California, he had not known when Jamie would arrive in New York, so everything was arranged at the last minute. "But I do wish your Mother to know that I thought of her, that I knew it would be my Mother's wish that she should be present, and that I did try to get in touch with her but had no means of finding out her whereabouts."

Even during the tour of the all-star *Two Orphans* company from the spring of 1904 until May 1905, with its many one-night stands — which in these years James O'Neill usually spared his wife by sending her ahead to the large cities — Ella accompanied her husband, and they, as always, included some of the unmarried or solitary actresses on their excursions. Sarah Truax, who replaced Margaret Illington as Henriette, was married to an actor, Guy Bates Post, but their careers had divided them; they were in different companies; and at this point they were not even in correspondence. (By 1907 they were divorced.)

Young as she was, Sarah found that James O'Neill, in the role of Chevalier Vaudrey (he had played Pierre in he New York run), with "his figure" so "erect and slender," his "speech so silvery" was so romantic in appearance that no one in the audience caught their discrepancy in years. She remembered gratefully, "Mrs. O'Neill traveled with us sometimes, and they were both very good to me." When, for the week of February 13 through 18, 1905, they reached Louisiana, Sarah Truax recalled, "They took me to the Old Absinthe House in New Orleans, and I tasted absinthe for the first time." Eugene O'Neill's parents were much more inseparable and more often entertaining others together than their son Eugene later imagined, away at boarding school as he was for most of those years.

Certainly James O'Neill was always careful not to leave his wife lonely and bored when forced to be away from her even a few days at a time. Notes such as one he wrote to his good friend William Seymour at the Punch and Judy Theater in New York on January 8, 1917, are typical. "I am going to New London for a few days and Mrs. O'Neill will be alone. I wonder if you can spare three seats for Wednesday night and give her a pleasant evening during my absence? If business is capacity we are too old friends for you not to simply tell me so."

George Tyler was cheered to learn how well Ella was coping with James O'Neill's tangled affairs after her husband's death in 1920. He told Eugene, "You see, she never had a chance before—your dear father loved her so much that he couldn't bear to see her be anything else than an ornament." James O'Neill did spare her all housework (cooking and cleaning) from the time of their marriage, but he had a thorough respect for her higher capabilities, and for those of women in general. When a number of men in the profession argued against allowing women members to run a fair to raise money for the Actors' Fund on the grounds that they would be "insulted" by other males, James O'Neill wrote at once from Lincoln, Nebraska, on March 12, 1892, on behalf of the "noble women of our profession, who have grandly carried the good work on so well." He declared, "Has it never occurred to the persons that are so strenuously defending the women, and who are so anxious to throw the mantle of their manly (?) protection around the weak, defenceless creatures, that these same women have not once asked for said defence, or expressed a single doubt as to their personal or moral safety. When a woman says she cannot defend herself, and cries for assistance, then is the time to offer it, and not till then."

Even before the fair opened, the women announced that they had collected almost $78,000 in tickets and subscriptions. James O'Neill pointed out that the "greatest testimony" to refute the opposition was "that women who have the ability and character to carry such a grand scheme to such a grand success in such a marvellously short time have nothing to fear from all the horrors pictured by the opposition."

In no way did James O'Neill treat his wife as anything other than a beloved comrade. She was always with him on what he spoke of as "his fixed habit of exploring every town he visits and photographing its curios." She also shared his enjoyment of gourmet dining wherever they happened to be. Ella's old convent friend Loretto Ritchie Emerson — as Loretto's niece Marion McCandless testified — saw her as perfectly at home in her husband's world. Miss McCandless told me, "My aunt, Loretto Ritchie Emerson, often spoke of the very happy marriage of the O'Neills. Ellen used to say to her that her children 'grew up on the road,' as she went with her husband on his stands about the country." Marion McCandless also quoted a letter she had received from George Tyler several years before she wrote to me. "He said James and Ellen O'Neill were one of the most beloved couples of the theater world; James noted always for his affability under the trying conditions."

CHAPTER ELEVEN

Jamie Tyrone

S ome of the "old sorrow" in this play for his father and mother had been already resolved by Eugene O'Neill when he began to write *Long Day's Journey into Night* in 1940. But the unresolved pain and grief and resentment he still felt for his brother James had never been. A little of it had emerged and been alleviated in the writing of his play *The Great God Brown* back in the 1920s, but the greater part of his divided feelings for the beloved brother who had brought about so much of the early turmoil in his life had never been resolved through his creative work. In the course of the struggle to resolve *Long Day's Journey*, Eugene had to achieve far greater conscious understanding of his brother's role in his life as well as a resolution of it by way of the poetic imagery of the play.

In fact, it seems that after the play was finished, Eugene O'Neill was not satisfied that *Long Day's Journey into Night* had given him total acceptance of both the good and the evil that had come to him from his brother, or had allowed him to achieve complete and loving forgiveness. At any rate, Eugene found it necessary to follow this play a few years after with another one centered on Jamie. He could triumph over all the sorrow only by creating a second epitaph for Jamie in *A Moon for the Misbegotten.*

In *Long Day's Journey into Night* Eugene O'Neill had put his bitter exasperation with his son Shane into his depiction of his father's disillusion in Jamie so that the play Jamie is not a twin for Jamie O'Neill. What was lost thereby was a sense of the brilliant promise James Jr. had demonstrated throughout the years of his schooling until he risked a sufficiently scandalous act of defiance of the rules to make even the Jesuits — trained in coping with weakness of the flesh — cut him off from the Fordham degree he came so close to achieving. Also, unlike Shane, Jamie never showed a disposition after he left Fordham to live idly on his father's money. It was Shane — not Jamie — who showed himself—as James Tyrone complains in the play—ready to "sit back like a lazy lunk and sponge on me for the rest of your life!"

As for the crucial point of Jamie's expulsion from Fordham, there is no exact record of his misconduct—only the ambiguous notation "Withdrawn by request." Whatever Jamie did, it was sufficiently bad to warrant a severe penalty. So in December 1899 James O'Neill Jr. vacated his illustrious position as editor of the school magazine and missed out on the Fordham degree he had nearly completed.

Apparently, in view of James O'Neill Jr.'s brilliant academic record and the respect the authorities felt for his father, they chose to arrange things with discretion. However serious the infraction of the rules, they were not out to crush this young man's entire future. Their repression of the scandal left Jamie perfectly free to transfer his credits to another university somewhere else, and so take his degree. Certainly that is the ending James O'Neill would have wanted for the story, and he must have endeavored to convince Jamie to do so. Jamie himself must have refused absolutely to go back to being a schoolboy for even one more year of his life.

Thus, seven years later, when Jamie's younger brother Eugene was suspended from Princeton at the end of his freshman year, he was following his brother's example in deciding to make that the end of his college career by withdrawing permanently from the university. Curiously, after both James O'Neill's sons had thrown away the college diploma he had so wanted for them, and both in the same careless way, James had his advance man Jimmy Byth issue a public statement on his two wayward heirs that made them appear in a flattering light.

"James O'Neill had no slightest intention of allowing either of his two sons, James O'Neill, Jr., nor Eugene Gladstone O'Neill, to go on the stage. Eugene Gladstone had no wish to do so. Last month he made his successful debut in the manufacturing business. But James O'Neill, Jr. was suspiciously silent upon the theme of his future field of usefulness. His father's suggestions about the law rebounded from a wall of discouraging silence. At dinner one night the young man timidly approached the subject.

"'Father, I—I've decided what profession I should like to adopt. You and Mama won't like it very well—at first—but—?'

"'You want to go upon the stage?' The boy nodded. The father sighed. 'Well, I'll give you a chance to begin,' said the actor. 'It will be a very small chance,' he resolved. James O'Neill, Jr. was assigned to the smallest roles in the James O'Neill Company. 'I gave him $20 a week, and almost nothing to do,' said the actor. 'But by a slip in my plans he was made understudy for the man who plays my son in Monte Cristo. The young man did not make good, and there was nothing to be done but let the understudy play it. My son played the son in Monte Cristo. He did so well that we had to let him go on playing it. His salary went from $20 to $50. That spoiled my plans and settled his future.'"

That James O'Neill had certainly hoped for a career in law for both his sons was true. But it was pure generosity that inspired James O'Neill to make it appear that Jamie had gotten a role in *Monte Cristo* in spite of, rather than because of, his father. Clearly what had taken place was that Jamie received a year's training in acting from his father (beginning sometime after he left Fordham at the end of 1899 and lasting through the August rehearsals in his father's company in 1901) by assigning him small roles and having him understudy some of the more demanding roles. Jamie's debut was announced in the *New York Dramatic Mirror* of November 2, 1901: "James O'Neill, Jr. made his debut as Albert in Monte Cristo in support of his father at Waterbury, Connecticut, October 23, and was successful in the part."

Unlike the Albert de Morcerf of the Dumas novel, the character in the Fechter version turns out to be in a surprise happy ending the son of Edmund Dantes by his lost love Mercedes. Thus the role seemed made for James Jr. Audiences loved the real father and son relationship behind the play one. When Jamie first appeared at McVicker's Theater in Chicago on February 17, 1902, a review of this spectacular version of *Monte Cristo* declared, "Last evening's entertainment was made particularly charming by the debut of James O'Neill, Jr., who, by his unusual resemblance to his father promises another generation of Monte Cristo." The critic of the *Dramatic Mirror* in Chicago reported in admiration of the father, "Mr. O'Neill is apparently years younger than the handsome young man who is his son both in real life and in the play, and the elder James was playing Monte Cristo when he told me of this same youth as a prattling baby." All of Jamie's reviews were favorable. Eugene (at De La Salle Institute in New York) wrote his cousin Lillian Brennan in New London, "Jamie has made a big hit" (as Albert) "and there are big notices about him in all the papers wherever they go."

So the ending of Jamie's debut season from October 1901 through May of 1902 was full of hope and promise for both father and son, and Jamie was at his most witty and charming when he and his father came to Liebler and Company's New York premises to plan for the next season. As written up for publicity shortly after, this is what took place.

"Mr. O'Neill and his son were smoking and chatting in William Connor's office when Connor remarked to 'Jamie,' as the young actor is known among his friends, that he soon would be as big a man as his father.

"'Oh, I don't know,' he replied, taking a deep breath and inflating his chest to its full capacity. 'On chest measurement, I think I've got the pater pushed way up stage.' O'Neill, Sr. observed that if Jamie were speaking figuratively he admitted everything, as he considered him the chestiest youngster he ever had met; but if it were a case of material inches — well. Mr. O'Neill stood erect and inhaled a bit of oxygen himself. Then he winked at Mr. Connor. At the psychological moment Herman Friedmann, who has charge of all the Liebler firm's 'paper,' entered the office carrying a wire tape measure.

"'Ah,' exclaimed young O'Neill, 'just the thing! If Mr. Friedmann will let us take his tape a moment we shall see.'

"'We shall see!' exclaimed the father, and immediately stripped off his coat and waistcoat. Jamie followed suit. Friedmann carefully measured the younger man's chest. Result, forty inches. The older man then threw back his shoulders and smiled. 'For the entire office force, Jamie,' he said, 'at the buffet across the street.'

"'Father' said the dutiful youth, 'you're on.'

"Friedmann stretched the tape around Mr. O'Neill's chest. Then he let out a link. Then he let out another link. Then he said: 'Forty-four and one-quarter inches!'

"'I especially stipulated the chest,' said Jamie, 'not the waist measurement.'

"'But this is the chest,' protested Mr. Friedmann. The thirty-eighth street elevator had to make two trips to accommodate Jamie's guests and for five minutes the Liebler and Company offices were closed while the Normandie buffet provided the largest single treat of the season. The check amounted to $6.90.

"'Present this bill with my compliments,' said the young O'Neill, 'to the elderly grey-haired gentleman at the other end of the line. He has a wallet filled with bank notes sewed to the inside of his shirt that increases his chest measurement exactly five inches.' Then he turned to his father and added: 'Pater, I hate to give you away. But $6.90 for a single high ball — this is too much for a poor young actor!'"

It looked as if Jamie was on his way. After his introduction to the public in 1901–2 with his father's company, he had been gotten a role for the coming season by Liebler and Company in *Audrey*, supporting Eleanor Robson. His father would be touring his company that year in *The Honor of the Humble*. *Audrey* opened November 17, 1902, in Richmond, Virginia, at the Academy of Music to crowded houses. The *New York Clipper* declared it an "immense drawing card." Yet that auspicious beginning of an independent acting career unshadowed by his father for Jamie went up in smoke only months after it began. As Eleanor Robson explained later, she became "seriously ill." "We had to close *Audrey* because my physician said I would be a nervous wreck if I continued playing." That, of course, was not Jamie's fault.

But the fact that he reverted to his father's company for the next seven years — that is, as long as his father had one — must certainly have been at least in part his choice, for he had begun well and had done nothing at this stage of his career to close opportunities to him. There were great personal advantages to touring with his father. Enormously popular as James O'Neill was, he was frequently feted by the Elks, Knights of Columbus, and fellow actors wherever he went, and as soon as Jamie joined his company, he was included by his father in all the invitations he received. That first season, for instance, at Evansville, Indiana, the *New York Clipper* of December 7, 1901, reported that "James O'Neill and his son were entertained by the Knights of Columbus of this city." When they reached St. Paul, Minnesota, on March 4, 1902, the *Clipper* of March 15 reported, "The Knights of Columbus gave a reception in their hall to James O'Neill and his son. A good program was presented consisting of musical numbers, a wrestling match, and a boxing bout. After the program was over refreshments were served." They certainly included lavish servings of the very best in alcoholic drinks. When they played South Bend, Indiana, Jamie and his father were entertained by the faculty and students of Notre Dame. As the *Dramatic Mirror* of March 29, 1902, recounted, James Jr. had been "educated at the University of Notre Dame and began his stage career on the University stage. Young O'Neill, his father, and the company were guests of honor at the St. Patrick's Day performance of *Twelfth Night*" by the students. Such entertainments were typical, and Jamie went everywhere with his father.

Besides, Jamie was also constantly included by his parents in their habitual dining at the most famous gourmet restaurants in any of the large cities in which they happened to be. Certainly the constant companionship of his mother on the road was for Jamie a chosen pleasure, for she was always his deepest attachment. At the same time, he was a free male adult and could also carry on what seems to have been his life program throughout those years: that of making as many sexual conquests as possible among the attractive girls to whom his position as an actor gave him access in all the great cities of the United States.

Thus Jamie was back with his father in the fall of 1903 touring in the role of Captain Sabattier to his father's Captain Gerard in *The Adventures of Gerard*, with nothing notable in his press notices except the report from St. Louis in the *New York Times* on December 17 that in his "thrilling sword play" with James Sr. at the Olympic Theater, "the veteran actor almost severed his son's right hand at the wrist." In March 1904 when he and his father returned to their home in

New London, Connecticut, for the rehearsals by Liebler and Company of the all-star revival of *The Two Orphans* with James O'Neill, Grace George, Clara Morris, Louis James, Kyrle Bellew, Margaret Illington, and Charles Warner, one of the supporting nonstar players was James O'Neill Jr. in the role of Lafleur, an impersonation that went unnoticed both at the New York opening and the tour that followed up to June 1905. On the other hand, his father was universally praised in the role of Pierre, the cripple, which he took at first, as "fine of method and intelligent and sympathetic" or as "so realistic" in the role "that he made us shudder." He was an actor "whose art always shines out." Later, when he took over Kyrle Bellew's role of the Chevalier Vaudrey, he was praised for his "courtly, fine, and finished impersonation."

When James O'Neill returned to a farewell tour in *Monte Cristo* for the 1905–6 season, he made some attempt to give Jamie experience in some of the more demanding roles. In the program for the West End Theater Christmas matinee of 1905, James Jr. is listed as playing Nortier. He must have failed in the part, for Jamie's career ended as it began with his playing the role of Albert de Morcerf, relying on his good looks and resemblance to his father to get by.

In fact, by 1906 some critics were saying that James O'Neill's son, though "much like his father," was "still far short of the high standard the older man has reached. The voice is not as smooth and even, and there is not the same magnetic presence. But the training that he is receiving will be invaluable, and something should be heard of him later." The following year, this same critic of the *Florida Times Union* declared that James O'Neill's company was "wholly competent" with the "one exception of the wonderful old actor's son." "James O'Neill, Jr.," the review continued, "has inherited none of his father's histrionic ability. He is decidedly weak, and his experience has not worked to improve him. Several of the climaxes were almost absolutely ruined by his stiffness, his lack of fire, his characterless speaking of the lines. When the heart of the father ceases to cloud the judgment of the actor and artist, James O'Neill, Sr. will drop James O'Neill, Jr. from his company; and the plays will be the better therefore."

Jamie's acting was very uneven. Sometimes he still received good reviews. The *Pittsburgh Leader* of April 16, 1907, declared that James Jr. "is a manly looking chap and did excellent work" as Albert de Morcerf in *Monte Cristo*. The *Pittsburgh Dispatch* of the day after that declared that Jamie "resembles his father in many respects and gives promise of better things in the future." But in these years he began receiving very bad notices. When Jamie was playing the villain Dr. Feneton to his father's Abbé Bonaparte in the play of that name, the *St. Louis Star* of September 7, 1908, declared of Jamie, "Heredity appears to have failed in his case."

Meanwhile, James O'Neill Jr. was busy with his truly chosen career of wine, women, and song. The extreme failures in his acting came from a growing tendency to go on stage, as Tom Dorsey Jr. expressed it, "all corned up," that is, drunk to the point where his never brilliant acting degenerated into expressionless repetition of the lines. Jamie's successes were all offstage in variations on the role of Don Juan. The *New York Standard* of October 5, 1906, gave a suggestion of one of Jamie's erotic successes by hinting that the "fine old actor," James O'Neill, has "a son old enough to be almost engaged to Elfie Fay." Elfie's father was Hugh Fay of Barry and Fay, vaudeville Irish comedians, and she had grown up in show business. By 1906 Elfie was already starring in "a riotous single" act as a "sprightly hoyden." Her "specialty" and "trademark" was the rendition of "The Belle of Avenue A" to the applause of all New York.

"Almost engaged" Jamie might well have been, but "altogether engaged" he never would be. Marriage was not what he was seeking when winning women. Nor were the great majority of his affairs such as could be given a respectable gloss for publication. The rumor of his conquest of Elfie Fay was just the barest tip of the iceberg. Buried beneath the surface was a veritable mountain of seductions, ranging from starlets to chorus girls and on down.

On the whole, Jamie took his position of being the junior of James O'Neill as a joke. The *New York Dramatic Mirror* of March 3, 1906, passed on the joke by announcing, "Lionel and John Barrymore and James O'Neill, Jr. have solemnly organized a society known as 'The Sons of Actors.' Lionel is the president, John the secretary, and the younger O'Neill the treasurer, and the trinity forms also the Board of Directors. The directors are busy just now stalking members." The two Barrymores went on to surpass their position as sons of Maurice Barrymore by a greater fame than their father's. But James O'Neill Jr. never approached even equaling his father.

Not having fulfilled any of his early promise as an intellect or as an actor, James Jr. was certainly a disappointment to his father. But by reading his own disappointment in his son Shane into his play, Eugene O'Neill gave James Tyrone Jr. failures that never belonged to his brother. Certainly up to 1912, the time of the play, and even beyond, Jamie could not be accused, as is James Tyrone Jr., of a lazy refusal to work. Until the spring of 1909, Jamie acted steadily in his father's company every year. Then in the fall of 1909, when James O'Neill disbanded his own company to accept the role of Monseigneur Saracinesca in *The White Sister* with Viola Allen, a play in which there was no subordinate role for Jamie, Liebler and Company placed James Jr. in their second road company for *The Traveling Salesman*.

The first company, which played in New York City until April 10, 1909, had more successful actors and went on to play to capacity houses in all the great cities of the United States, starting with Chicago. The second company acting that popular melodrama was aimed strictly at small-town America, with one-night stands requiring grueling travel from town to town, crossing back and forth over state boundaries. A typical section of their schedule read like this: "Great Barrington, Massachusetts, March 2, 1909; Pittsfield 3; North Adams 4; Gardner 5; Fitchburg 6; Norwich, Connecticut 8; New London 9; Willimantic 10; Middletown 11; New Britain 12; Meriden 13; Winsted 15; Derby 16; Waterbury 17; Bridgeport 18; South Norwalk 19; Peekskill, New York 20; Wilmington, Delaware 22; Frederick, Maryland 23;" et cetera.

It was by no means easy work moving from town to town and from theater to theater, often by night trains to makeshift accommodations. Nevertheless, Jamie worked steadily through the whole tour all through 1910 and 1911. Then he joined his father for the equally grueling twice-daily performances on the Orpheum circuit of the vaudeville version of *Monte Cristo* beginning in September 1911 and concluding mid-March 1912. Only after January 1915 when *Joseph and His Brethren* closed and James O'Neill was no longer touring with his own company so that jobs did not fall into Jamie's lap, did the younger O'Neill fall idle. "The lazy lunk" ready to sponge off his father had not yet appeared in Jamie at the time Eugene O'Neill set the action of *Long Day's Journey into Night*. Only in the very last years of his father's life did Jamie descend into unremitting alcoholism and irremediable unemployment.

Rather than striving to become a better actor, Jamie aimed his ingenuity at making clever bets on racehorses. This choice, like many others in his life, came out of what he found at hand in his father's way of life. James O'Neill himself had no passion for gambling, but he loved fine horses and many of his close theatrical New York friends including Connor and Tyler at Liebler and Company enjoyed the races and heightened their interest by bets on which horse would win. When James O'Neill returned to New York at the end of his season in May 1903, he went along "for the company" with his sporting friends to a bar where it was possible to place money on the races. The Brooklyn Handicap was on. After placing their bets, Tyler and Connor began to talk of the turf and to tease O'Neill over his innocence of it. James O'Neill confessed—as was reported shortly afterward—that "the only thing he knew about the races was that there was a prominent jockey named O'Neill, who, he believed, was distantly related to him." His tablemates told him that this very jockey would ride one of the horses in the Handicap that day. Immediately O'Neill reached into his pocket and "pulled out a considerable sum," asking his companions to place his money on the jockey O'Neill to win the race.

They objected, "But O'Neill isn't a horse. O'Neill is the jockey, and the horse he is to ride stands no show to get in the money."

"Ah," O'Neill asked, "what is the name of the horse?"

"Irish Lad."

"Irish Lad!" exclaimed O'Neill, pulling out still more money to be placed on O'Neill and his mount. "Irish Lad and O'Neill is too good a combination to miss. You can't beat them."

He was immediately attacked by all his friends, scolding his "reckless waste of money." They suggested he place the bet "across the board" to increase his almost impossible chances. James O'Neill insisted on a straight bet, repeating, "They can't beat an O'Neill on Irish Lad." One of the company offered him an additional personal bet that he would lose all his money. James O'Neill accepted that bet too. In the end, the knowing ones were amazed and confounded to learn that Irish Lad with O'Neill riding him won the Handicap, paying odds of twelve to one.

Thereafter it was not unusual for James O'Neill to run into New York from New London for a day to attend the races. One year — so Eugene reported long afterward — James O'Neill hired a coachman for New London who owned several racehorses himself. With his love of splendid horses, James O'Neill went into partnership with him thereafter, using the farm he had bought at Bound Brook (later Zion), New Jersey. As Eugene O'Neill informed his friend Marion Welch in September 1905, he and his family were staying at his father's farm in New Jersey with "a breeder of race horses." With frequent visits there, both Jamie and Eugene learned all about racing from the inside.

Eugene (and probably Jamie with him) became adept at studying the racing form sheets. With his fine memory, Eugene knew their contents by heart. One day the former coachman took the boy to the Sheepshead Bay track and introduced him to a famous trainer, Al Weston. "They started to talk horses, of course," Eugene recalled long afterward, "and the minute they'd mention a name I'd break in and say, 'Oh, yes: Laddie Z, by Buzzfuzz out of Guinevere; ran second at Morris Park, June 16th; fourth at Sheepshead, July 10th.' I knew them all; I couldn't help it. After an hour of this, Weston gave me a hard look and said, 'Kid, either you'll be a jockey or you'll get yourself killed.'" With all these contacts with racing men and with the racehorses on their New Jersey farm, it is no wonder that Jamie became addicted to gambling. Always putting himself unconsciously in rivalry with his father, and never winning except verbally and fictitiously through his wit, Jamie developed a lust for magical victories. He couldn't direct himself to striving for supremacy as an actor, so he placed his hopes on luck and an absolute faith in his own cleverness. Ultimately, when the death of his father released Jamie from his compulsive but eternally losing battle for supremacy over him, James Jr. was actually able to use his brilliance in the mathematics of probability to improve his chances.

Eugene O'Neill confided to his friend Harold DePolo on January 10, 1922, that one "bit of news" about Jamie would surprise him: "He hasn't had a drink in almost a year and a half now." (That is, from the time of their father's death on August 10, 1920.) "Fact, I swear to you! My mother got him to go on the wagon and stick—and he has stuck. Another bit of info will more than surprise you. His sobriety has had a wonderful effect on his judgment of the ponies. He follows a system of his own with religious rigidity, has accumulated quite a small bankroll in reserve, and spends hours a day in intensive doping. He has been beating them for the past year almost."

So Eugene O'Neill was using his own memory of his brother after their father's death to create James Tyrone's response to Jamie's teasing quote of *Othello*, "If it takes my snoring to make you remember Shakespeare instead of the dope sheet on the ponies, I hope I'll keep on with it." The passion for gambling came early to James Jr., but his devotion of hours each day to study of the racing form sheets came long after 1912, the time set for James Tyrone's remark. Like other aspects of James Tyrone Jr.'s character, it was altered in significance by being taken out of the chronology of its inspiration.

Eugene O'Neill achieved a resolution for his turbulent feelings toward his brother in part by giving him credit for the positive inheritance Jamie had given him, along with the negative. In the play O'Neill makes clear his debt to Jamie for a love of contemporary poetry and a desire to create it. In the final act, Jamie Tyrone expresses the loneliness and anguished loss of the three men of the family at Mary Tyrone's detachment from and indifference to them when she is under the influence of the drug. At the very finale of the last act, Jamie quotes with intense sorrow Algernon Charles Swinburne's "A Leave-Taking" with its heartbroken refrains, "She would not hear" and "She would not know."

Moreover, he made Jamie Tyrone fully conscious of his ambivalence toward the younger brother he introduced to dissipation at a dangerously early age. In a moment of truth, Jamie himself warns Edmund to watch out for his own jealous compulsion—despite his love—to "stab you in the back." Nevertheless, with all Eugene O'Neill's effort to extract the love and good wishes from the destructive in his brother's contradictory feeling for him, Eugene had arrived

— if not in full conscious awareness — at a complete understanding of Jamie's need to see to it that his mother and father's "pet" failed as dismally in life as he had.

This understanding appears in the curious half-farcical story Jamie Tyrone tells of his evening at the local brothel. In pity he had selected Fat Violet because she was about to be given "the gate," having become too fat to attract customers, and having lost her chief asset, her ability to play the piano, by her tendency to become "too boiled to play." Both these attributes echo curiously the associations with Mary Tyrone at the start of the play when she is flattered with "how fat and beautiful" she looks, or teased for being "so fat and sassy." Also, as the long day progresses she recalls her promise as a pianist and mourns because her hands have become too crippled to allow her to play.

So the story of Jamie weeping over Fat Violet and at the same time scorning her as the "fat girl in a hick town hooker shop" suggests that Jamie is plagued by an indelible association of the mother he loves and admires with prostitutes. He himself, recalling the first time he caught her with a needle, says he had not dreamed that any "women but whores took dope." Thus, just faintly hinted, but certainly indicative of Eugene O'Neill's inner knowledge, is the idea that Jamie O'Neill's resort to prostitutes and compulsion to seduce scores of women came as an unconscious revenge on the mother he loved for her disillusioning addiction.

Moreover, the farcical Fat Violet scene suggests that Eugene O'Neill knew that Jamie O'Neill's compulsion to introduce his fifteen-year-old brother to prostitutes came of his need to make him share in both the revenge and the disillusionment. Certainly by writing this encounter of Jamie Tyrone with the prostitute, Eugene had come to a conscious perception of the suppressed hatred and vengeance mixed with pity and lust that undermined Jamie's relations with women and pushed him to a taste for conquests of tarts and women of the streets. At any rate, when Eugene followed up this play with another giving even greater forgiveness and understanding for his brother as Jamie Tyrone — A Moon for the Misbegotten — O'Neill would have Jamie confess explicitly to the revenge he has taken against his dead mother with a particularly degrading "pig" of a prostitute on the days of the long train journey carrying his mother's body from California to New York for her funeral and burial.

CHAPTER TWELVE

Edmund Tyrone

I t is notable that Eugene O'Neill made himself, as the character Edmund Tyrone, the most guilty, if innocently so, of the four Tyrones. At any rate, in this play, it is Edmund, by way of his incipient tuberculosis, who frightens his mother into a relapse of her drug addiction. That, in turn, drives the three male Tyrones into drunkenness. In this way Edmund triggers all the tragedy of the one-day play. Despite the switch in names that keeps the "Eugene" of the play safely sheltered from all blame as his mother's dead baby and allows him to treat himself in the character Edmund more objectively, Eugene O'Neill certainly was aware that he could design Edmund's guilt only by fictionalizing on a fairly large scale. He knew that he had almost no information on his maternal grandfather, and that he would have to imagine the facts he needed to depict a fatality in Edmund's sickness. In fact, even where Eugene O'Neill thought he knew the facts about his grandfather, he demonstrated his ignorance, as he did by attributing his Uncle William Joseph Quinlan's profession of wholesale grocer to his grandfather, when Thomas Joseph Quinlan's liquor and cigar store would have fit the fatal influence of alcohol in the family much better.

O'Neill was perfectly conscious of the fact that he was ascribing his wife Agnes's loss of her father, Edward (Teddy) Boulton, killed by tuberculosis at the very time their marriage was breaking up, to his mother in the play, so that she would be especially terrified of the tuberculosis in her son. As has been already seen, Thomas Joseph Quinlan's obituary in the *Cleveland Plain Dealer* of May 26, 1874, declared that Quinland died "after a short illness," which excludes a long disease like tuberculosis. Also, there is no evidence of a relapse on Ella O'Neill's part in December of 1912, when Dr. James Alexander Miller diagnosed Eugene's attack of pleurisy as "a very favorable case" of tuberculosis so that it did not appear life-threatening, even with the fear of consumption at the time, so Eugene O'Neill really manufactured for himself in this autobiographical play a guilt of which he was never guilty.

The answer to this riddle is that an overwhelming guilt was certainly a key autobiographical fact in O'Neill's life although even with all his insight, he could not always pinpoint what aroused the feeling in him.

Curiously enough, while giving his play a fictional guilt, Eugene O'Neill excluded from his play and the character of Edmund a very real guilt of which he was fully conscious. He represented his earlier compulsive drinking, but not the resulting distress he had caused the women he loved by seeking oblivion. As has been seen, friends of his such as Hutchins Hapgood testified to his need to blot out reality, as did others who witnessed it at the time. Malcolm Cowley told me of having to put O'Neill to bed in Greenwich Village during the early years of Prohibition, and recalled to others Eugene's flight from Ridgefield to the Hell Hole when Wallace reported Eugene had holed up in one of the back rooms and "drunk himself into a coma." In the play O'Neill attributes this old guilt that lost him Beatrice, brought misery to his marriage with Agnes, and almost lost him Carlotta, not to himself as Edmund, but to the father, James Tyrone. Eugene O'Neill certainly knew that James O'Neill never drank to the point of losing self-control. Nevertheless, the needs of his play won out over truth. Eugene O'Neill used his recollections of his own shocking disgraces in early loves to give Mary Tyrone a devastating disillusionment right at the start of her romantic marriage — a disillusionment that his own mother never experienced, but the women he loved in the years before he conquered his alcoholism certainly had.

In the play O'Neill had Edmund refer to his suicide attempt, but he erased the fact that he, Eugene, had been driven to it by his belief at the time that he had ruined his hopes of true love forever. There is no mention in *Long Day's Journey into Night* of his miserable marriage to the pregnant Kathleen Jenkins, his subsequent flight first to Honduras and then to Argentina, nor to the ugly and degrading staged adultery in the brothel on December 29 and the early hours of December 30, 1911, which left him desperate enough to take his life. The references to Argentina in the play treat his going there, as O'Neill had always treated it in interviews, as if it were prompted by his own romantic impulse, and as if it had nothing to do with the marriage to Kathleen or his father's attempts to rescue him from it.

Eugene O'Neill certainly excluded mention of that first marriage in all his accounts of his early life. Nevertheless, his omission of the marriage from the play was probably necessitated as much by artistic considerations as by any wish of his that it had never taken place. The focus in the play rests sharply on emotional forces within the immediate family. All the tensions, conflicts, and shifting alliances are determined by interaction among the four Tyrones: mother, father, and two sons. The offstage characters, the deceased grandparents and the still-living Shaughnessy, McGuire, and Fat Violet, are only there for what they reveal of the family and take no part in either the one-day tragedy or the four Tyrones' tragic straying from ideals. A wife for one of the sons, even a divorced wife, would have broken the concentration on how forces from the family past have alienated the four of them forever from what they wished to be.

As for the chief guilt Eugene O'Neill did take upon himself in the character of Edmund — causing his mother's addiction by his birth — the only certainty is that O'Neill believed it, although there is medical doubt that birth pains last long enough to make for addiction. Yet even the play declares that James Tyrone did not discover Mary's drug-taking until long after it began. There is every reason to suspect that Ella O'Neill's addiction could have begun during her long illness after the death of her baby Edmund in 1885, rather than after Eugene's birth in 1888. Also, there is no necessity for the doctor who prescribed it to have been a cheap one, as in the play. Morphine was standard treatment for severe pain at the time. Only years later did it become apparent that most addictions had begun with a physician's legitimate prescription. O'Neill's belief may or may not be true — but the brevity of the pain in a successful birth like O'Neill's throws much scientific doubt upon its validity. The affectionate recall by Elizabeth Murray, Eugene's nurse in those first weeks of his life of Ella, his "dear mother," suggests that at that time Ella O'Neill was her usual charming self, not a woman muddled by drugs. Also, since Ella breast-fed Eugene throughout his infancy (as attested in the records of Gaylord Farm), she appears to have been thought in good health at the time.

The character of Edmund is fully as tragic as those of the other three Tyrones. The end of the play is full of Edmund's bleak feeling of a hopelessly ruined life from his knowledge that he is consumptive. Yet by 1940 when he began writing, no one knew better than Eugene O'Neill that his own tuberculosis had led, not to ruin, but to the happy ending of a quick return to health and a rebirth into a rich new life as a devoted playwright.

O'Neill was depicting very truly his own dark outlook after his diagnosis, despite the excellent prognosis he had been given. Certainly he was sincere when he told Agnes's father Teddy Boulton that the first weeks in a sanitorium "are the devil's own for getting one at the bottom of depression." In fact, all the photographs of O'Neill with other patients at Gaylord Farm in those early months show him scowling resentfully at the camera, immortalizing his misery.

So there is no hint of the coming of what he would consider his rebirth as a playwright at Gaylord Farm in *Long Day's Journey into Night*. There is no hint of his reconciliation with his father, nor of his father's pride in him as America's most promising dramatist in the year or two before his death. Nor is there any hint in the play's image of James Tyrone of Eugene's final realization, written to Agnes at his father's deathbed, that his father had been "a good man, in the best sense of the word — and about the only one I have ever known." There is even less suggestion of Eugene O'Neill's ultimate decision that the best test of what his father had attained was "the great affection and respect that all bear him who knew him."

Also, there is only the slightest hint in *Long Day's Journey*, expressed as a seemingly hopeless longing, of the fact that his mother would, as she actually did, ultimately free herself totally from drugs. No more had Eugene O'Neill given any hint that during the years after his birth, there were very many years, by far the majority, in which Ella, with all her charm and beauty, had remained untainted by them.

A great work of art cannot stay factually true to the complexities of life. Tragedy cannot express the awe and pity it conveys to an audience for very real agonies in the human condition if it muddles together all the joys and achievements and prides with the old sorrows. Eugene O'Neill was perfectly sincere, nevertheless, when he said this play of "old sorrow" had been written "in blood." He had truly suffered over and pitied and regretted all the personal traits, forces out of their past, and chance events of life that had separated him and his beloved ones forever from the ideals and dreams they had hoped to fulfill. He had suffered as much for his mother and for all the women he had loved when he represented the play father as falling into his own former habit of drinking himself comatose as if he had represented it in the character representing himself. He had felt just as guilty projecting himself into the play father as into the younger son. He was not exculpating himself by transposing it, merely using the facts where they would have the greatest dramatic effect. The unwary biographer who raids a so-called autobiographical play for the facts of an author's life will end up disseminating a mass of misinformation.

Certainly Eugene O'Neill's life story has been raddled with "facts" and foolish interpretations by biographers who took all the events in *Long Day's Journey into Night* as literally true. James Tyrone and Ella Tyrone and their two sons have much of the atmosphere of their originals, even if they take features from other people and actions done by others. *Long Day's Journey into Night* is profoundly true, but never as a literal record of the family of Eugene O'Neill. Its truth lies in the universality of the human inability to achieve fully all the ideals and dreams of youth, in the picture it gives of the way a family's past may determine its present and future, in its analysis of the intrinsic innocence of much guilt, and in its compassionate view of inevitable human regret and loss. Had O'Neill written a perfectly accurate account of his youth and family, he would never have created the immensely moving and revealing tragedy that *Long Day's Journey into Night* ultimately became.

CHAPTER THIRTEEN

The Black Widow

On October 13, 1940, Eugene O'Neill finished the second draft of *Long Day's Journey into Night*. On November 29, 1945, he made sure his publishers, Random House, agreed legally to his stipulation that his contract for *Long Day's Journey into Night* include the clause, "Publication shall not take place until twenty-five (25) years after my death." On June 13, 1951, he reminded Bennett Cerf that the play "is to be published twenty-five years after my death" with the added stipulation "but never to be produced as a play." He had appointed his "darling Carlotta" to become his literary executor and see that all his wishes were carried out, and he died on November 27, 1953, in the conviction that she would do so.

But it all turned out differently than he had hoped. If his "darling Carlotta" had sat down and decided that she would consistently negate what he wanted for this play and all the others in her power, she could not have brought about the opposite of his wishes more consistently and thoroughly than she did. She had started out well by giving José Quintero permission to produce *The Iceman Cometh* at the Circle in the Square. His excellent and intimate representation rescued the play from its unfortunate Broadway debut by the Theater Guild in 1946 and gave it its deserved reputation as one of the greatest of O'Neill's plays. Already at this point Carlotta was taking her first step contrary to her husband's wishes demonstrating her absolute power as his literary executor.

Only a year and a half after O'Neill's death on November 27, 1953, she must have already decided to wield that power, for she notified Random House that they were to break the seal O'Neill had placed on *Long Day's Journey into Night* as a first step to publishing the play. Bennett Cerf thereupon read it, saw what a painful and unflattering revelation it gave if looked upon as autobiography, and became convinced that O'Neill's consistent orders up to the time of his death that the play was not to be opened and published until twenty-five years after his death represented the author's indelible wishes and must be adhered to. Carlotta, taking advantage of her total legal control, thereupon broke the contract with Random House for refusal to carry out her orders. Apparently, she then talked with Donald Gallup, librarian of the Yale American Literature Collection, as to what publisher he advised her to try. So it came about that, on his advice, astonishingly enough, although it was a small university press generally publishing books aimed at a very limited readership, with none of the resources for publicity of a commercial house, Yale University Press announced, as newspapers all over the United States reported on June 21, 1955, that it would publish Eugene O'Neill's *Long Day's Journey into Night* on February 20, 1956. (Typical of their underestimate in their inexperience of publishing a major author, they timidly published only five thousand copies in their first edition, which naturally were entirely sold out well before publication date.)

Left with the problem of explaining why she did the opposite of what O'Neill wanted, Carlotta created an explanation that converted O'Neill, postmortem, to her point of view. During an interview with Seymour Peck and Brooks Atkinson, she said in answer to Peck's reminder of the twenty-five-year ban O'Neill had placed on publication: "Well, I might as well get this over." When she and O'Neill had come to New York at the end of 1945, she said, O'Neill had told Random House he wanted them to promise not to publish *Long Day's Journey into Night* until twenty-five years after his death, and they agreed. Then "about 1952–53," when she complained of lack of money, he told her, "We've got a nest egg" and informed her it was *Long Day's Journey into Night*. She told Atkinson and Peck that she had then asked, "What about the twenty-five-year restriction?" and Eugene announced, "Oh, well, that's all over now; we don't have to do that" because Eugene O'Neill Jr. was then dead, and "it was he who asked me." As she recalled, Eugene Jr. had told his father he did not think that the play should be published or produced, "because it puts me in a bad light. It shows the kind of family I came from." Quite apart from how out of character this supposed reply of Eugene Jr. is, it is also decisively contradicted, and by his father himself, in an account of his son Eugene's first reading of *Long Day's Journey into Night* that O'Neill wrote into his *Work Diary* on September 4, 1941, immediately after the reading. "Eugene reads *Long Day's Journey Into Night*— greatly moved, which pleases me a lot." The following day he gave him *The Iceman Cometh*, and wrote afterward that Eugene "was again much moved." On the 12th of September, O'Neill wrote, "Eugene leaves for Montana in eve — a son who is also a friend! — hate to see him leave."

Clearly Eugene Jr.'s reaction was very different from Carlotta's story. In fact, months later Eugene Jr. was still writing to his father of his admiration of *Long*

Day's Journey into Night. On February 2, 1942, his father replied, "I'm glad you continue to remember *Long Day's Journey into Night* with fine appreciation." Eugene Jr. was all for the play and very far from ashamed of it or wanting it suppressed. But Carlotta had found she could make the dead say whatever she wanted them to. Eugene Jr. had committed suicide on September 25, 1950, almost a year before Eugene O'Neill wrote Bennett Cerf on June 15, 1951, to remind him that *Long Day's Journey into Night* was to be published only "twenty-five years after my death — but never produced as a play." Eugene Jr.'s death had not brought about any change in his father's directions for the play, for his son had had nothing to do with his request for the delay in publication.

Carlotta had gone against only one of O'Neill's wishes at that point. She went on to break the second — his wish never to have it produced as a play — and she did so in record time. It happened that Dag Hammarskjold, the United Nations secretary general, got in touch with her to ask in behalf of Karl Ragnar Gierow, managing director of Sweden's Royal Dramatic Theater, if there were an O'Neill play available they might perform. At once Carlotta sent Gierow a copy of *Long Day's Journey into Night.* She said that just before her husband's death, he had told her he wanted the Swedish Royal Dramatic Theater to be the first to produce the play. As she explained later to Louis Sheaffer, "A few weeks before Gene died, he told me one day of how grateful he was to the Swedish theater. 'They have done my plays all along,' he said, 'more often than anyone else, and better, and seemed to enjoy doing them. I'd like them to be the first to do *Journey.*' And that's how it was." Apart from the absurdity of her story that O'Neill wanted the first appearance of what he considered his finest play to come out in a Swedish translation, there was also his prohibition of any production to be pushed aside. Nevertheless Carlotta declared that in giving the play to the Swedish, she was "carrying out one of her husband's last wishes."

Meanwhile, she was working for an American production to come about. It was announced July 1, 1956, that Jo Mielziner with Mildred Dunnock and Karl Malden had acquired the rights to produce the play. But they were in no hurry to mount the production, with Mielziner then in a musical starring Ethel Merman, Dunnock at the Stratford, Connecticut, Shakespeare Festival, and Malden in Hollywood. In no mood to wait, Carlotta took the play from them. Playing the great lady graciously showering benefits, she gave José Quintero the rights to produce and direct *Long Day's Journey into Night.* He was "stunned," he said. "What money she could have had from a richer, more established impresario than I! She could have had a quarter million dollar advance. She gave me complete directorial freedom, no do's and don'ts. 'I trust you' was her only comment." So early in November 1956, *Long Day's Journey into Night* opened at the Helen Hayes theater with Fredric March as James Tyrone, Florence Eldridge as Mary Tyrone, Jason Robards as Jamie Tyrone, and Bradford Dillman as Edmund Tyrone to great success and the award of a Pulitzer prize in May 1957.

O'Neill had refused production for reasons he stated over and over again — because he could not bear the compromises of the commercial theater, and because he found particularly distressing the deformation his characters underwent even at the hands of the better actors. In this play, where the characters represent his beloved father, mother, and brother, as well as his youthful self, the thought was unendurable. In fact, even in this good production, and even in the smallest details, his conceptions underwent strange alterations. For instance, in his stage directions, O'Neill tells us that James Tyrone wears a collarless shirt "with a thick white handkerchief knotted loosely around his throat." The handkerchief was no peculiarity of his father. In hot weather — and the play takes place in very hot weather — any common workman in his shop in those years would tie a pocket handkerchief around his neck to keep the perspiration rolling down his face and neck from soaking his shirt. As O'Neill specified, there was nothing picturesque or romantic about it. Tyrone is dressed for work, for gardening. On Frederic March the handkerchief was transmogrified into an ascot, the garb of an English gentleman of leisure nattily attired for the racetrack. Similar changes all the way, trivial in themselves, resulted in a stage character very different from the image of the totally unpretentious James O'Neill captured in the written play. As for the twenty-five-year delay O'Neill requested, his friend George Jean Nathan's recollection rings true: "O'Neill had confided to me, personally, that regard for his family's feelings — chiefly his brother's and mother's — had influenced him to insist upon the play's delay."

Surely his wife Carlotta also knew that as well. But she had the legal power to do as she wished. As she exulted to Brooks Atkinson and Seymour Peck, Eugene O'Neill had "made a literary trust and paid me the greatest compliment he could have done" and had made "the will in which I have complete and absolute control of everything, and he said to me (as I told you a little while ago) that I could publish it if and when I pleased but the only thing he insisted upon was . . . " and at this point, again attributing it to O'Neill, she let out one of her central purposes in having the play published at once, her desire to publicize the love the great man had felt for her and the emotional dependence he had on her support. She said that what O'Neill had insisted upon was that the play be printed (as she ordered) with "an inscription to me," which she said he had written "to be put in that play." Actually, O'Neill wrote her various inscriptions to various manuscripts of the play—all of them love letters of gratitude—and she selected for *Long Day's Journey* a particularly flattering one, which she declared he had insisted had to be published with the play. As an intimate inscription and gift to her on their anniversary, as it actually was, it tells that her love gave him the faith to work with "old sorrow" in painful recollections of his family, so that he could "face my dead at last and write this play—write it with deep pity and understanding and forgiveness for all the four haunted Tyrones." Used as a dedication to the play in the front of the book, as Carlotta arranged it, it had the unfortunate result of predisposing critics to see the play as faithful family biography and personal autobiography, rather than as the universal human tragedy of the impossibility, with the chances of life and pressures out of the past, for anyone to live faithful to his ideal of what he wished to be and to achieve.

Thus when Brooks Atkinson reviewed the book on February 17, 1956, he declared, "Essentially, *Long Day's Journey Into Night* is not so much a tale as O'Neill's remorseless attempt to tell the blunt truth about his family as a matter of artistic conscience." Atkinson found it "devastating," because "it is personal and as literal as a drama can be." Other critics followed his lead. No wonder, then, that biographers would believe they could use the play as a quarry for accurate facts about the family. But any who did so were badly misled. O'Neill had a larger purpose than a literal biography of his family. He aimed at revelation of a wider truth that he had perceived in his own suffering as one of them and in his compassion for theirs. The play was a truthful human tragedy, but it was not meant to replicate family history. He used facts flexibly and attributed to his characters events experienced by other people. He mixed himself and Carlotta into the father and mother of his play. As David F. Perkins, who had acted with James O'Neill in *The Three Musketeers* and *Virginius*, declared after seeing *Long Day's Journey into Night*, it was surely "the finest of all" Eugene O'Neill's plays, but Perkins was not clear "how these critics agree that the Tyrone family is a factual, actual reflection of Eugene O'Neill's own family life. To those of us still living who knew and admired James O'Neill, Sr., all this is incomprehensible. It stirs us to anger." Just this anger by people who had known the O'Neills, and unfortunate misreading by critics as literal autobiography was what Eugene O'Neill had hoped to avoid by delaying publication for twenty-five years, by which time the theme of his play would have shed its personal associations and could address itself to humanity as a whole.

A Moon for the Misbegotten

CHAPTER FOURTEEN

The Epitaph

Eugene O'Neill's last play arose directly from the two intimate plays about his youth, *The Iceman Cometh* and *Long Day's Journey into Night*. Indeed, he had just finished *Long Day's Journey* when he got his first idea for the new play, and he actually hijacked for it one of the characters from that play—his brother Jamie—and took his story line from the comic story of his father's tenant, called Shaughnessy in his family play. Thus his first note for the new play in his work diary dated October 28, 1941, reads: "S. [Shaughnessy] play idea, based on story told by E. [Edmund] in 1st Act of 'L.D.J.I.N,' except here Jamie principal character & story of play otherwise entirely imaginary, except for J.'s [Jamie's] revelation of self." Immediately O'Neill became convinced, "This can be strange combination comic-tragic—am enthused about it." He got straight to work on it, calling it now for himself "Dolan play," after John Dolan, the actual tenant of James O'Neill who modeled for Shaughnessy, and then, later, changing the name to Hogan as in the published play. He had finished an outline and begun the dialogue on November 10, 1941.

Showing how thoroughly this play was saturated with the themes of ideals and pipe dreams that had nourished the two earlier plays, O'Neill found a title for it expressive of an ideal, calling it first "Moon of the Misbegotten" and then "A Moon for the Misbegotten." The moon is traditionally the image for romantic love, and as first conceived, this play was to concern the romantic ideals of a man and a woman, their divided and contradictory desires of romantic love, and how those contradictory ideals of love made a conventional happy ending between them impossible. (In the final form of the play, this theme remained central.)

By November 26, 1941, when he completed a first draft of his first act, he was writing in his work diary, "getting great satisfaction this play—flows." But his creative push broke with the events of December 7, 1941. He wrote, "WAR! Japs blast Pearl Harbor! (Now the whole world goes into the tunnel!)." He became "glued to the radio" in the next days. Nevertheless he was "determined to finish 1st d. [draft] of this play, war or not." So he labored on, but kept noting, "too much war on mind," or "little done—mind on war." When he finally finished a first draft of *A Moon for the Misbegotten* on January 20, 1942, he wrote, exhausted, "had to drag myself through it since Pearl Harbor and it needs much revision—wanders all over place." Not until a year later, January 3, 1943, did he finally reread it and decide, "want to get this really written— real affection for it—can be fine, unusual play," and set to work, fighting his faltering health all along the way, and arriving at a very different revised draft that did not wander, and which placed a much stronger emphasis on the character of Jamie.

Certainly in many ways the character takes on both traits and story of the Jamie in *Long Day's Journey into Night*. But as history, this play is even less trustworthy than the family one. For instance, *Moon for the Misbegotten* not only mentions Jamie Tyrone's being expelled from university, but also tells of the prank that caused it. The character recalls it in the first act of *Moon for the Misbegotten*, and it fits entirely into the comical, at times almost farcical, tone of that act before the tragic undertones of the drama emerge. According to Jamie, he passed off a prostitute as his sister to the Jesuits, and she let the secret out by concluding her remarks to the priest accompanying them around the campus by saying, "Christ, Father, it's nice and quiet out here away from the damned Sixth Avenue El. I wish to hell I could stay here!" Presumably that put her out, and Jamie with her. As comedy this is funny, and it is plausible, but it cannot be the real story of what happened to Jamie O'Neill at Fordham University. For one thing, with James O'Neill's habit of making friends with the priests teaching his sons, and with his fame and charm, all the Jesuits at Fordham must have known that their brilliant and promising student was the elder of James O'Neill's two sons. James O'Neill Jr. was editor-in-chief of the literary magazine *The Fordham Monthly* as well as winner of almost all prizes for excellence in his studies. He could never have introduced a bogus sister to the faculty, all of whom knew his family well—certainly well enough to know there was no sister. In Jamie Tyrone's retelling of the scene, the prostitute's words don't reveal conclusively that she is a prostitute; she is not misbehaving. And it is unlikely that the student with her would be expelled on the basis of her taking names in vain, particularly if he were a brilliant student at the top of his class. Whatever the actual cause of James O'Neill Jr.'s expulsion, the Jesuits discreetly suppressed all details of Jamie's crime. They even arranged it so he could have transferred the credits of his three successful years at Fordham to another university and taken his degree despite this transgression. Jamie's choice was to end his higher education with his exit from the Jesuits.

In *A Moon for the Misbegotten* Jamie Tyrone has all of Jamie O'Neill's love of poetry and readiness to quote the avant-garde poets of his day, such as Algernon Swinburne and Ernest Dowson. Although Eugene O'Neill speaks of himself in *A Moon for the Misbegotten* only as the distant brother he actually was in the fall of 1923, his own heritage from Jamie in familiarity with the poets of the decadence directed him as he wrote. He had always felt strong identification with his brother in poetry and creativity. Also, he saw his brother, the person who had turned him from his childhood dreams and taught him knowledge of drink and prostitutes, as almost a part of him. Eugene O'Neill certainly was conscious of that feeling when he wrote his first play drenched in the atmosphere of their relationship, *The Great God Brown*, in which one character appropriates the personality of another. Eugene always saw his dissipated self in the admired image of his witty, charming older brother who started him indulging in prostitutes and chorus girls when he was only fifteen years old. In the family play, Jamie calls him his Frankenstein — something he created altogether. In *The Great God Brown* he had seen himself as hiding behind his brother's mask, as if he were secreted within his outer personality.

In *Long Day's Journey into Night* O'Neill had created the strange story told by Jamie of his night at the local brothel. Very delicately he had suggested a resemblance between the pathetic prostitute Fat Violet who has lost her ability to play the piano and his mother with her crippled fingers, so that Jamie's resort to the prostitute serves as an unconscious revenge on the mother under drugs. At this point Eugene O'Neill must have been awakening to the thought that Jamie's wasted life, dissipated among prostitutes and tarts, and his need to have his young brother follow his path, came from an obscure urge to revenge himself on his mother.

In *A Moon for the Misbegotten* Eugene was perfectly clear that Jamie Tyrone's penchant for prostitutes came from an urge to work out his rage and pain, contempt, and pity on a proxy figure. He had Jamie realize consciously what he has been doing. The perception was certainly true for O'Neill, but the story he designed to express it must be largely fictional.

Eugene O'Neill had received a letter from Mrs. Libbie Drummer to Mrs. Phillips, a long-time friend of the O'Neill family, which Mrs. Phillips had then sent on to Eugene. The letter presents Mrs. Drummer's detailed account of the death of Ella in Los Angeles, and Eugene took from it Jamie's agonizing confession to Josie that his dying mother knew he had relapsed into drinking, "saw I was drunk," and was glad to die because of it. Mrs. Drummer had declared that the most pitiful part of Ella's death was that "I think she knew he was drinking before she died and realized everything and was helpless." So this much of Jamie Tyrone's confession is true for Jamie O'Neill. The character's most shocking revelation, however, is that he hired a prostitute for the entire train trip carrying his mother's body back from California to New York. He recalls that this "pig" became for him a proxy for the dead woman: "It was as if I wanted revenge—because I'd been left alone—because I knew I was lost, without any hope left—that all I could do would be drink myself to death." Certainly Eugene O'Neill looked upon his brother's seductions as an unconscious revenge on his mother for her drug addiction and, at the same time, a working out of his pity and love.

But the prostitute story remains in the realm of fiction. According to Ella O'Neill's friend Mrs. Drummer, Jamie O'Neill had been seen off on the train by one of the nurses who had cared for his mother. She reported to Mrs. Drummer afterward that "he had ten bottles of whiskey with him" in his private compartment. Mrs. Drummer commented, "I was so worried. I did not know if Jamie would ever reach New York alive. He was in dreadful condition." Actually, when the train reached New York, Will Connor and his nephew had to search the entire train at Grand Central Station before they found Jamie finally "in a drunken stupor, with empty bottles all around, beyond knowing them," and unable to do anything but "mumble incoherently." He remained so "broken up" and alcoholic that he could not attend his mother's funeral on March 10, 1922. The story of a blonde pig on the train was surely fictional, but it expressed a profound truth for O'Neill.

Certainly he himself had used prostitutes for revenge during his months of drunken dissipation after being jilted by Beatrice Ashe, and he had put his doing so into his play Welded when he had its protagonist, furious at his wife, declare to the prostitute he has picked up, "You have the power—and the right—to murder love! You can satisfy hate!" So although Jamie is the only protagonist of A Moon for the Misbegotten, Eugene O'Neill was so powerfully present in him that the play serves even more as his own epitaph than that of his dead brother.

Jamie O'Neill was too cynical to feel Dowson's bitter disillusionment when he woke after a night's dissipation to realize that romantic love was lost in the past and "the dawn was grey." Instead, it was Eugene who was haunted like Dowson by the irrevocable loss of genuine feeling, for it was he who had experienced a shocking destruction of his childhood faith in love and romantic ideals as a young boy. The disillusionment of gray dawns with prostitutes had haunted him all his life thereafter. He had shown his understanding of it in the poem he wrote right after his attempt at suicide, "The Lay of the Singer's Fall." It tells of a poet who became invaded by a devil of doubt who undermined his faith in love and ideals at the moment he learned the meaning of sin, so that he had nothing left to live for. In Eugene O'Neill's world, his brother had played the mocking skeptic, the Mephistopheles, and had given him the knowledge of sin. And it had been in the image of his brother that all his disillusioning dissipations had always been carried out. So although it had indeed been his brother who had set out to drink himself to death after their mother died, Eugene O'Neill was fully with him in his rush to destruction as protagonist of A *Moon for the Misbegotten.*

The play is set in September 1923, when his brother Jamie, like Jamie of the play, had almost succeeded in drinking himself to death, as he had been doing from the day his mother collapsed in California. But Jamie O'Neill had by that time done such destruction to himself with dangerous Prohibition whiskey that he was blind and confined in the Riverlawn Sanitorium at Patterson, New Jersey. Jamie Tyrone was still destroying himself in New London in September, and already dead in his heart if not yet in his life. As such he is one of the two misbegotten of the play, and Eugene O'Neill filled the play character with his own regret for lost innocence and damaged ideals. So all he seeks in his tormented guilt is forgiveness and peace in the innocence of his childhood ideal of love. The other misbegotten of the play, Josie Hogan, the woman born too big and powerful to fit into a male-dominated world, seeks consummation of her humiliating and self-slandered virginity through her genuine love for Jamie. Thus her romantic dream places her at cross-purposes with her beloved, who seeks only release from the self-loathing he has experienced in the gray dawns after nights of dissipation with sluts. As he tells Josie, he shrinks from "the aftermath that poisons you." There have been, he says, "too many nights — and dawns. This must be different." The great scene of A *Moon for the Misbegotten* offers a different night illumined by a genuinely romantic moon that cannot be extinguished into a tawdry gray morning.

Eugene O'Neill found it by his own creation of a resolution of what Jung called the "dual mother image" of mythology and dreams — both an expression of the human unconscious. This Jungian concept had been one of the subthemes meant to recur in O'Neill's planned great cycle of eleven plays. In it the longing to return to the womb in "order to be born again" from a mother symbolic of renewal and life contrasts with the "terrible mother," expressive of the danger of "drowning" in one's "own source," of finding within only death, the peace of nonexistence. Both mother images appear in the surviving draft of *More Stately Mansions* and also in the scenario O'Neill wrote for the play to follow it, "The Calms of Capricorn," which also survived by sheer accident.

In *More Stately Mansions* the dual mother is represented by the womblike Chinese summer house in the garden, which has come to symbolize for Simon his mother's identity. He is both lured by it and terrified of losing himself within. Ultimately, Deborah, his mother, saves him from madness and death by shutting herself up alone in her own depths behind the locked door of the summer house. The dual mother in the scenario for "The Calms of Capricorn" appears in Ethan's ambivalence toward the sea, the mother of life, which he both loves and hates. For him, a victory over the sea by making her carry his clipper ship at record-breaking speed will give him power to possess her and she in return will give him, he says, "freedom and rebirth." But if she turns into a "devil mother" and overcomes his ship with "storms and calms and fogs," he will throw himself to her to swallow and spew "out in death." In the same scenario, O'Neill gave Ethan's mother Sarah a mystical vision of her meaning for her beloved husband Simon, who has just died. She declares that she is overcome with pride because her "heart has borne the man [she loves] into life, and in [her] heart he's become a man" yet "always remained a child, and at the last his death is only a return behind the gates of birth to sleep at peace again forever in the love" of her "heart." It was this mystical perception of the woman as eternal mother bearing her man, by way of her love, into both the gift of life and the endless peace of death that gave O'Neill his idea for the major scene of *A Moon for the Misbegotten* and his own unique unification of the dual mother image into one beneficent source of endless love giving birth to both life and repose.

In the fourth act Josie is able to give a night that, as she says, will end like the promise of God's peace in the sorrow of the soul. She is seen at dawn hugging the deathlike figure of Jamie against her breast, asleep in the love of her heart. So as the great virgin mother of life she has given her child a dawn in which he can awake "at peace with myself," free at last from all the "sick remorse" of his wasted life.

So this last play of all, like the other two set at his rebirth as a playwright, is filled with O'Neill's coming to terms with death. For every minute that he struggled to complete these last three works, he certainly knew he was dying as a creative artist. Looking through his *Work Diary* at any point in those last years, one can see recurring signs of the approaching end. On June 12, 1942, he wrote that he was "at new low." Again and again he noted that he has had "short shift" in his work because he "fades out." Morning after morning he noted, "bad night, prostate pain," and day after day, using the current erroneous diagnosis, he declared "Parkinson's bad." July 28, he confessed, "Tough game — take sedatives and feel a dull dope — don't take, and feel as if maggots were crawling all over inside your skin." August 2, he reported, "in addition to other troubles develop painful hip." August 6, "nothing much done — feel too sick." August 10, "sinking spell — all in," and so on, day after day. Working on his projected play "The Last Conquest" in December, he told himself, "no go — decide will have to quit on this again — or on anything else — one of my old sinking spells is on me — lower than low — mind dead." The next to the last day of December, he admitted, "Parkinson's terrible — got fit in a.m. when I thought I'd hop right out of my skin — just as well I have no will to work because couldn't make it anyway."

Yet only four days after that he resolved to get A *Moon for the Misbegotten*, left in its unsatisfactory first draft, "really written." He certainly was anticipating his own death as a creative artist as he crafted his protagonist's death. On January 31, 1943, when he finished a second draft of A *Moon for the Misbegotten*, he wrote, "What I am up against now — fade out physically each day after 3 hours — page a day because work slowly even when as eager about play as I am about this." With the lack of coordination resulting from his neurological problems, he found it a "constant strain to write." So apparent to him was the approach of the end that he spent part of his time after writing, "destroying old stuff" he had no time to perfect. Thus this last play of all is really an epitaph for both his dead brother and for himself manifestly dying as a creative artist. He as well as his brother — who had actually died on November 8, 1923, not two months after the action of this play — share in Josie's final benediction, "May you have your wish and die in your sleep soon, Jim, darling. May you rest forever in forgiveness and peace." After A *Moon for the Misbegotten* was finished in the spring of 1943, Eugene O'Neill was already dead at heart, even as Jamie in his play. But he had years of cruel affliction to suffer before his last breath on November 27, 1953, granted him the peace and forgiveness and eternal rest he desired.

Abbreviations Used in the Notes

Basso	Hamilton Basso, "The Tragic Sense," *New Yorker*, February 8, 1948.
Berg	Henry W. and Albert A. Berg Collection, New York Public Library, Astor, Lenox, and Tilden Foundations.
Bryer	Jackson R. Bryer, editor, *"The Theatre We Worked For": The Letters of Eugene O'Neill to Kenneth MacGowan* (New Haven: Yale University Press, 1982).
Correspondence	The Correspondence of Agnes Boulton O'Neill and Eugene O'Neill, Houghton Library, Harvard University.
Fales	The Fales Library, New York University.
Floyd	Virginia Floyd, *Eugene O'Neill at Work* (New York: Ungar, 1981).
Gelb I	Arthur Gelb and Barbara Gelb, *O'Neill* (New York: Harper, 1962).
Gelb II	Arthur Gelb and Barbara Gelb, *O'Neill: Life with Monte Cristo*, edited by Glenn Young and Greg Collins (New York: Applause and Cinema Books, 2000).
International	International Institute of Social History (Internationaal Insituut voor Sociale Geschiedenis), Amsterdam.
Karsner	David Karsner, *Sixteen Authors to One* (New York: Copeland, 1928).
Mullett	Mary B. Mullett, "The Extraordinary Story of Eugene O'Neill," *American Magazine*, November 1922.
O'Neill Poems	*Eugene O'Neill Poems 1912–1944*, Edited by Donald Gallup (New Haven: Ticknor and Fields, 1980).
Princeton	Manuscripts, Princeton University Library.
Random House	*The Plays of Eugene O'Neill*, 3 vols. (New York: Random House, 1967).
Shaughnessy	Edward L. Shaughnessy, "Ella, James, and Jamie O'Neill," *The Eugene O'Neill Review*, Fall 1991.
Sheaffer I	Louis Sheaffer, *O'Neill: Son and Playwright* (Boston: Little, Brown, 1968).

Sheaffer II	Louis Sheaffer, *O'Neill: Son and Artist* (Boston: Little, Brown, 1973).
SL	*Selected Letters of Eugene O'Neill*, edited by Travis Bogard and Jackson R. Bryer (New Haven: Yale University Press, 1988).
Sweeney	Charles F. Sweeney, "Back to the Source of Plays Written by Eugene O'Neill," *New York World*, November 9, 1924.
"The Accursed"	Emma Goldman, "Donald Vose: The Accursed," *Mother Earth*, January 1916.
Vorse	Mary Heaton Vorse, "Eugene O'Neill's Pet Saloon Is Gone," *New York World*, May 4, 1930.
Work Diary	*Work Diary, 1924–1943*, transcribed by Donald Gallup, preliminary edition, 2 vols. (New Haven: Yale University Library, 1981).
Yale	Collection of American Literature, Beinecke Rare Book and Manuscript Library, Yale University.

Notes

A note on methodology: For ease of reading, I have silently corrected and normalized punctuation and spelling in quotations from primary sources. Dialogue from various sources is generally quoted directly, whereas the intervening narrative is often paraphrased.

The Iceman Cometh
Chapter One. Riddle in *The Iceman Cometh*

page 7 blend of memories
I have shown the blending of memories from an author's life, from people he has known, and from lives he has read about throughout my recent book, *Creating Literature Out of Life: The Making of Four Masterpieces* (University Park: The Pennsylvania State University Press, 1996).

page 7 the "Policy King"
Adams is called the "convicted policy king" in "Sing Sing for Adams," *New York Daily Tribune*, April 25, 1903, and again in the headline "Inquest on 'Al' Adams: Coroner Will Subpoena Former Policy King's Debtors," October 3, 1906. See also "Al Adams a Suicide, Following Misfortunes," October 2, 1906, in which the *New York Times* declares that Adams was known as the "Policy King."

page 7 "the Jimmy the Priest—"
Since O'Neill was jotting notes for his own eyes only, he abbreviated the reference to "The Jimmy the P.—H. H.—Garden idea." Entry of June 6, 1939, Eugene O'Neill's *Work Diary, 1924–1943*, transcribed by Donald Gallup, preliminary edition, 2 vols. (New Haven: Yale University Library, 1981), in the collection of Yale University Library, 2:351. Hereafter cited as *Work Diary*.

page 7 They assume that
For example, see Louis Sheaffer, *O'Neill: Son and Playwright* (Boston: Little, Brown, 1968), 189–90, hereafter cited as Sheaffer I; and Arthur Gelb

and Barbara Gelb, *O'Neill* (New York: Harper, 1962), 161; hereafter cited as Gelb I.

page 7   his seafaring days

I do not include the two sea voyages to Honduras and Argentina that James O'Neill, Eugene's father, arranged to get him to jobs in those countries, only those Eugene himself signed on for as a sailor, starting with the voyage Buenos Aires to Durban, South Africa, at the beginning of 1911, and ending with his last voyage, South Hampton to New York on the S.S. *Philadelphia* arriving August 26, 1911.

page 8   a major investor

The *Boston Traveler* for November 24, 1909, referred to James O'Neill as "shrewd in business affairs" and declared that the year before he "embarked in a manufacturing and mercantile business in New York"—which must have referred to Henry L. Brittain's company and makes it appear that James was the principal backer or perhaps the only backer. In fact, the investment seems to have been made in the name of Eugene's mother, Mary Ellen, "Ella," for in his letter home to his parents from Honduras on November 9, 1909, Eugene asks, "How is Brittain making out? I suppose when I see you again that Mama will have all her money back. What? Well, here's hoping she will." *Selected Letters of Eugene O'Neill*, edited by Travis Bogard and Jackson R. Bryer (New Haven: Yale University Press, 1988), 18–19. Hereafter cited as SL. A note by the editors assumes, I believe erroneously, that the "money back" refers to Ella's having invested in the gold-prospecting that Eugene had joined—but the logic of the writing makes it clear that Eugene is referring to Brittain, whose company had fallen into difficulties. Of course, James had many investments, and he certainly had invested in Earl Stevens's expedition as well as Brittain's company and was able to get Eugene in on it because of his power as investor, just as he had gotten him his job with Brittain.

page 8   between Dey and Fulton Streets

According to New York City directories of the time, Dey Street came at 191 Broadway and Fulton Street at 207 Broadway, so 194 would have been between the two on the side of the even numbers.

page 8   Jimmy the Priest's

The saloon was functioning in 1907, but according to Louis Sheaffer, Jimmy Condon—the proprietor who gave his nickname to the place—took over in 1908. That, of course, was the year O'Neill, working nearby for Brittain, would have become a regular customer. Sheaffer I, 189.

page 8   the Garden Restaurant

When James C. Warren testified before the Supreme Court at White Plains, New York, on June 10, 1912, in *Kathleen O'Neill vs. Eugene O'Neill*,

for the divorce, he declared that on the night of the adultery, he, Edward
Ireland, Edward Mullen, Frank Archibold, and Eugene O'Neill met at the
Campus Restaurant on 104th Street and Columbus Avenue and went from
there to the Garden Restaurant at Fiftieth Street and Broadway. The discrepancy of this address in comparison with the actual one for the Garden
Hotel and Restaurant at Twenty-seventh Street and Madison Avenue probably came because Warren was citing it as a known hangout of O'Neill, but
not one Warren was actually acquainted with. He hoped by listing several
consecutive saloons, the others not named, to show that the group had
moved, casually and without design, from the Campus Restaurant to the
house of prostitution at 140 West Forty-fifth Street, where the adultery was
to have taken place. So Warren placed the Garden Restaurant farther uptown than it actually was because the address at Twenty-seventh Street and
Madison would have been out of the way of the progression from uptown
and would have thrown doubt that the adultery had come about naturally
and had not been staged — as it actually had been — to supply evidence for
the divorce.

page 8   "old drunken Garden days"

Telling of how he used to meet all the old circus men, poultry men, and
horse breeders who showed at the old Madison Square Garden at the bar of
the Garden Hotel, Eugene O'Neill declared that he became an habitué
there "some time after" he discovered Jimmy the Priest's (November or
December of 1907). The listing of it in evidence for *Kathleen O'Neill vs.
Eugene O'Neill* shows that the drunken days there must have started soon
after if he was known to hang out there by the end of 1911. "A Eugene
O'Neill Miscellany," the *New York Sun*, January 12, 1928. O'Neill's reference
to the "old drunken Garden days" comes in a letter to his wife Agnes about
getting a dog for Shane: "All say wise bet is to wait for dog show next month
when good bargains can be had. Jamie knows several dog men well from old
drunken Garden days. They will tip us off." The letter dates from some time
in the week or two before Idle Inn opened on December 20, 1921, because
in the same letter O'Neill tells her that Ben-Ami will be acting in it and
Robert Edmond Jones is doing the sets for it. The Correspondence of Agnes
Boulton O'Neill and Eugene O'Neill, Houghton Library, Harvard University. Hereafter cited as Correspondence.

page 8   during trips to New York into 1918

Agnes Boulton refers to such stays at the Garden Hotel in *Part of a Long
Story* (New York: Doubleday, 1958), 91, 127, 268.

page 8   "dry as dry"

Letter of O'Neill to Agnes Boulton O'Neill [December 1?, 1919],
SL, 98.

page 8   "Hell Hole 1915"
          Eugene O'Neill Poems 1912–1944, edited by Donald Gallup (New Haven: Ticknor and Fields, 1980), 76, 77. Hereafter cited as *O'Neill Poems.*

page 9   Hotel Ansonia
          In an interview in 1955 with Arthur McGinley I learned of the events of the summer of 1906 and of the O'Neills at the Hotel Ansonia. Since James O'Neill knew everyone in the hotel, according to McGinley, when he and Eugene joined his family there after James and Ella O'Neill's return from abroad, the O'Neills must have been staying there for some time before they sailed for Europe in May. In "James O'Neill Points a Moral for Young Actors," the *New York Telegraph* of December 30, 1905, announced that James was "Monte Cristoizing at the West End to crowded houses" during the holiday period. I assume he began his sojourn at the Hotel Ansonia on Broadway and Seventy-third Street then because it was comfortably near the theater. The Theatre Collection of the Museum of the City of New York preserves a program for the week of *Monte Cristo* at the West End Theater beginning with a matinee on Christmas Day, Monday, December 25, 1905. James O'Neill's "Dates Ahead" in the *New York Clipper*, January 20, 1906, include Jersey City from January 1 through 6; Paterson 8; Atlantic City 10, 11; Trenton 12; Plainfield 13. The session at the Harlem Theater was 15–20, where he "packed the house" both matinee and evening. The Ansonia was a convenient base for all these places.

page 9   preparing for a trip to England
          The *New York Dramatic Mirror*, May 19, 1906, announced, "James O'Neill and Mrs. O'Neill will sail for Europe on the Caronia on May 22, to be gone until August." The July 14, 1906, issue says that James "is now in Dublin." On August 4, 1906, the *Mirror* reported, "James O'Neill has just returned from a vacation spent in Europe to prepare for his tour next season in a new play, *The Voice of the Mighty* by James Slevin."

page 9   opened in Chicago
          James O'Neill's fall tour is listed in the *New York Clipper* as "Chicago, Ill. Aug. 27–Sept. 1; St. Louis, Mo. 3–8; Springfield 10; Joplin 11; Kansas City 13–15; Topeka, Kan. 17; Leavenworth 18; St. Joseph, Mo. 19; Lincoln, Neb. 20;" etc.

page 9   Al Adams, who lived in a luxurious suite
          Materials on Adams's drinking and loneliness are in many reports, most particularly "Al Adams a Suicide," *New York Daily Tribune*, October 2, 1906.

page 9   kindly to a man "under a cloud"
          For instance, right after the pugilist Jere Dunn was acquitted of a charge of murder, the *Chicago Herald* censured both the actors McKee Rankin and James O'Neill for associating with Dunn. Many people I interviewed spoke

of how James was always genially ready to include all kinds of people in a group having drinks at a bar — even such a disreputable person as a prize fighter suspected of murder.

page 10 a "runner" for Zachariah Simmons
"Al Adams a Suicide," *New York Daily Tribune*, October 2, 1906. Before that, Adams had been a brakeman on the New York, New Haven, and Hartford Railroad.

page 10 "The governor wasn't half as bad"
Quoted in "Al Adams a Suicide, Following Misfortunes," *New York Times*, October 2, 1906.

page 10 Dr. Irvine, the prison doctor
"Thinks Adams May Die," *New York Daily Tribune*, April 29, 1903. At this time Adams was sixty, but, Irvine said, was "much older than his years."

page 10 "the disgrace and grief." "the shame he had tried"
"Al Adams Ends Outcast Life," *New York Sun*, October 2, 1906.

page 11 "his daughters did not make." "his sons were not allowed"
"Al Adams a Suicide, Following Misfortunes," *New York Times*, October 2, 1906.

page 11 "happy life with my." "dwelt together"
"Al Adams to 'Seal His Past,' Chose Suicide." *New York World*, October 2, 1906.

page 11 if he "were paupered." would breakfast. a "sealed book"
Ibid.

page 11 Boardman and Company. M. J. Sage and Company
"Al Adams a Suicide, Following Misfortunes," *New York Times*, October 2, 1906.

page 11 Eugene came to know Al Adams
Although there is no direct evidence that either James or Eugene O'Neill knew Al Adams, the indirect evidence is overwhelming. They were all staying at the Hotel Ansonia from December through August 1905–6, the O'Neills on and off, and all were given to congregating at the bar. Moreover, Arthur McGinley recalled that James O'Neill knew everyone in the hotel at the beginning of August. Also significant is the appearance of Al Adams's story in *The Iceman Cometh*. O'Neill told Robert Sisk in a letter of October 13, 1940, of the play, "All the characters are based on people I once knew or knew of, although none of them is an exact portrait of anyone." Collection of American Literature, Beinecke Rare Book and Manuscript Library, Yale University. Hereafter cited as Yale.

page 11 being "hounded" unfairly
The manager of the Hotel Ansonia, W. E. D. Stokes, reported Adams as saying, "The newspapers and police have hounded me until I think I'll kill

myself" on the day before his suicide. "Al Adams a Suicide," *New York Daily Tribune*, October 2, 1906.

page 11   Walter off to Mexico
             "Adams Estate $8,000,000," *New York Daily Tribune*, October 9, 1906. "Al Adams Ends Outcast life," *New York Sun*, October 2, 1906.

page 11   they quarreled so fiercely
             "Al Adams a Suicide," *New York Daily Tribune*, October 2, 1906.

page 11   As Eugene O'Neill understood it
             In his pencil notes for *The Iceman Cometh* (Yale), under the heading "Al Adams," after noting the two lawyer sons, O'Neill wrote, "Another son sentenced 6 months in jail, 1904, for assaulting father." Apparently O'Neill was refreshing himself on dates and facts of Adams's life. Either his source was not fully accurate, or the statement of the sentence was correct but did not mention the later withdrawal of charges by Adams. The fact that Louis was held only a few days on Blackwell's Island is noted in "Al Adams a Suicide," *New York Daily Tribune*, October 2, 1906.

page 12   based on "Al Adams's son"
             This is quoted from O'Neill's pencil notes for *The Iceman Cometh* at Yale. In his pencil first scenario (also at Yale) for the first scene, O'Neill refers to Willie Oban as "Adams," and he calls Willie's raffish sailor song "Adams' song." The fact that he gives no first name suggests again that the character was a composite of all O'Neill knew of the sons, not a portrait of any one.

page 12   "at Harvard and at Heidelberg"
             Pencil notes for *The Iceman Cometh*, Yale.

page 12   as his father had advised, law
             One of James O'Neill's favorite stories was of how, during his barnstorming days as a very young actor, the company he was in collapsed in Illinois. As he told it, "While in Monmouth a wealthy old gentleman, the head of a prosperous law firm, took a great fancy to me. He invited me home to dinner, and offered to adopt me if I would agree to give up the stage, and study law in his office." James O'Neill turned down the offer for love of the theater, but he added, "I've regretted it ever since." Asked, "Why," he declared, "Because I look upon law as the foundation of all success." Interview with James O'Neill, *New York Dramatic Mirror*, February 2, 1895. The same story is told in an interview in Lewis C. Strang, *Famous Actors of the Day in America* (Boston: Page, 1900), 140. No wonder James wanted Eugene to study law.

page 12   "son of Monte Cristo"
             When his first plays were produced, Eugene O'Neill was thought of very much as his father's son. The headline in the *Philadelphia Public Ledger*, March 16, 1920, on the tryout of his play *Chris Christopherson* read

"Sea Story 'Chris' by Monte Cristo's Son / Premiere at the Broad of Drama by Eugene O'Neill, James's Boy."

page 13   "hatred and defiance." "resentment"

The diagram O'Neill made for Gilbert Van Tassell Hamilton is reproduced in Sheaffer I, 506. As I point out in *Eugene O'Neill's Creative Struggle: The Decisive Decade, 1924–1933* (University Park: The Pennsylvania State University Press, 1992), 216, Sheaffer's transcription of O'Neill's comments are flawed, partly because of the difficulty of the handwriting and partly because Sheaffer was never altogether in tune with O'Neill's ideas so that his conjectures are often askew. However, this very valuable document was made public through Sheaffer's tact in dealing with Dr. Hamilton's widow.

page 13   "In the days you speak of"

Letter to Arthur McGinley, December 10, 1932. I transcribed the original letter when it was in the possession of Arthur McGinley. It is reproduced in SL, 408, but I differ with the editors on the transcription. O'Neill had told McGinley that the year before James O'Neill died, he and his father had become "good friends." So, as I transcribe him, O'Neill declared, "I wouldn't have made any such crack later on." The editors of SL transcribe it "have made any such crash later on." Also, they transcribe the place where the crack was made as "Dondero's," whereas I believe it should be "Dandero's."

page 13   "Papa." "crooked old bucket-shop"

Eugene O'Neill, *The Iceman Cometh* (New York: Random House, 1946), 14, 56.

page 13   "King of the Bucket Shops"

Ibid., 37.

page 13   "younger son is at college"

Brooklyn Eagle, April 25, 1907.

page 13   Returning from an alcoholic binge

In a letter to the *New York Times* of November 28, 1953, Professor Edward Hubler corrected an article in the *Times* of that date on Eugene's Princeton career, which repeated the legend that he was expelled for heaving a brick through the stationmaster's house. (A variant of that myth has O'Neill throwing a bottle of beer through President Wilson's study window on campus.) The information in Hubler's letter came from Dean Fine, who had been head of the disciplinary committee in the spring of 1907, by way of Dean Christian Gauss, who had asked him about it later. Hubler said there was no record of how long the suspension was to hold.

page 14   He even was granted a degree

O'Neill could have had an honorary degree from Princeton if he had wanted one. To Saxe Commins, who asked if he were interested, O'Neill confided his opinion that honorary degrees were "Crap cum laude."

(Letter of February 24, 1943, manuscript in the Princeton University Library. Hereafter cited as Princeton.) O'Neill told Terry Helburn of the Yale degree: "Would have refused that one except Baker wanted me to accept." (Letter of March 12, 1938, Theater Guild Collection, Yale.) To George Jean Nathan, O'Neill declared that the Yale honorary degree "was unquestionably Yale's way of showing its appreciation and relief that he had gone, instead, to Princeton and Harvard." George Jean Nathan, *Encyclopaedia of the Theatre* (New York: Knopf, 1940), 295.

page 14   really a "scapegoat"
Willie thinks he can force the district attorney to open Pat McGloin's case because he has seen his father's papers and remembers "a lot of people." O'Neill, *The Iceman Cometh*, 57.

page 14   "Remember, they get you"
Ibid., 180.

page 14   the grafting police chief
Among O'Neill's pencil notes for *The Iceman Cometh* at Yale is one on Al Adams as "friend, Chief of N. Y. Police 1898 until office abolished in 1901."

page 14   ejected long ago for graft
Hope recalls his dead wife Bessie's saying that McGloin is "the biggest drunken grafter that ever disgraced the police force." O'Neill, *The Iceman Cometh*, 55.

page 14   died in jail
Telling of how his father was locked up, Willie says he "pined in confinement. And so he died." Ibid., 37.

page 14   one of his large revolvers
In "Al Adams a Suicide," the *New York Daily Tribune* (October 2, 1906) reported, "The large bullet had crashed through his head, tearing out some of the brains and part of the skull, and then going clear through a partition and embedding itself in a panel of the outer hall."

page 15   more than eight million dollars
"Adams Estate $8,000,000," *New York Daily Tribune*, October 9, 1906. Part of the estate consisted of a three-quarter interest in the Karsch brewery, which, the *Tribune* said, "controls more than a hundred corner saloons."

page 15   "contemptible swindler." "the organized theft"
Editorial, October 2, 1906. An editorial in the *New York Daily Tribune*, April 22, 1903, called Adams a "contemptible swindler" and declared that his robbery of the poor was "complete and utterly remorseless." When Adams was sentenced to Sing Sing on April 21, 1903, Justice Scott said that the crime and sorrow Adams had brought about could "never be atoned for nor blotted out." Scott probably had in mind the murder of Charles S. Macfarlane, an official of the "anti-Policy Society" by one of Adams's henchmen, William Spencer, who "shot him dead" in the Criminal Courts Building. "Al Adams a Suicide," *New York Daily Tribune*, October 2, 1906.

page 15   "In a deep sense"
            Eugene O'Neill said this in his general press conference for *The Iceman
            Cometh* production, and it was reported in many newspapers. My quote
            comes from Marguerite Young, "O'Neill Ready to Junk Man in Favor of
            Ants," *New York Herald Tribune*, September 3, 1946.

Chapter Two. The Proxy Suicide

page 17   those two reckless fictionalizers
            See "Literary Personalities: Eugene O'Neill," *The World of George
            Jean Nathan*, ed. Charles Angoff (New York: Knopf, 1952), 39–40, and
            Agnes Boulton, *Part of a Long Story* (New York: Doubleday, 1958),
            202–4. Nathan was entirely scrambled on the date and facts. He tells of
            O'Neill's sharing a room with Joe Smith—on whom O'Neill based Joe
            Mott in *The Iceman Cometh*—at the Hell Hole and declares that this
            room was the famous Garbage Flat. But Joe was one of O'Neill's black
            friends, and in the first years that O'Neill knew him he was still a power as
            a Tammany politician, "Boss of the Ninth Ward," with a white mistress, and
            hardly down to sharing a room. See Smith's delineation by Mary Heaton
            Vorse, "Eugene O'Neill's Pet Saloon Is Gone," *New York World*, May 4,
            1930. Hereafter cited as Vorse. The Hell Hole did not rent rooms,
            although in later years O'Neill sometimes slept over in Tom Wallace's
            "zero flat" above the saloon along with the bartenders Lefty and Chuck.
            See, for instance, O'Neill's letter of January 22, 1920, to his wife Agnes,
            SL, 106. The Garbage Flat was down the block from, not in, the Hell Hole.
            O'Neill said that it was on Fourth Street between Washington Square and
            Sixth Avenue, whereas the Hell Hole was on the corner of Fourth Street
            and Sixth Avenue. His roommates there were Terry Carlin and Jack
            Druilard, not Joe Smith. See O'Neill's letter of November 30, 1943, to
            J. J. Douthit, SL, 547.
                Nathan also has O'Neill's cronies at Jimmy the Priest's collecting money
            from his father and getting drunk on it to celebrate his survival—impos-
            sible because James O'Neill was not in New York then, but on tour in the
            Midwest.

page 17   wildly improbable substitutes
            This humorous ploy of Nathan in 1932, when he wrote this account, was
            used by O'Neill himself seven years later in *The Iceman Cometh* (23), when
            he had Larry describe Harry Hope's fifteen-cent whiskey as "cyanide cut
            with carbolic acid to give it a mellow flavor."

page 17   "miserable foggy." "in the middle"
            Reproduced in Virginia Floyd, *Eugene O'Neill at Work* (New York: Ungar,
            1981), 8. Hereafter cited as Floyd.

page 17   Recently biographers have given
           See especially Arthur Gelb and Barbara Gelb, *O'Neill: Life with Monte Cristo* (edited by Glenn Young and Greg Collins, New York: Applause and Cinema Books, 2000; hereafter cited as Gelb II). The Gelbs characterize this note for *Exorcism* as "compelling evidence" that the suicide took place in March. Gelb II, 331–32.

page 17   overdose of Veronal
           Veronal, a hypnotic, might have been prescribed to O'Neill for insomnia, but it was also used to treat severe alcoholism. It is still in use.

page 18   a prodigal son return
           From the *New York Times* review of *Exorcism* quoted in the *Boston Transcript*, April 5, 1920.

page 18   woken up one morning
           Hamilton Basso, "The Tragic Sense," *New Yorker*, February 28, 1948, 37. Hereafter cited as Basso.

page 18   "five bucks" into a "thousand"
           Kyle Crichton, "Mr. O'Neill and the Iceman," *Collier's*, October 26, 1946, 19. David Karsner in *Sixteen Authors to One* (New York: Copeland, 1928), 114, reported O'Neill as saying simply that he "found himself broke in New Orleans." Hereafter cited as Karsner.

page 18   "When I survey"
           Letter at Cornell University Library.

page 18   Edward Mullen, Frank Archibold
           These materials on the adultery and the divorce come from *Kathleen O'Neill vs. Eugene O'Neill*.

page 19   "mangled" version
           Report in *Variety* from Denver, dated February 14, 1912. He had been receiving $1,250 weekly.

page 19   "two-a-day." seven days a week
           The facts about the vaudeville tour of *Monte Cristo* are in "James O'Neill Recalls Boston Memories," *Boston Transcript*, October 20, 1913.

page 19   "soul-crushing"
           Report in *Variety* from Denver, dated February 14, 1912.

page 19   a recent biography
           Gelb II.

page 19   reported in the *New London Day*
           The feat was published again in the column on New London, "Twenty-Five Years Ago," on July 22, 1937.

page 19   according to Charlie Thompson
           Charles Thompson related this in his unpublished autobiography "Another Connecticut Yankee," quoted in Sheaffer I, 226. See the Louis Sheaffer Collection, the Library, Connecticut College.

page 20 "a friend of mine, a Liverpool"
Perhaps both O'Neill and Driscoll were wearing their American Line jerseys when they met at Jimmy the Priest's. Letter of O'Neill to Ralph E. Whitney, SL, 515.

page 20 "thought a whole lot"
Louis Kalonyme, "O'Neill Lifts Curtain on His Early Days," *New York Times*, December 21, 1924.

page 20 the fall of 1916
In a note on the first draft of "Tomorrow" at Princeton, O'Neill said that he wrote three short stories at this time: "Tomorrow," "The Hairy Ape," and "The Web."

page 20 two weeks of December 1921
On the first longhand draft of "The Hairy Ape" at Princeton, O'Neill noted after "Curtain" on the last page of the play that it was begun December 7 and finished December 23, 1921.

page 21 floating near the Statue of Liberty
Sheaffer (I, 203, 494) drew these details from a police report and Christopherson's death certificate, New York City Health Department Bureau of Records.

page 21 "was found frozen"
Charles F. Sweeney, "Back to the Source of Plays Written by Eugene O'Neill," *New York World*, November 9, 1924. Hereafter cited as Sweeney.

page 21 A. Toxen Worm
Information on Aage [the first name that Worm understandably suppressed in the United States] Toxen Worm appears on various dates in issues of the *New York Dramatic Mirror*. In the *Mirror* of April 27, 1895, he is spoken of as "formerly the well-known critic of the Pittsburgh Dispatch," who has been doing advance and press work for James O'Neill for the last two seasons. The December 28, 1895, issue speaks of Worm's "B.A. from the University of Copenhagen." By the September 18, 1897, issue he has become "business representative of James O'Neill" and has just returned August 28 from Denmark to St. Louis, where he attended "to business for Mr. O'Neill" and revisited "the scenes of his boyhood." (The "business" was most likely private investments rather than any theatrical concerns of James O'Neill.) By the issue of April 11, 1908, Worm had been a member of Liebler and Company for a year and had just been elected governor of the Friar's Club. In the May 22, 1912, issue he reminisces of how once long ago he "superintended the pastimes of Christian IX of Denmark's grandchildren, including George of England, Czar Nicholas of Russia, and the present King of Denmark."

page 21 "to work in the Boer"
March 1904. *The Iceman Cometh*, 35. The date when the actors in the Boer War Spectacle landed in America is in a program for the St. Louis

"Great Boer War Spectacle" performed in the Theater Library of the New York Public Library.

page 22   "a strong yen." "because in the distant"
Letter of O'Neill to Terry Helburn, July 13, 1928, SL, 306.

page 22   three dollars a month
Early interviews—such as those of Sweeney or of Louis Kalonyme, "O'Neill Lifts Curtain on His Early Days," *New York Times*, December 21, 1924—give this sum as the monthly rental. Later articles convert it to three dollars a week because, with inflation, three dollars a month seemed impossibly cheap to them. Of course, they did not take into account the drop in the real value of the dollar since 1911. See, for instance, Basso (1948) and Tom Prideaux, "Most Celebrated U.S. Playwright Returns to Theatre," *Life*, October 14, 1946, 106.

page 23   "Tomorrow" was published
In a letter to Eugene O'Neill of March 30, 1917, Waldo Frank, editor of *The Seven Arts*, agreed to publish "Tomorrow" if O'Neill would cut an O'Henry-style surprise ending that O'Neill had used to conclude the story. In it, O'Neill had Art discover that, ironically, right after Jimmy's suicide, Jimmy had been given notice that he had inherited "the bulk" of his Aunt Mary's estate estimated at "twenty thousand pounds." Frank thought this postscript weakened the tragedy, and O'Neill agreed to cut it. In a letter of April 2, 1917, Waldo accepted the altered story for fifty dollars. (Letters of Waldo Frank to Eugene O'Neill, Boulton Collection, Yale.) I have supplemented the published "Tomorrow" with O'Neill's longhand script at Princeton, which is very valuable for canceled autobiographical passages and for his original placing of the story, as, in his words, taking place in "the winter of my great down-and-outness." I have also used a typescript of "Tomorrow" in a folder labeled "Rialto Service Bureau—Mimeographing and Typing" in the Henry W. and Albert A. Berg Collection, New York Public Library, Astor, Lenox, and Tilden Foundations (hereafter cited as Berg). My quotes are from the longhand script unless otherwise noted.

page 24   "fine title 'The Iceman Cometh'"
Work Diary, 2:351 (June 7, 1939).

page 24   periodical drunk
As described in *The Iceman Cometh*, a periodical drinker or drunk is one who stays sober all year except for one (or perhaps two) relapses into total alcoholism, each relapse occurring around the same date each year and lasting several weeks.

page 24   "Jimmy Tomorrow." "leader of our"
O'Neill, *The Iceman Cometh*, 35.

page 24   "dear personal friend"
O'Neill told Ralph Sanborn (letter of May 1930, Sheaffer I, 214, 494) that he held "Tomorrow" in "high affection" as a record not only of a "dear personal friend" but also of "a section of my life."

page 24   "at liberty." "past three seasons"

Because I had already found Jimmy's real name from the clipping of Richard Little's article on James O'Neill in the *Chicago Record Herald* in the Robinson Locke scrapbook on James O'Neill in the New York Public Library, I was able to cull these two notices on Jimmy Byth when I examined the many bound volumes of the *New York Clipper* and the *New York Dramatic Mirror*, week by week, from 1866 through 1920 for information on James O'Neill. This first is from the *Mirror* for August 10, 1895. A season for a traveling company would run from September through the following May, so Byth probably began as advance man for *The Devil's Auction* in September 1892.

page 24   "booking representative of the Hopkins"

New York Dramatic Mirror, June 11, 1898.

page 24   Boer War broke out

Hostilities began in October 1899.

page 24   Richard M. Little

Richard M. Little, "Haunted by the Ghost of Monte Cristo," *Chicago Record Herald*, February 9, 1908.

page 25   a Germanic spelling, "Beith"

Angoff, 40–41.

page 25   John G. Nagle.

Little refers to Nagle consistently but incorrectly as "Magle." In quoting I have corrected the name, using the spelling that appears on theatrical programs during the years Nagle worked for James O'Neill.

page 25   he was clearly of Scottish origin

Talking of Jimmy's enthusiastic response to his questions on O'Neill, Little wrote, "Mr. J. Findlater Byth in spite of his proud Scotch lineage looked as if he wanted to embrace me." Little hyphenates "Findlater-Byth," but that device (arising from property inherited from the female line when the husband would add the property owner's name—that is, his wife's maiden name—to his own because women were legally unable to own property) was not correct for Byth's family and never was used by him when he advertised in the *New York Dramatic Mirror*.

page 25   "[I was there] merely"

Little's article has several uncorrected printer's errors. This is clearly one of them, for these words were left out, garbling the passage and destroying its meaning.

page 25   "career as a wartime Reuters correspondent." "fraud, an innocent harmless one"

Sheaffer I, 130. Sheaffer based his idea of Byth's fraudulence not only on the question of working for *Reuters*, but also on what was said about his upper-class Scottish origins. Assistants of Sheaffer, working in England, unearthed a record for the birth of a James Bythe in 1866, not in Scotland but in Church Town, a hamlet of Cornwall. This Bythe was also born not among the gentry, but as the son of a poor upholsterer in a lowly mining town. So Sheaffer concluded that this was O'Neill's Byth and that he had lied about being an educated Scot. My own opinion is that Sheaffer was given the birth record for the wrong Byth. Both Byth and James were very common names and there would have been many James Byths in those days to confuse with the one who became an advance man for James O'Neill.

A lower-class boy who grew up in a provincial Cornish village would never have emerged with an upper-class accent as Jimmy Byth was said to have by the only two people who reported the speech of the real man, that is, Richard Little and Eugene O'Neill. Also, it is unlikely that Eugene O'Neill would have been way off, as Sheaffer thinks he was, in believing Byth to have been a university man and "a highly educated man" with a knowledge of "literature and the classics," as he describes the character Jimmy in "Tomorrow." In *The Iceman Cometh*, Eugene tells us of Jimmy, "His speech is educated, with the ghost of a Scotch rhythm in it. His manners are those of a gentleman" (6).

page 25   Reuters was strictly an English agency
Some American journalists, such as J. E. Pearson, who were reporting for American pro-British newspapers, did work for *Reuters* and march with the British army.

page 25   went in for summary execution
Only after the war was over did the British become less severe. For instance, the Irish rebel from Australia, Arthur Lynch, who was caught fighting with the Boers, was at first sentenced to death and only later reprieved to life imprisonment. See T. Fisher, *The Afrikaners* (London: Cassell, 1969), 157.

page 26   slanted their reports
Arthur Conan Doyle in *The Great Boer War* (London: Smith, Elder, 1902), 126, was bitter over the fact that "continental papers" invariably rejoiced over British defeats. "France, Russia, Austria and Germany were equally venomous against us," he complained. Because the British blundered by charging in open ranks against guerilla-style hidden Boers, almost all of whom were marksmen, English defeats—with high casualty rates—were continual in the first year of the war.

page 26   "firsthand experience in Africa"
Sheaffer I, 130.

page 26   General Piet Wetjoen
Apparently Eugene O'Neill arrived at the surname for his character Piet Wetjoen by blending the names of two famous Boer guerilla generals: Christiaan De *Wet* and Commandant Ben Vil*joen*. De Wet's younger brother, renowned as was his brother Christiaan for daring, was named Piet, thus providing the character's first name. In O'Neill's notes for *The

Iceman Cometh at Yale in which he listed the names of the real people on whom he based his characters, he wrote, apparently referring to his General Wetjoen, "Viljoen."

page 26   "work in the Boer War spectacle"
O'Neill, *The Iceman Cometh*, 35.

page 26   program for the reenactment
The Theater Library of the New York Public Library at Lincoln Center has a program for the Great Boer War Spectacle at St. Louis.

page 27   one from each side
Captain Lewis seems to have come in large part, not from one of the English fighters in the Boer War whom O'Neill knew, but from an English resident at Jimmy the Priest's whose name was Major Adams. At any rate, in his notes at Yale for the characters of *The Iceman Cometh*, O'Neill listed "Major A.—same as life—." O'Neill makes much of Captain Lewis's scar from a native spear wound, so he must have been a professional soldier dating back to the Zulu War—well before the Boer War broke out. Perhaps Captain Lewis combines Major Adams's experiences with those of one of the English combatants in the Boer War whom O'Neill came to know later at the Garden Restaurant.

page 27   from the "blue" of the story to "big brown"
As the story appeared in *The Seven Arts* of June 1917, Jimmy had "faded blue eyes." Perhaps the "brown" eyes of Jimmy in *The Iceman Cometh* came from his face "like an old well-bred gentle bloodhound's" and the fact that his eyes were "more bloodshot than any bloodhound's ever were" (6). With all the bloodhound images, the blue eyes would have been a jarring note even if Jimmy's eyes actually had been blue.

page 27   reading and taking notes
The notes that he took on his reading are at Yale, pages 31–32.

page 27   Pretoria, not Cape Town
When the Boer leader Paul Kruger escaped from South Africa in September 1901, he fled by train from Pretoria to Lorenço Marques in Mozambique and from there by ship to Europe. Winston Churchill, a correspondent for the *Morning Post*, was captured at the start of the war by the Boers and imprisoned in the Staatsmodel Skool at Pretoria. Escaping on December 12, 1899, Churchill hid out among the sacks on a goods train to Lorenço Marques and from there took steamer to Durban. See Doyle, *The Great Boer War*, 510, and Brian Roberts, *Those Bloody Women: Three Heroines of the Boer War* (London: Murray, 1991), 72.

page 27   "some English paper"
O'Neill, *The Iceman Cometh*, 35.

page 28   "beautiful and she played"
Ibid.

page 28   "The suicide really happened"
Letter to George Jean Nathan of February 8, 1940, SL, 501.

Chapter Three. The Anarchist Contingent

page 29   *anarchist* covered a wide range
Most of the names for these parties already existed. The socialists were established in the United States as a legal party committed to legal methods. Among the group at Provincetown were Marxists, Bakuninites, Tolstoyans, socialists, revolutionaries, and total pacifists, as well as many people who would not be considered radical today because most of the reforms they were fighting for are now respectable liberties. At that time, however, Emma Goldman and Margaret Sanger were being jailed simply for lecturing on birth control. Others were promulgating nothing more radical than the eight-hour working day or the right to form unions.

page 29   *Bread and Butter*
The version I read is the typescript Eugene O'Neill submitted for copyright to the Library of Congress. In a pencil list of the plays he had written up to 1921 that O'Neill made for Kenneth MacGowan, O'Neill described *Bread and Butter* as a four-act play written in 1914, "afterward destroyed." A verifax copy of this list is in the Special Collections, University Of California at Los Angeles, Library.

page 30   the anarchist Ferrer School
Francisco Ferrer was a Spanish educator who designed and established one of the first progressive schools, the Escuela Moderna, on the principle that education should be in itself life experience by doing, rather than simply learning about how things are done. His school embodied the ideas of Rousseau, Pestalozzi, Froebel, Kropotkin, and Tolstoy. In 1909 Ferrer was executed by firing squad at Barcelona on a charge, of which he appears to have been entirely innocent, of conspiring to assassinate the king of Spain. Some six years later, in his honor, at least twenty Ferrer schools were established in the United States, including one for children at Stelton, New Jersey, and the one largely for adult education in New York City. See Joseph Deitch, "A School in a Class by Itself," *New York Times*, March 8, 1981, 2, and Paul Avrich, *The Modern School Movement: Anarchism and Education in the United States* (Princeton: Princeton University Press, 1980).

page 30   advertisement in the December 1915 issue
Henri and Bellows were announcing room in the class for a few more students (352).

page 30   unpaid volunteer worker
At the last minute O'Neill had decided against returning to Harvard for Professor Baker's advanced class in playwriting so as to take a job as drama critic
in New York City for a Midwestern theater magazine projected by a friend
from Baker's class, Colin Ford. (See Sheaffer I, 315, 318.) Although O'Neill
received salary for a couple of months, the plan collapsed for lack of funds,
so O'Neill was again living on an allowance from his father and free to work
for *Revolt* when it got under way in December 1915.

page 30   weekly anarchist magazine *Revolt*
O'Neill told of working for *Revolt* in a letter to Beatrice Ashe, July 25,
1916, SL, 73. I have photocopies of all issues of the magazine from the
originals in the International Institute of Social History (Internationaal
Instituut voor Sociale Geschiedenis) in Amsterdam. Hereafter cited as
International.

page 30   evicting them at once
The story is told in a column titled "The Offices of Revolt Raided by the
Police," in the January 1, 1916, issue, 6, telling its readers that the loss was
about fifty dollars and the police found no bombs, for theirs were "made of
metal which couldn't penetrate into the skulls of these minions of stupid-
ity." Actually, they lost a week's issue because of the move, their next one
coming out two weeks later, January 15, 1916.

page 30   he knew classical Greek
So said Jack Johnson, "Cape Cod Literati Misses O'Neill," *Boston Herald*,
August 20, 1939. Johnson describes Havel as "a Greek scholar and poet."

page 30   docking on December 7, 1900
Richard Drinnon, *Rebel in Paradise: A Biography of Emma Goldman*
(Chicago: University of Chicago Press, 1961), 67.

page 31   "narrowly escaped." "Federal pen"
O'Neill's letter to Beatrice Ashe, July 25, 1916, SL, 73.

page 31   should have been "Polyandrous"
In pencil notes for a "Biography of Spiritual Adventure," George Cram
Cook labeled Polly so. In these same notes Cook described Hippolyte
Havel as "A Gypsy. Revolutionist. Hater of Bourgeois Pigs. A pure soul."
In Berg.

page 31   anarchist colony at Stelton, New Jersey
The colony had grown up around the Ferrer Modern School for children
established in homage to the anarchist educator, Francisco Ferrer.

page 31   "To drink much and often"
Hutchins Hapgood, *A Victorian in the Modern World* (New York: Harcourt,
Brace, 1939), 328.

page 31   only he does not know it
O'Neill, *The Iceman Cometh*, 12.

page 31   Anarchist Forum for
           The other discussion leaders for 1916 were Harry Kelly, Leonard D. Abbott,
           and Gussie Miller. They met at 8 p.m., and each leader guided the group
           for a month. Havel was scheduled for March.

page 31   Commemoration Meeting
           Revolt, January 15 and January 22, 1916, 8. Other speakers were Robert
           Minor, Leonard D. Abbott, Bernard Sernocker, Pietro Allegra, Pedro Es-
           teve, Elizabeth Gurley Flynn, Karl Dannenberg, Gussie Miller, William
           Shatoff, Harry Kelly, and Michel Dumas.

page 31   International Protest Meeting
           It is advertised in the January 29, 1916, *Revolt*, 8.

page 32   "dressed in threadbare"
           O'Neill, *The Iceman Cometh*, 4.

page 32   "a stick, conventional black"
           Hapgood, *A Victorian in the Modern World*, 328.

page 32   "crinkly long black hair"
           O'Neill, *The Iceman Cometh*, 4.

page 32   "long black hair." "very small"
           Mabel Dodge Luhan, *Movers and Shakers*, volume 3 of *Intimate Memories*
           (New York: Harcourt, Brace, 1936), 48.

page 32   "small man" with "tiny"
           O'Neill, *The Iceman Cometh*, 4.

page 32   "intelligent brow"
           Luhan, *Movers and Shakers*, 48.

page 32   "high and imaginative"
           Hapgood, *A Victorian in the Modern World*, 198.

page 32   pug nose and a "high forehead"
           O'Neill, *The Iceman Cometh*, 4.

page 32   "wild little man." "perpetual state." "mean, vindictive." "irrationally
           condemnatory"
           Hapgood, *A Victorian in the Modern World*, 426, 198.

page 32   "Capitalist swine!"
           O'Neill, *The Iceman Cometh*, 11.

page 32   "They talk like goddam"
           Luhan, *Movers and Shakers*, 90.

page 32   "glasses bigger than." "Bourgeois! Voting!"
           Art Young, *On My Way*, quoted in Max Eastman, *Enjoyment of Living*
           (New York: Harper, 1948), 439.

page 33   "Don't be a fool!"
           O'Neill, *The Iceman Cometh*, 11, 34, 104, 249.

page 33   "a dollar a day"
           In *Revolt* (February 5, 1916, 4), the editors declare that the expenses of the
           paper are fifty dollars a week and that "Hippolyte Havel gets a dollar a day

for expenses." Most of the money went to the printers. The price for a year's subscription appears on the masthead page of every issue.

page 33   "would ask me for." "characteristically asked me"
Hapgood, A *Victorian in the Modern World*, 330.

page 33   the poet's native German
In a letter to his daughter Oona, July 14, 1939, O'Neill told her that he had once "passed a German exam" required for entrance to Princeton, which he found "hard to believe now when I can scarcely read a word of it" (SL, 489). At Harvard in 1914 he bought French and German grammars to refresh the French and try for a reading knowledge of German because there were no translations into English of the best contemporary playwrights who wrote in those two languages. The French came easily, but O'Neill was doubtful of the German from the start and soon gave up on it. Letter to Beatrice Ashe [November 8, 1914], SL, 38.

page 33   the translation of his poem "Revolution"
See my discussion later in this chapter on the question of O'Neill's possession of back files of *Mother Earth*. The poem is on pages 1–3 of the March 1910 issue.

page 33   "The day grows hot — oh, Babylon!"
The German of this line of "Die Revolution" is "Der Tag wird heiss." The poem is dated 1851, so it came in the repressive years after the unsuccessful revolutions of 1848.

page 33   "unsuccessful struggle." "one reason why." "by tinkering with"
Oliver M. Sayler, "The Real Eugene O'Neill," *Century Magazine*, January 1922, 358–59.

page 34   "there are too many things"
Karsner, 119.

page 34   "man's rebellion against his environment"
David Karsner, "Eugene O'Neill at Close Range in Maine," *New York Herald Tribune*, August 8, 1926, *Sunday Magazine*, 6.

page 34   "that these unfortunate men lost"
W. W. Robinson, *Bombs and Bribery* (Los Angeles: Dawson's Book Shop, 1969), 24. The McNamaras had essentially the idea of bombing buildings put up by nonunion labor. John J. McNamara, James's brother, was secretary of the International Association of Bridge and Structural Iron Workers (Indianapolis). He was charged with dynamiting the Llewellyn Iron Works in Los Angeles, and James Barnabas McNamara was charged with dynamiting the Times building. The William J. Burns Detective Agency exerted pressure on the McNamara's associate, Ortie McManigal, to save himself by informing against them (3–6).

page 34   Donald Vose
My account is largely based on Emma Goldman's "Donald Vose: The Accursed" in the January 1916 *Mother Earth*, 353–57. Hereafter cited as

"The Accursed." The account of Vose's testimony is in "Schmidt Found Guilty," *New York Times*, December 21, 1915, 4.

page 35 "not agreeable." "his high pitched"
"The Accursed," 354.

page 35 anarchists could rent inexpensive rooms
Goldman's goal was to provide low-cost or free shelter to fellow anarchists.

page 35 Vose somehow always had money
Goldman said that she had received many messages that Donald Vose was "spending a great deal of money on drink." "The Accursed," 355.

page 36 "the perjured Burns' spy"
Terry Carlin's letter was directed to Tom Barker, Labor Temple, Los Angeles, and published in the January 22, 1916, *Revolt*, 6.

page 36 Schmidt's defense attorney
It is not Carlin's normally elegant prose but rather legal avoidance of loopholes that designed a phrase like this: "I have never been in that place with either one or both of them, nor have I ever been there." The *New York Times*, January 13, 1916, 22, says that the motion for a new trial was denied, and that after his conviction, Schmidt had read a statement denying any part in the Times building explosion. Nevertheless, he spent the rest of his life incarcerated at San Quentin.

page 36 silence it at once
The last issue of *Revolt*, February 19, 1916, 4, announced that the Chicago anarchist paper *Alarm* had been silenced and those who published it arrested. *Revolt* offered free copies of their paper to *Alarm* subscribers, but their turn for suppression was next.

page 36 "a complete hate." "the sort of thing Bob M." "clearly saw through him"
Letter of Saxe Commins to his Aunt Emma Goldman, September 23, 1925, Emma Goldman Collection, International.

page 36 "Bob M — Anarchist — incorruptible fanatic"
O'Neill, pencil notes for *The Iceman Cometh*, Yale.

page 37 "from Coast drunk." "Farm school"
Pencil scenario for *The Iceman Cometh* dated June 1939, Yale. The handwriting of the scenario is difficult to decipher. The boy's name looks like "Potter" but may possibly be "Porter."

page 37 Bob Minor came from pioneer
My materials on Bob Minor come from Joseph North, *Robert Minor: Artist and Crusader* (New York: International Publishers, 1956). For Minor's ancestry see pages 12–13. Minor married Lydia Gibson, an artist and poet on the *Masses* in 1922 when he was thirty-eight years old. Ultimately he became a leader in the American Communist Party.

page 37 "one of the few unusual"
"The Accursed."

page 37   "After all, I'm from"
O'Neill, *The Iceman Cometh*, 128.

page 37   "shifting eyes." "not agreeable"
"The Accursed."

page 37   "personality is unpleasant"
O'Neill, *The Iceman Cometh*, 21.

page 37   actual facts that feed into fiction
For instance, I have shown in my *Creating Literature Out of Life* how Tolstoy used the tragic duel that ended Alexander Pushkin's life for the opening episode in *War and Peace* of Pierre's disastrous marriage (134–38).

page 38   his mother and the other betrayed anarchists
In the actual betrayal by Donald Vose, Matthew Schmidt had not been the only victim. Vose had also informed earlier on David Caplan, a chicken farmer in Washington State. The Burns detectives waited until they were ready to arrest Schmidt to make their arrest of Caplan on a charge of being implicated in the Times bombing. The trial of Schmidt took place as *Revolt* began publication in December 1915. The trial of Caplan came later. In O'Neill's story the arrests resemble more the Haymarket bombing in Chicago years earlier than the McNamara case. In the Haymarket story a whole group of anarchists were arrested and convicted largely, it appears, on evidence of their being anarchists rather than evidence of involvement in the bombing.

page 39   defending Terry Carlin. "the only uncompromising." "evidently warmly liked"
Hutchins Hapgood, "The Case of Terry," *Revolt*, February 19, 1916, 6. Hapgood withheld no punches. He declared that a great number of so-called anarchists were just as "unjust," just as "arbitrary and despotic" as the privileged people they attacked — and that this could be seen in those who condemned Terry without evidence.

page 39   the Garbage Flat. "fondly." "a nice even carpet"
The flat was paid for by Jack Druilard, who shared it with Terry Carlin and O'Neill. O'Neill, letter to J. J. Douthit, November 30, 1943, SL, 547.

page 39   "hulk of a wreck." "the trio were inseparable"
The source for the initial stop at Truro is Jack Johnson, "Cape Cod Literati Misses O'Neill," *Boston Herald*, August 20, 1939. One of the odd bits of misinformation that has been revived recently is the assertion that Eugene O'Neill did not meet John Reed for the first time in the summer of 1916, nor did he come to Cape Cod with Terry Carlin. As John S. Bak declares in "Eugene O'Neill and John Reed: Recording the Body Politic 1913–1922," *The Eugene O'Neill Review*, Spring/Fall 1996, Reed and O'Neill's was not a "providential" meeting in 1916 but "in fact a renewal of a friendship begun two and a half years earlier in the winter of 1913" (17).

Bak's source for this statement is what he calls the "definitive" biography of O'Neill by the Gelbs (Gelb I [1962]), who declare also that it was Reed, not Carlin, who brought O'Neill to Provincetown in 1916 (Gelb I, 262, 308). The Gelbs in turn got this misinformation from Sonya Hovey, wife of Carl Hovey, editor of the *Metropolitan* magazine (Gelb I, 263).

From O'Neill's letter to Dr. David Russell Lyman of December 20, 1912 (SL, 21), we know that O'Neill entered Gaylord Farm Tuberculosis Sanatorium in Wallingford, Connecticut, Christmas Eve 1912. From his father's letter to Dr. Lyman and Lyman's reply on May 30, 1913, we know that O'Neill left the sanatorium cured in June 1913. So January, February, and March of the winter of 1913 are excluded for a meeting of Reed and O'Neill unless John Reed traveled to Connecticut to visit O'Neill at the tuberculosis sanatorium — quite apart from the fact that the Mexican Revolution (which Bak, the Gelbs, and Mrs. Hovey thought O'Neill was going to report with Reed) did not begin until late March 1913.

So that leaves November and December of 1913 for the only time when this supposed winter meeting of O'Neill and Reed could have taken place. But according to many sources, O'Neill was in New London, Connecticut, for all the rest of 1913 and throughout winter, spring, and summer of 1914, carrying out a regime of writing and sleeping outdoors prescribed by the sanatorium. In the summer of 1913, O'Neill was with his family at 325 Pequot Avenue in New London and he transferred to the Rippin's rooming house across the road for the fall and winter. According to his letter of May 7, 1914 (to Jesse Rippin, SL, 21–24), he returned to the family home when his father returned from his tour at the end of May.

O'Neill's letter to Dr. Lyman in the summer of 1914 declares, "I have gone in swimming in this Long Island Sound at least once a week ever since I left Gaylord last June. I haven't missed a single week" (SL, 25).

O'Neill's bout of tuberculosis involving a lengthy cure at a sanitorium and a long regime of rest afterward makes it quite impossible that O'Neill was in New York, where he might have met John Reed in any of the winter months of 1913, or that he would have thought of undertaking an arduous reporting trip to Mexico at that time. One of the reasons Bak (18) was eager to accept the Gelbs' assertion about the 1913 meeting was his conviction that an "important literary exchange took place" between Reed and O'Neill beginning with the writing of O'Neill's *The Movie Man*, which Bak thought was written in 1914, as do the Gelbs. But in a list of his plays up to 1921 that O'Neill made for Kenneth MacGowan, O'Neill declared that he wrote that play in 1916 (a copy of the list is in Special Collections, University of California at Los Angeles Library).

The evidence supports the conclusion that Terry Carlin brought O'Neill to Cape Cod and that O'Neill met Reed there for the first time in the

summer of 1916. Many firsthand witnesses have testified to this, and one letter written at the time also supports it. O'Neill and Carlin had been rooming together all that spring of 1916 in the Garbage Flat, and they continued
their companionship when they came to Cape Cod, first at Truro and then,
after O'Neill's first play had been accepted by the Provincetown Players, at
a rented studio over John Francis's Grocery Store in Provincetown for the
remainder of the summer.

O'Neill had no need of Reed's work on Mexico to conceive *The Movie
Man* in 1916. As early as 1913 (unquestionably through his father's film connections) O'Neill was earning money.by writing scenarios for *Moving Pictures*—so he told Dr. Lyman in his 1914 letter. He thus had his own connections to film people three years before he met Reed, and during the
Mexican Revolution. He could easily have picked up from any one of them
the story of the film-bribed Mexican general that he used in the play.

Of course, O'Neill also followed avidly coverage of the Mexican Revolution in newspapers and magazines, so he knew a lot about the war, whether
or not John Reed's articles in the *Metropolitan* were among those he read.
It seems certain that *The Movie Man* grew out of O'Neill's personal, life
knowledge, rather than from whatever information he might have gotten
out of an acquaintance with Reed. As for Sonya Hovey's remembrance, she
was clearly mixing up Reed and Mexico in 1913 with the fact that in the
fall of 1916 Reed brought O'Neill to Carl Hovey's attention by submitting
O'Neill's short story "Tomorrow" to him. Although in his reply on October 11, 1916, Hovey agreed with Reed that O'Neill could write, he rejected
the story as too slow-moving for the *Metropolitan*'s readers. (John Reed Collection, Harvard.)

page 39   "put the bite." "it will probably amuse"
Hapgood, *A Victorian in the Modern World*, 396.

page 40   "trampishly with an older man"
Harry Kemp, "Out of Provincetown: A Memoir of Eugene O'Neill," *Theatre Magazine*, April 1930, 22.

page 40   "Terry Carlin and O'Neill"
Letter of Hutchins Hapgood to Mabel Dodge, July 1, 1916, Luhan, *Movers
and Shakers*, 478. "Bayard" refers to Bayard Boyesen, the poet.

page 40   O'Neill took Terry into his home
There are many references to Terry in O'Neill's letters to Agnes and hers to
him from 1919 through 1921. Even before they owned the remodeled Coast
Guard Station at Peaked Hill Bar, and they would rent a cottage in
Provincetown for the year, Terry stayed with them for long stretches. In a
letter to O'Neill during his November 1919 trip to New York, Agnes reported Terry's assurance that Christine Ell could get "all she wants" of Prohibition whiskey and so she, with other of the Provincetown Players, might

"stage you a real party." A few days later (letter dated "Friday") Agnes told him that Terry was holding the baby Shane while she wrote for the noon mail, and "He does it like an expert too." In this letter, Terry sends word to Hutch Hapgood and Hippolyte Havel that he will be back in New York after Christmas (Correspondence).

Terry was still with them in Provincetown when Agnes wrote to O'Neill in New York on January 11 and 12, 1920 (Correspondence), that Terry was sorry he had not accompanied O'Neill to New York. In a letter later that January O'Neill told Agnes she should urge Terry to come to New York because "Hutch has made all arrangements for Terry to have a room in town here." O'Neill wanted them to have Peaked Hill Bar "entirely to ourselves until August 1st at least." But Terry was still in Provincetown on February 6, 1920, for O'Neill wrote her on that day telling her to get rid of both Shane's nurse, Mrs. Clark, and Terry with "any stall" she could think of on the day in the week to come that O'Neill would return so that that day and night would be "just our very own" (Correspondence).

A year later, in a letter of May 4, 1921, when his friend Saxe Commins was fixing his teeth in Rochester, New York (Saxe was still a dentist at that time), Agnes wrote him that she couldn't come to him because she did not like "to leave Shane with Clark for 2 weeks — out there — even with Terry." By June 24, 1921, Terry had his own shack in Provincetown. In a letter later that summer when Agnes was visiting her family, O'Neill wrote her that he had met Terry at Francis's Grocery Store in Provincetown and, learning he had been "tortured to death by the mosquitoes in his swamp villa," brought Terry back to Peaked Hill Bar with him. A few days later (August 11, 1921), O'Neill wrote her that "Terry went back to his shack yesterday. I wanted him to stick around but I guess he pined to return to his brewing. I'm regretful. It's comforting to have him about when you're not here. He has a quality all his own" (Correspondence).

By June 11, 1933, O'Neill was sufficiently worried about Terry's age and alcoholic deterioration to think he might be best off put into a "Home" at payment where he would get "real care." O'Neill thought it would not be good for Terry to join Bohemian friends at Truro for that would "mean booze — and a little more booze and what mental control he has will be gone and he'll be a total wreck." (Letter to Harry Weinberger, SL, 415–16.)

page 40   O'Neill sent an SOS. "dope out" an ideal
Letter of O'Neill to Saxe Commins dated June 1937, Princeton.

page 40   "library of Anarchist-Syndicalist"
Letter of O'Neill to Saxe Commins, July 24, 1937, Princeton.

page 40   O'Neill had already read
In a letter to his Aunt Emma Goldman, September 23, 1925 (International), Saxe told her that when her book *My Disillusionment in Russia* (Garden City, New York: Doubleday, Page, 1923) was published — in a version badly

mutilated by cuts — O'Neill had told him that he had read it and asked, "But why was it amputated?" Saxe added that he "explained the rotten circumstances."

page 41   "unfortunate mother of"
"The Accursed."

page 41   "be brave." "the heroic figure"
Ibid. In his play, O'Neill had Parritt say sardonically that his death will give his mother, always a ham, the chance "to play the great incorruptible Mother of the Revolution" (248). Surely this touch comes straight out of Emma Goldman's advice to Gertie Vose to play the role of Gorky's Mother in his novel of that name, given at the conclusion of her article "The Accursed."

page 41   "old, worn, bruised"
Ibid.

page 41   mature radical leader Emma Goldman
In Winifred L. Frazer's *E.G. and E.G.O.: Emma Goldman and "The Iceman Cometh"* (Gainesville: University Presses of Florida, 1974), Frazer saw the character of Rosa Parritt as based entirely on Emma Goldman. Knowing something of O'Neill's association with *Revolt* and by interpreting O'Neill's play, I believe Rosa Parritt is instead a composite of several different people: Terry Carlin's early love Marie, plus Gertie Vose as seen by Emma Goldman, Emma Goldman herself, and just a touch of Rosa Luxemburg.

page 41   "the most terrible blow." "torture, agony." "give ten years"
"The Accursed."

page 41   "If he doesn't know you"
Letter of Saxe Commins to his Aunt Emma Goldman, September 23, 1925 (International).

page 41   "Hutch and I sat up"
Letter of O'Neill to Agnes dated "Monday evening" from January 1920 (Correspondence).

page 41   "and her boy by another"
Hutchins Hapgood, *The Spirit of Labor* (New York: Duffield, 1907), 284.

page 43   "She is seriously ill"
Hutchins Hapgood, *An Anarchist Woman* (New York: Duffield, 1909), 179–80.

page 43   "If an oyster can turn"
Ibid., 203.

page 43   "If I cannot have"
Ibid., 215.

page 43   "I once thought that"
Ibid., 257.

page 43   "She loved me intellectually." "she began cruelly"
Ibid., 263.

page 43 "human solidarity." "I quit my fanatical"
Ibid., 305.

page 43 "I am very 'crummy'"
Ibid., 240.

page 43 "I am willing to let"
Ibid., 302–3.

page 44 "Nirvana is very welcome"
Ibid., 159.

page 44 "Old Cemetery"
O'Neill, *The Iceman Cometh*, 111.

page 44 "thin, dark, handsome"
Eastman, *Enjoyment of Living*, 565.

page 44 his "gaunt" face
O'Neill, *The Iceman Cometh*, 4.

page 44 O'Neill made Larry flea-bitten
In the word of the play, "lousy." Ibid., 5.

Chapter Four. Ward Heelers, Pimps, and Prostitutes

page 45 July 28 and 29
The dates of his first production can be calculated from his letter of "Tuesday," July 25, 1916, to Beatrice Ashe (SL, 71), in which he tells her the productions are scheduled for Friday and Saturday of that week.

page 45 "jitney Tammany politician"
O'Neill, *The Iceman Cometh*, 36.

page 46 "boss of the Ninth." "the conscious dignity"
Vorse, 7M.

page 46 "some of the gang"
Letter to Agnes O'Neill, "Tuesday a.m." [December 2?, 1919], SL, 99.

page 46 Joe Smith was certainly a little "shabby"
Vorse.

page 46 "future play." "'Joe'—tragic-comedy"
Except that I have written out O'Neill's "Prohib." I quote the note exactly as O'Neill made it in "Summer—1921" now at Yale. Under the note are the two possible titles for the play: "White" and then "Honest Honey Boy." This note has been reproduced with arbitrary changes in Floyd. A decade later—on May 25, 1932—O'Neill noted while working on *Days without End* (called at that point "Without Endings of Days") that he had also made "notes & outline old Joe Smith idea play" on that day. (*Work Diary*, 1:129). Only seven years later he took up Joe Smith's story again for *The Iceman Cometh*.

page 46   "Honey Boy" popular in 1907
O'Neill made a list of songs with their dates for his player piano on an en-
velope, labeled "1st Roll, 2nd Roll, 3rd Roll." On the 3rd Roll, the fourth
song is "Honey Boy (1907)."

page 46   "Joe S.—Jovial cynic"
Pencil notes for *The Iceman Cometh*, Yale.

page 46   "it would not be wise." "good humor"
The first of these two passages in O'Neill's preliminary descriptions of the
characters for *The Iceman Cometh* is crossed out by O'Neill in the first longhand draft typescript of the play, Yale.

page 47   a knife "slash"
O'Neill, *The Iceman Cometh*, 5.

page 47   "seem as delighted"
Letter of O'Neill to Agnes O'Neill, "Tuesday a.m." [December 2?, 1919], SL,
100. I take issue with the transcription of this passage by the editors of SL.
They have transcribed it as "They urged me to send all their blessings to
you on 'The little girl.'" The word "on" makes the passage meaningless. It
should be a dash, so the passage reads "blessings to you—'the little girl.'"
Also, their "Jim Martin" (99) should be, I believe, "Jim Martini." I correct
a third error in their transcription of this letter in a later note.

page 47   a token South African population
I am sure that O'Neill's choice of the table at which the Joe Smith character was to be placed was barely conscious, certainly not meant to strike an
audience allegorically.

page 47   "at least a dozen"
Vorse.

page 47   "old circus man." "ticket wagon"
Sweeney, 5M.

page 47   President Vilbrun Guillaume Sam in Haiti
In O'Neill's note for *The Emperor Jones* in the Wilderness Edition of his
plays, he declares that the story about President Sam of Haiti that his old
circus friend told him gave him the first idea for *The Emperor Jones*. My account of the real story of President Sam comes from Arthur C. Millspaugh,
Haiti Under American Control: 1915–1930. (Boston: World Peace Foundation, 1931), 34–35.

page 47   historical novels of Sir Walter Scott
For instance, in *Old Mortality* (New York: Dutton, 1911), 177, Scott tells of
how John Grahame of Claverhouse was thought to have supernatural (Sa-
tanic) defenses so that "many a Whig that day loaded his musket with a dollar cut into slugs in order that a silver bullet (such was their belief) might
bring down the persecutor of the holy kirk, on whom lead had no power."
See also *Guy Mannering*.

page 48   "of the tropical forest." "prospecting for gold"
Note on *The Emperor Jones*, Wilderness Edition.

page 48   a year later
Between the first idea for the play of the silver bullet and the second idea of the tropical forest, O'Neill says in his note for the Wilderness Edition that a half year passed. Between the forest idea and the third idea of the Congo drum beat, he places a full year. If he began writing in the fall of 1920, he must have gotten the first idea sometime late in 1918.

page 48   O'Neill kept in his pocket. "I knew all the circus"
As O'Neill told Sweeney in November 1924 (5M), "My friend, by the way, gave me a coin with Sam's features on it, and I still keep it as a pocket piece."

page 48   "knows all the old circus jokes"
"George M. Cohan at Home: In Which Broadway's Song-and-Dance Man Discusses O'Neill," *New York Times*, September 10, 1933.

page 49   with the "grimy smears"
Letter of O'Neill to Beatrice Ashe dated "Thursday" [October 8, 1914], SL, 30.

page 49   asked Eugene's friend Art
This story was told by McGinley a number of times, as for instance in "Columnist Recalls Eugene O'Neill as Dreamy Reporter in New London," *New Haven Evening Register*, November 28, 1953.

page 49   "hootch." "He had a quart"
Letter of O'Neill to Eugene O'Neill Jr., April 28, 1944, SL, 552–53.

page 49   "close pals." "He and I got in some." "Get Art alone"
Ibid.

page 50   "You have the power"
Welded in *The Plays of Eugene O'Neill*, 3 vols. (New York: Random House, 1967), 2:473. The collection is hereafter cited as Random House.

page 50   "ladies of the evening"
So O'Neill told Ruth Gilbert when she asked if there was a part she could play in *The Iceman Cometh*. "Ruth Gilbert Grows Up from One O'Neill Play to Another," *Brooklyn Eagle*, November 24, 1946.

page 50   "You wouldn't find any"
Jack Gaver, "Broadway: O'Neill Talks of New Plays," *Newark (New Jersey) News*, September 4, 1946.

page 50   "Some 'hard' ladies"
Letter to Agnes O'Neill, "Tuesday a.m." [December 2?, 1919], SL, 99. The editors have read the second sentence as "Where this latter got his jug." I read it as "Where this latter got his jag," a slang reference to his drunken state. As can be seen in the next note, O'Neill also used "jag" for intoxication in *The Iceman Cometh*.

page 50   one of those "polite jags." "a coupla all-night"
O'Neill, *The Iceman Cometh*, 73, 64.

page 50   "imaginative creation." "a periodical drunk"
Letter of O'Neill to George Jean Nathan, February 8, 1940, SL, 501.

page 50   "never knew" a Hickey. "all of them"
Letter of O'Neill to Kenneth MacGowan, December 30, 1940, in Jackson R. Bryer, editor, *"The Theatre We Worked For": The Letters of Eugene O'Neill to Kenneth MacGowan* (New Haven: Yale University Press, 1982), 258. Hereafter cited as Bryer.

page 51   "encourages Jimmy Tomorrow and Tom." "real meaning of what"
Pencil notes for *The Iceman Cometh*, Yale.

page 51   "Dear Old Big Heart"
Letter of O'Neill to Beatrice Ashe, "Tuesday," July 25, 1916, SL, 73.

Chapter Five. The Vital Impulse for *The Iceman Cometh*

page 53   fed up to his "teeth"
Letter of O'Neill to Lee Simonson [May? 1934], SL, 435.

page 53   alimony payments
In a letter to Lawrence Langner of October 23, 1941, Yale, O'Neill declared that if alimony was not made tax deductible, he intended to retire from all productions.

page 53   minimum alimony was
See John Chapman, "The Lady-Killer and The Playwright's Daughter," *New York Sunday News*, June 20, 1943. O'Neill also gave Agnes and the children the Bermuda home the couple had recently bought together.

page 53   afford to remarry
Only after World War II, when O'Neill's lawyer arranged a single lump sum payment to her and terminated yearly payments, did Agnes remarry.

page 53   if he earned $50,000
Letter of O'Neill to Sisk, November 28, 1941, Yale.

page 53   only as published books
As early as his letter to Simonson [May?, 1934], SL, 435, O'Neill had announced, "I think I shall permanently resign from all production and confine my future work to plays in books for readers only." When O'Neill first conceived his cycle of one-act plays *By Way of Obit*, he decided it was "for book more than stage perhaps" (*Work Diary*, 2:395).

page 53   trilogy of God plays
For *Dynamo's* production, O'Neill had talked much of the theme of the trilogy about the death of God and the attempts to find God in science, love, and money, with the result that all the critics had mistaken the theme of the

entire trilogy for the theme of its first play, *Dynamo*. So O'Neill dropped it to write the trilogy *Mourning Becomes Electra*. After its production, he wrote the second play of the God trilogy, with the idea of letting that fact about *Days without End* be known only after the production of the third play (see note at "four plays became five" later in this chapter). But that was never written as part of the God trilogy. Instead, that became the last play of his great unfinished cycle of plays, *A Tale of Possessors Self-Dispossessed*.

page 53   directive power of the past

O'Neill told Robert Sisk in a letter of July 3, 1935, SL, 447, that the cycle was "a broadening of the Electra idea." He was always conscious of the essentially musical structure of all of his plays, particularly *Mourning Becomes Electra*, through his use of the "rhythm of recurrent themes" (*Work Diary*, 2:228).

page 54   "What is a man profited"

O'Neill, as reported by Jack Gaver, said that the Bible (Matthew: 16:26) gave the theme of his nine-play cycle best, using these words. "Eugene O'Neill Goes Back to Stage After Layoff of 12 Years," *San Francisco News*, September 5, 1946.

page 54   four plays became five

The history of the cycle's growth is clear from O'Neill's *Work Diary*. On February 3, 1935, O'Neill wrote, "decide new first play of Sara—Harford—marriage—parents." At this point he is calling the entire cycle *A Touch of the Poet*. On July 9, 1935, he made notes for a "6th Play, as yet unentitled." (The published *Diary* has the misprint "entitled," 2:225.) On August 29, 1935, O'Neill made notes for a "7th Play," which he revealed on September 2, 1935, to be his third God play, formerly entitled "Bessie Bowen" (2:229). On September 7, 1935, he was "playing around with idea new first play," making eight in all (2:230). On June 7, 1936, he decided "a 9th play may be necessary" (2:256).

page 54   double-length plays

When O'Neill finished the first draft of the first play of the cycle called *Greed of the Meek* on December 23, 1937, he declared it "longer than 'Strange I'" (for *Interlude*), and he decided that the trouble was that he had tried "to get too much in these plays for single length" (*Work Diary*, 2:309). When he finished the first draft of *More Stately Mansions* September 8, 1938, he found it "as long as Strange Interlude" (*Work Diary*, 2:328). On October 20, 1940, he found the first plays of his cycle not only too long but also "too complicated," with "too many interwoven themes and motives, psychological and spiritual." His solution on October 22 was to write four plays to replace the two. Thus he ended by "expanding Cycle to eleven" (*Work Diary*, 2:391).

page 54   "Will never live to do it"
           May 21, 1941, *Work Diary*, 2:408.

page 54   not "really" sick. "pipedream that keeps us." "hopeless hope"
           When I cite plays before *The Iceman Cometh*, I refer to Random House. For
           The Straw quotes see Random House 3:350, 415.

page 54   "their own hopeless hopes." "It is the dream"
           Mary B. Mullett, "The Extraordinary Story of Eugene O'Neill," *American
           Magazine* (November 1922), 118. Hereafter cited as Mullett.

page 54   "toy mountains." "meaningless nothingness." "the walled garden"
           Hardy's quotes are from the first four drafts of *Days without End*, begun
           May 15, 1932, and finished March 3, 1933, when O'Neill began a fifth draft,
           eliminating Hardy and using masks. Longhand script at Yale, page 12.
           There are seven drafts of the play in all.

page 55   "spiritual significance"
           O'Neill told Mullett, 118, of the "spiritual significance which life attains
           when it aims high enough."

page 55   "a study in the workings"
           Angoff, *The World of George Jean Nathan*, 397. Nathan's essay "On Two
           Dramatists" is reprinted from *The Theater Book of the Year*, 1946–47.

page 55   "pleasantly engrossed in"
           Since the published *Dynamo* had been revised into a play different from
           the one produced by the Theatre Guild, I have taken my text from the type-
           script sent for copyright to the Library of Congress. There is also a type-
           script in the Berg Collection (New York Public Library) as well as a long-
           hand script at Yale.

page 56   "no plot in the ordinary sense"
           Barrett Clark reported that O'Neill told him this on an afternoon in
           March 1946 in New York. *Eugene O'Neill: The Man and His Plays* (New
           York: Dover, 1947), 151.

page 56   "I want to make life reveal"
           Letter of O'Neill to Kenneth MacGowan, December 30, 1940, Bryer, 256–
           57. MacGowan thought O'Neill ought to cut the first act of *The Iceman
           Cometh* drastically. O'Neill replied that unless one knew "the souls of the
           seventeen men and women" in his play, one would not find what Hickey
           does to them so "profoundly disturbing."

page 56   "I think I'm aware"
           "The Ordeal of Eugene O'Neill," *Time*, October 21, 1946, 71–78.

page 56   "The philosophy is that"
           Karl Schriftgiesser, "The Iceman Cometh," *New York Times*, October 6,
           1946, 1–3.

page 57   "After all, an ideal is"
           Letter of O'Neill to Lawrence Langner, August 2, 1938, SL, 480.

page 57   to accept—free of all delusions

From statements that O'Neill made before the production of *The Iceman Cometh*, it is clear that his iceman symbolized death. As O'Neill declared in a press conference quoted by Marguerite Young in "O'Neill Ready to Junk Man in Favor of Ants," *New York Herald Tribune*, September 3, 1946: "In a deep sense the iceman is death, who 'cometh like a thief in the night.'" As Karl Schriftgiesser reported, O'Neill declared, "The surface meaning of *The Iceman Cometh* stems from the sardonic wisecrack, often repeated by one of the characters, who tells people he has left his wife safe at home with the iceman." But as the play "proceeds the 'iceman,' who started a ribald joke, takes on a different, deeper and even terrifying meaning and before the end becomes Death itself." Of course, once an audience learns that Hickey's wife is lying dead in the arms of the iceman, they have virtually an explicit definition of the iceman as death.

Nevertheless—purely on the basis of the word *cometh*—a wholly different interpretation, for which there is not a jot of evidence either in or out of the play, has been offered and widely accepted by some. For example, Cyrus Day, in "The Iceman and the Bridegroom," *Modern Drama*, May 1958, 3–9, asserts that O'Neill is really referring ironically to the announcement of the coming of Christ as a "bridegroom," in Matthew (25:6) in the parable of the virgins. Day states that O'Neill was probably stimulated to do so by the title of Waldo Frank's 1938 novel, *The Bridegroom Cometh*. From this assumption, Day asserts that O'Neill meant his iceman as a foil to the bridegroom of Christianity, because he brings the opposite of eternal life. O'Neill—he believes—has an "anti-Christian undertone in mind" for his play. Although the only explicit bridegroom in the play is Chuck, the pimp-bartender in his pipe dream of marrying the prostitute Cora, Day pulls in his iceman-Christ-bridegroom.

Day offers as evidences for his interpretation what he calls a number of "tantalizing resemblances" to the New Testament in the play. He equates the Last Supper with Harry Hope's birthday dinner, which, he says, Hickey leaves "as Christ does, aware that he is about to be executed." But in the play Hope's party takes place the night *before* the night on which Hickey makes his confession and is taken away by the police. So Day's resemblance rests on a confusion in his understanding of the play's time scheme.

Day also thinks that "Hickey as savior has twelve disciples," and that since Donald Parritt is twelfth on O'Neill's list of characters, he is Judas Iscariot. But in actuality there are thirteen male characters beside Hickey: Harry Hope, Ed Mosher, Pat McGloin, Willie Oban, Joe Mott, Piet Wetjoen, Cecil Lewis, James Cameron, Hugo Kalmar, Larry Slade, Rocky Pioggi, Don Parritt, and Chuck Morello. Judas was one of the twelve disciples, but Hickey has thirteen.

Day's questionable numerology extends to his other "resemblances." He believes that because there are three of them, the three whores in the play represent the three Marys (the Virgin Mary, Mary Magdalene, and Mary the mother of James). From there he concludes that O'Neill was introducing "concealed blasphemies" into his play and was laughing "in secret at the critics who supposed that he had written a compassionate play in *The Iceman Cometh.*" Day says the play is completely nihilistic, and so do such of his followers as Judith E. Barlow in her book *Final Acts: The Creation of Three Late O'Neill Plays* (Athens: University of Georgia Press, 1985), 57, who gives complete credence to what she calls Day's "seminal essay."

page 57   lay aside his opus magnus
In his *Work Diary*, 2:206, on New Year's Day, 1935, O'Neill told himself that he had "grand ideas for this Opus Magnus if can ever do it—wonderful characters!"

page 58   he thought himself "jinxed"
O'Neill thought that perhaps all his ill health came of the hot, humid climate of Sea Island, Georgia, and he was jinxed there. (*Work Diary*, October 3, 1936, 2:269.)

page 58   devastating neurological disorder
At first the doctors (and O'Neill with them) described his illness as nerves, then as neuritis, and then for many years as Parkinson's disease. After his death and postmortem, it appeared to have been cerebellar degeneration, but there was no agreement as to whether it was hereditary or alcoholic. It might shed some light on the cause to bear in mind that O'Neill's alcoholic bouts were intermittent rather than constant, and that from 1926 until his death in 1953, he abstained from alcohol (except for about three brief relapses).

page 58   "bilious attack." "gastritis." "continual vomiting"
There are at least nine references to bilious attacks in the *Work Diary* in May and June 1936 (2:254, 257, etc.). During July, August, and September he was taking Dinatol for the biliousness. The gastritis and vomiting had started well before February 1936 and continued through February, March, and April 1936, when he was calling it "stomach upset." From February on there are also many references to extreme depression.

page 58   "whole person sick"
October 7, 1936, *Work Diary*, 2:260. During 1936 O'Neill made several trips to New York City from Georgia for treatment by Dr. Draper at Doctors Hospital.

page 58   Sophus Keith Winther
On July 6, 1933, when O'Neill finished reading Winther's book on his work, he declared it "best yet done, all around," *Work Diary*, 1:165. The Winthers visited O'Neill at Sea Island, Georgia, from August 25 to 29, 1936 (2:264).

page 58   "sick-stomach." "nerves bad." "movie news people." "Hell of a chance"
November 8, 1936, *Work Diary*, 2:271–72. The bad nerves came on November 11, one day before the news that he had received the Nobel Prize.

page 58   "A little [more] excitement"
The telegram was sent in answer to congratulations by Theresa Helburn and her husband to "Mr. and Mrs. Oliver Opdyke" on November 15, 1936. Theater Guild Collection, Yale.

page 58   "very sick, weak and woozy"
December 23, 1936, *Work Diary*, 2:275–76. On December 26, Dr. Dukes sent him to Merritt Hospital for observation.

page 58   "terrible cramp"
Work Diary, 2:276. On December 27, Carlotta had joined O'Neill in the hospital, as they both had flu.

page 58   "bad pain kidneys." "pain prostate." "caffeine, adrenaline"
January 6, 1937. Also January 9, 11, 12, 1937, *Work Diary*, 2:276–77.

page 58   "attacks dyspepsia." "creative mind alive"
May 16, 20, 23, 29, 1937, *Work Diary*, 2:287–88, 290.

page 59   "sinking spells"
Writing on April 16, 1880, to his friend Edmund Gosse to tell him about his severe illness in California and about Dr. Bamford, who brought him through it, Robert Louis Stevenson listed among the appalling symptoms of his pulmonary hemorrhages, "sinking fits in which I lost the power of speech." Since Eugene O'Neill began referring continually to having "sinking spells" from the time he arrived, sick, in California and during all the time thereafter that he lived there, I suspect that having "sinking fits" (of which, Stevenson appears to be quoting his California doctor) or "sinking spells," as O'Neill always called them, was a diagnosis peculiar to California doctors. (Possibly there was something in the California climate that brought on spells of total prostration lasting a few days in persons suffering chronic ill health, as were both Robert Louis Stevenson and O'Neill during their residence in the San Francisco area.) David Daiches, *Robert Louis Stevenson and His World* (London: Thames and Hudson, 1973), 49.

page 59   ubiquitous invader of the homes
In the Middle Ages the men with universal access to homes when husbands were away were the friars. The same kind of jokes were therefore made about them as were made about icemen in a later age.

page 59   "mad tortured." "Go! Get the hell"
O'Neill, *The Iceman Cometh*, 248.

page 59   "a denial of any other." "had locked myself in"
Quoted in Croswell Bowen, *The Curse of the Misbegotten: A Tale of the House of O'Neill* (New York: McGraw-Hill, 1959), 316. Bowen was

reproducing his own earlier article "The Black Irishman," in *P.M.* (November 3, 1946), 13–17.

page 59   "New London family one"
Work Diary, 2:351.

page 60   "long but grand!" "one of best plays"
Work Diary, 2:357, 367.

page 60   "moments in it"
Letter of O'Neill to George Jean Nathan, February 8, 1940, SL, 501.

page 60   "the best." "suddenly strip the secret"
Letter of O'Neill to Lawrence Langner, August 11, 1940, SL, 511.

page 60   O'Neill recalled his fruitless struggle
In a letter to Dudley Nichols, December 16, 1942, O'Neill declared himself an optimist for a United Nations victory, but "a pessimist about any intelligent, greedless peace." Peace, he knew, was always "made by and of men, and if men have changed at all spiritually since the last war, it is for the worse." He saw no statesmen "noble-minded" enough "to make an unselfish peace, and then keep on waging it," SL, 537–38.

page 60   "swinish British Tories"
Letter of O'Neill to George Jean Nathan, June 15, 1940, SL, 507.

page 60   "Only a blathering"
Letter of O'Neill to George Jean Nathan, October 1, 1939, SL, 496.

page 60   "a favorite bit." "impressive ghostly quality"
Letter of O'Neill to Lawrence Langner, May 13, 1944, SL, 556–57.

page 61   "It is as deeply moving."
Letter of O'Neill to Norman Holmes Pearson, July 30, 1942, SL, 532.

page 61   "finest values would be lost"
Letter of O'Neill to Eugene O'Neill Jr., April 28, 1941, SL, 517.

page 61   "because now we need"
Letter of O'Neill to Norman Holmes Pearson, July 30, 1942, SL, 532.

Chapter Six. Broadway — On and Off

page 62   agreed on Dowling to direct
Letter of O'Neill to Lawrence Langner [January 22, 1945], SL, 568.

page 62   the huge Martin Beck Theater
James Barton's delivery of Hickey's final soliloquy failed in part because his voice was inadequate for a theater so large. On opening night he spent the special dinner intermission for the critics clowning with friends and thus had no strength left for the final soliloquy. Ultimately he developed laryngitis and had to be substituted by E. G. Marshall (transferred from acting Willie Oban). Marshall was so much better than Barton as Hickey that the guild cast him in the role for the road tour in the spring of

1937. "O'Neill, Barton Draw: Actor Cut But Paid," *New York News*, March 8, 1937.

page 63   the excellent acting

The cast at the Circle in the Square was Farrell Pelly as Harry Hope, Phil Pheffer as Ed Mosher, Albert Lewis as Pat McGloin, Addison Powell as Willie Oban, William Edmonson as Joe Mott, Richard Abbott as Piet Wetjoen, Richard Bowler as Cecil Lewis, James Greene as James Cameron, Paul Andor as Hugo Kalmar, Conrad Bain as Larry Slade, Peter Falk as Rocky Pioggi, Larry Robinson as Don Parritt, Patricia Brooks as Pearl, Gloria Scott Backé as Margie, Dolly Jonah as Cora, Joe Marr as Chuck Morello, Jason Robards as Hickey, Mal Thorne as Moran, and Charles Hamilton as Lieb.

page 63   destroy the drama's emotional build

According to Jack Gaver, *The Iceman Cometh* was not a financial success "despite the extraordinary publicity." He said it was "still in the red after 136 Broadway performances and a tour." *Curtain Calls* (New York: Dodd, Mead, 1949), 154.

page 63   "hungry enough" to roast

On opening night, October 9, 1946, according to Mark Barron, "Eugene O'Neill Will Roam No More: Imposing list of Plays Prepared" (*Fort Worth Star-Telegram*, October 13, 1946), the critics were allowed a leisurely dinner with the curtain rising at 5:30 and an intermission from 6:30 to 7:45 p.m. Thereafter, as O'Neill told Earl Wilson, there would be only a half-hour intermission after the first act, with the curtain rising at 8:00 and coming down at 11:30. "Eugene O'Neill Talks about his New Play," *New York Post*, August 2, 1946.

page 63   too many cuts

Bryer, 256–57.

page 63   "Take him giving us"

Robert Sylvester, "O'Neill Sets Aside Drama for Staging 25 Years After Death," *New York News*, June 10, 1946.

page 64   a considerable disappointment

Saxe Commins's wife, Dorothy, had been a concert pianist and was a fine musician. She transcribed the "Sailor Lad" song from O'Neill's singing it to her. "My voice," O'Neill told her, "croaks like a frog." (Interview with Dorothy Commins, December 17, 1964.) When O'Neill inscribed a copy of *The Iceman Cometh* to her with thanks for her "collaboration," he wrote, "It's sad the actor who sang it can't sing at all, although he acts finely." (Dorothy Commins's inscribed copy in her home at Princeton.)

page 64   rewrite the ending

A typescript of *The Iceman Cometh* with an inscription to Carlotta at Yale appears to be the production script, as it has a list of the properties to be used in the play at the back. It has the altered ending with the singing reduced to a snatch of the "Sailor Lad" song, followed by the derisive laughter of the other pipe dreamers.

page 64   "convert to death"
O'Neill, *The Iceman Cometh*, 258.

Long Day's Journey into Night
Chapter Seven. The "One-Day Play"

page 67   "outside" the cycle. "mind for years"
Eugene O'Neill told Dudley Nichols in a letter of October 13, 1940 (Yale), that the two "outside" plays had been "on my mind for years." As he told Clayton Hamilton in a letter of March 25, 1941 (Berg), he had felt "a sudden necessity to write plays I'd wanted to write for a long time." He had told George Jean Nathan in a letter of February 8, 1940 (SL, 500), that he would recognize in the first of these outside plays "material I have talked about using ever since you've known me."

page 67   "house-with-the-masked-dead"
Work Diary, 1:105.

page 67   "revisit Pequot Ave"
Ibid., 1:104.

page 67   "New Idea for Play."
Ibid., 2:290.

page 67   "attempt to go on." "the dead (his mother)"
These notes were part of O'Neill's ideas for the one-day play that I transcribed from the original manuscript at Yale. They are dated June 18, 1937. Floyd, 250.

page 67   "very, very young"
Letter of O'Neill to Jessica Rippin [postmarked May 7, 1914], SL, 23–24. He tells her that he has been piqued by her calling him "very, very young" and replies that she is herself no candidate for a home for the aged.

page 68   "A Long Day's Insurrection"
This and the following titles are listed in O'Neill's pencil scenario for *Long Day's Journey into Night*, Yale.

page 68   "Diary of a Day's Journey." "A Long Day's Journey"
These titles are on a separate sheet of "Notes and Diagrams for Long Day's Journey," Yale.

page 68   "Get better title"
Work Diary, 2:372.

page 68   "Dogs do not fear"
"Last Will and Testament of Silverdene Emblem O'Neill." Typescript sent by Carlotta O'Neill to Carl Van Vechten, January 19, 1941, Berg. O'Neill wrote this as an effort to get Carlotta to assuage her grief by

adopting another Dalmatian. Inevitably it also expressed his feelings toward death at the time, conditioned by the writing of *The Iceman Cometh.*

page 68   August 1912

Eugene O'Neill, *Long Day's Journey into Night* (New Haven: Yale University Press, 1956), 11. Hereafter cited as *Long Day's Journey.*

page 68   "summer, 1912"

The Iceman Cometh, vii, 3.

page 68   "have something within us"

Oliver M. Sayler, "The Real Eugene O'Neill," *Century Magazine,* January 1922, 358–59.

page 68   "I see life as a"

Letter of O'Neill to Mary A. Clark, August 5, 1923, SL, 181. Mary Clark had been one of the nurses who cared for him at Gaylord Farm.

Chapter Eight. The False in the True

page 70   "written in blood"

So O'Neill declared in his *Work Diary,* January 5, 1940, 2:368.

page 70   Eugene had scrapbooks

James O'Neill's scrapbooks are now at Yale.

page 70   very few facts

Eugene O'Neill did have his parents' marriage certificate. As he told Lawrence Estavan, who was supervising a book on the San Francisco Theater, January 15, 1940, SL, 499, it was "one of the few records of my parents in their early days that I possess."

page 70   "best" wedding gown. "never mind"

Long Day's Journey, 114.

page 70   May 25, 1874

The record of Thomas Joseph Quinlan's death is in the Probate Court of Cuyahoga County, New Court House, Cleveland, Ohio. Contrary to the date indicated in the record (May 25), I believe the newspaper account, which said he died at three o'clock in the morning of May 26, to be accurate. For a death during the small hours of the morning, very often the night is taken as a unit beginning with dark of the previous day.

page 70   Ella Quinlan married James O'Neill

I have a copy of the marriage certificate, with all information from the American National Shrine of St. Ann.

page 71   how his parents met

Long Day's Journey, 105.

page 71   simple and unpretentious

Ibid., 13.

page 71   only thirteen years old

From Mary Ellen Quinlan's baptismal certificate, Saint Patrick's Rectory, 640 Grand Avenue, New Haven, Connecticut; she was born August 13, 1857, and baptized August 23, 1857.

page 71   the Saturday matinees

James O'Neill had had a hard time convincing Ellsler to introduce Saturday matinees at the Academy, though these proved even more popular than evening performances. When again in Cleveland some forty years later, James O'Neill recalled, "From the first the matinees were successful, and in a short time the stars who came along, and who were engaged only for evening performances, were furious that they were not allowed to play and take the lion's share of the profits." Also, James O'Neill recalled that he had told Ellsler "these matinees would educate people and bring up a new generation of playgoers and they did. They were so popular that I have seen women and children sitting on the steps before the doors opened, eating their lunches. There were no reserved seats. It was first come first served and as the price was only a quarter the whole family came." William E. Sage, "St. James O'Neill, Patron of Matinee Girls." *Cleveland Leader*, February 23, 1910. There are also contemporary references to the matinees at Ellsler's Academy of Music in Cleveland. The *New York Clipper* of December 16, 1871, reported the matinee with Miss Effie Ellsler as Fanchon in *Fanchon the Cricket* the following afternoon. It also told of the stormy weather on December 8, when a surprisingly good house came and "Mr. James O'Neill and Bella Golden met with a warm and hearty reception on entering the stage." Also, the *Clipper* of December 30, 1871, announced that *The Streets of New York* was given "at the Christmas matinee."

page 72   leading man at McVicker's

James O'Neill recalled, "I was terribly frightened at the idea of being leading man to the great stars of that day"—that is, Edwin Booth, Charlotte Cushman, Salvini, and Barry Sullivan. "It was splendid training, and I think I laid the foundations of my fortune in those two years I put in at McVicker's. Chicago people took kindly to me and flattered me constantly. I remember one night that when I was playing Othello to Booth's Iago I got an ovation at the end of act three which staggered me. Colonel Sharpe, who now presides over the destinies of McVicker's theater, came to me that night and told me that he had never known a round of applause in that house to last so long as did that which greeted me at the curtain's fall. So you see, I have good reason to love Chicago." *Chicago Chronicle*, February 28, 1897.

page 72   he returned to Cleveland

The *New York Clipper*, June 21, 1873, reported that "James O'Neill of McVicker's Theater, Chicago has taken summer quarters at the Cliff

House, Rocky River, Cleveland, O., where he will remain until the opening of next season, when he returns to Chicago." The *Clipper* for August 2, 1873, reported that a dramatic group "under the name of John Ellsler's Company" and whose stockholders were James O'Neill, Will E. Chapman, Charles R. Rogers, and James B. Curran, was playing summer theater in and around Cleveland. "Their business so far has been very good, notwithstanding the excessively hot weather."

page 72   far away in California

The year 1875 was one of "panic" throughout the United States. Hooley moved his company to San Francisco as a measure to save his Chicago theater from bankruptcy. James O'Neill answered the question of why he left McVicker's in an interview with the *New York Dramatic Mirror*, February 2, 1895, "R. M. Hooley offered me a larger salary. . . . When Mr. Hooley went to San Francisco he took me with him for a special engagement of three months." That engagement "lengthened into a year."

page 72   "scandal of that woman"

Long Day's Journey, 86.

page 72   "Nettie was a very nice." "got mashed"

"The World's a Stage," *Chicago Tribune,* September 9, 1877. The *Tribune* reprinted the interview with Pop Seaman from the *Chicago Post.* The slang terms *got mashed* for *fell in love,* and *masher* for a man who caused women to fall in love with him have gone out of the language. The term *masher* survives but now signifies a pervert who throws himself against women in public places.

page 72   the name of Zucker

The reporter for the interview misspelled it as "Zooker." I have corrected it. The most likely Zucker in Cleveland in 1871 to be having an affair with an Irish girl and to be in possession of a pistol he was ready to use would be Israel Zucker, listed in the directories as having a saloon at 19 Liberty Street (also his residence). Also in Cleveland for 1871–72 was an Abraham Zucker, listed as "gent." with a residence at 41 Charles Street. The following year, he had a Frederick Zucker, a clerk, and H. Zucker, a salesman, boarding with him. All in all, it's much more likely that Mr. Israel Zucker, owner of a saloon, was the Cleveland Zucker enamored of the Irish Nettie. Apparently Zucker had genuine feelings for Nettie—who seems to have been willful and fickle. For 1871–72 I used the *W. S. Robson and Company's Cleveland Directory.*

page 73   she was only fifteen

When Nettie's son, Alfred Hamilton O'Neill, sued James O'Neill for money on March 6, 1897, he described his mother at the time of her alleged marriage to James O'Neill as "a mere child of only about fifteen years of age and wholly inexperienced in the ways of the world." See *Alfred H. O'Neill v. James O'Neill*, Chancery Bill No. 162,025, Circuit Court of Cook County, Illinois.

page 73   "brought him out"
"The World's a Stage." The interview with Pop Seaman declares that Seaman said he put O'Neill on the boards in Cleveland (from which O'Neill had come to Chicago). This would have been the reporter's error for Cincinnati, where James O'Neill actually began his acting career at the Cincinnati National Theater.

page 74   Nettie had been intimate
See the reply to Nettie's allegations submitted by James O'Neill's attorney Frederick Crane as reported in "The Actor's Reply to the Woman Claiming to Be His Lawful Wife," *New York Times*, September 19, 1877, reprinted from the *Chicago Tribune* of September 16.

page 75   the bad publicity
James O'Neill declared at once of Nettie's accusations, "If you want to put the whole thing into a sentence, you may say I got into a scrape when I was a young man, and I find I am not quite out of it." He explained that it was "an old scandal that has been tagging me around ever since I began to acquire a certain degree of prominence in my profession." "James O'Neill in a New and Highly-Emotional Role," *Chicago Tribune*, September 8, 1877.

page 75   "I think the whole thing." "Her statements are untrue"
Ibid.

page 75   settled out of court
On Friday morning, December 7, 1877, the *Chicago Inter-Ocean* ("Jim O'Neill's Other Wife") interviewed Pop Seaman at his apartment on Harrison Street, asking if the settlement was on a money basis. He answered "Yes, it was; papers were signed, and the whole thing settled." On December 8, 1877, the *Inter-Ocean* reported from a "reliable source" that "Jim O'Neill paid $550" and legal expenses.

page 75   Elizabeth Robins
All of the information on the incident comes from the Elizabeth Robins diaries and letters in the Fales Library, New York University. Hereafter cited as Fales.

page 76   Lillian West. "a clever comic opera singer"
The revelation that Lillian West was actually Mrs. Harry Brown came from the *New York Dramatic Mirror*, January 9, 1892. When Lillian West became the theater reporter of the *Chicago Evening News*, under the pen name "Amy Leslie," she reported in the July 10, 1909, issue that Ella Quinlan O'Neill "had been my seatmate at college for a year and was almost a child when she married O'Neill."

page 76   "Ella Quinlan never seemed"
Ibid.

page 77   Daisy Green. Loretto Ritchie Emerson
            Marion McCandless, who was in charge of alumni at St. Mary's College
            and author of a history of the *Holy Cross Alumnae Association, Family Por-
            traits* (Notre Dame: St. Mary's College, 1952), told me of Ella's schoolmates
            in a letter of January 17, 1955. Loretto Ritchie Emerson was Marion
            McCandless's aunt. McCandless called Ella's friend who became a nun
            "Daisy" Green, but that must have been a nickname, for Miss Green is
            listed in *Family Portraits* (454) as "Rosemary Green (Sister M. Evarista
            C.S.C.)." According to Marion McCandless, "She and my aunt and Ellen
            were great friends." There were only eleven in her graduating class, so Ella
            Quinlan was doing well to keep in touch with three of her college friends.
            Lillian West graduated the year before Ella.

page 77   "playing in the front yard"
            This is information given to me in a letter of February 1955 by Loretto
            Ritchie Emerson's daughter, Helen Emerson (Mrs. Edward E. McIntyre).
            I have placed this episode in February 1893 because it is the only time dur-
            ing Eugene O'Neill's early childhood that James O'Neill was playing for a
            fairly long period in the American Southwest, and Texas in particular.
                According to the *New York Clipper* of January 28, 1893, James O'Neill was
            playing in *Fontenelle* at Dallas, January 30, 31; Fort Worth, February 1, 2;
            Waco, 3; Austin, 4; San Antonio, 6, 7; Galveston, 8, 9; Houston, 10, 11. From
            January 12 through 18 James O'Neill played at the St. Charles Theater in
            New Orleans, Louisiana. According to the *Clipper* of February 18, 1893,
            James O'Neill's production was performed "in a spirited and heroic man-
            ner, and to the satisfaction of a large audience."
                Fontenelle was set at the court of Louis XV with Madame Pompadour as
            one of the characters played by a grandniece of the great Charlotte
            Cushman, with whom James O'Neill had acted as a young man in Chicago.
            (See the *New York Dramatic Mirror*, July 23, 1892.) According to the *Mirror*
            of September 3, 1892, she was to wear a ball dress made by M. Herrmann
            "heavily embroidered in gold, decorated with rhinestones. Mr. Herrmann
            recently presented to Mr. O'Neill a piece of embroidered silk which was
            originally part of a costume worn by Pompadour herself. Mr. O'Neill in
            turn has presented it to Miss Cushman, who will carry it as a handkerchief
            in one of the scenes." Audiences of the day demanded great display in
            costumes and scenery in theater.

page 77   born on August 13, 1857
            The baptismal certificate for Mary Ellen Quinlan (baptized August 23,
            1857) from St. Patrick's Rectory, New Haven, also gives the date of birth.

page 77   transferred to Cleveland
            Thomas J. Quinlan first appears in the New Haven City Directory for
            the year 1856–57 as confectioner, 67½ Grand Street, where he continues

through 1857–58 and then disappears thereafter. Thomas J. Quinlan first appears in the *Cleveland City Directory* for the year 1859–60 as "news dealer" at 173 Ontario Street. From 1861 through 1867 the address for his business is 174 Ontario Street, where he is listed in full as "dealer in books, stationery and fancy goods; also bread, cakes and confectionery." By 1868–69 he becomes "city circulator" for the *Cleveland Plain Dealer* and moves his home to what was first called "Kinsman Street" and then, from 1870–71 on, "Woodland Avenue."

page 77   Bridget's sister Elizabeth

That Bridget Quinlan and Elizabeth Brennan were sisters is clear from the records of their deaths in New London. We know that when Bridget Quinlan died in July 1887, her daughter Ella O'Neill was abroad with her husband. In reply to a letter from A. M. Palmer, who was writing a history of the Union Square Theater and wanted information, James O'Neill told him on May 17, 1887, "I sail for the other side June 9th and while there shall visit Ireland the land o me birth and expect to gather some points of my early life" (Letter in the Theater Collection, Harvard University).

According to the *New York Clipper* of May 28, 1887, "James O'Neill's family will accompany him abroad. He will visit only Ireland and Great Britain." So soon after the death of their baby Edmund in 1885, while left in the care of his grandmother, James and Ella O'Neill would not have left Jamie behind. So this trip included "family," not just wife. The *Clipper* of August 20 reported, "James O'Neill sailed for home from England August 12. His season will open September 5 in New England." So when Ella's mother died on July 28 or 29, none of her intimate family were immediately available for consultation, and it was probably James O'Neill's New London lawyer who gave the information on Bridget Quinlan's death for the record. Certainly, it was someone who knew little, for the record is full of errors.

For one thing, Bridget Quinlan's death record gives the date of her death as July 28, with a small c above it, which might mean *circa*. The *New London Telegraph* of 30, 1887—which clearly had better information — reported: "In this city, July 29, 1887, Mrs. T. J. Quinlan. Funeral from the residence of Mrs. William Brennan, Ocean Avenue, Monday morning at 8:30."

The death records of both Bridget and of her sister Elizabeth three years later (December 29, 1890) give the names of the two sisters' parents as Patrick and Anastasia (but with peculiar and different spellings in both), and the records are even more different as to their maiden name. Bridget Quinlan's name before marriage is given as Lundigan and Elizabeth Brennan's (which seems the correct one) as Landrigan.

Bridget Quinlan's age at death in the record is given as sixty years, but the tombstone in St. Mary's cemetery (replaced with a single stone for the whole family by Eugene O'Neill years later) gives the birth of Bridget as 1829, which would make her fifty-eight years old at her death in 1887. Also, the place of residence at death is incorrectly given in the record as Ireland. In those days before air travel, only a miracle would have brought her coffin from Ireland to New London in time for her funeral four days later (August 1).

page 78   Thomas Joseph also left relatives

The sponsors for Ella Quinlan's baptism are listed as Andrew Quinlan and Mary A. Quinlan. They are not in the *New Haven Directory* for 1858–59 but were probably living nearby. It is not known whether Andrew Quinlan was brother or cousin or uncle to Thomas J. Quinlan. Whatever the relationship, the family of Andrew probably stayed on the East Coast when Thomas Joseph went to Cleveland. The Quinlan family had come a few years earlier from Tipperary, Ireland.

page 78   to join her elder sister in New London

Certainly Bridget Quinlan and William Joseph Quinlan were not in Cleveland for 1876–77, for they are not in the directory for that year. I assume they went to New London but—since there is no direct evidence of their whereabouts—they might just as well have gone to New York City. New London is more probable in part because propriety in 1976 might not have placed the engaged couple in close daily contact at New York, whereas a New London residence would still allow comfortable visits from James O'Neill to New London or from Ella Quinlan with her mother to New York. Also, since Ella's Aunt Elizabeth and Uncle Thomas Brennan were the only participants at the private wedding ceremony in New York City, aside from Ella's mother and brother and the bride and groom, they were likely in close rapport with them during the year before the marriage. Besides, after her husband's death, and after her son had made an independent start in the world, Bridget Quinlan made her permanent home in New London near her sister Elizabeth; she died there in July of 1887 while Ella O'Neill was abroad in England and Ireland with her husband.

page 78   a visit back to Cleveland

The *New York Dramatic News* of June 23, 1877, announced that "James O'Neill has gone for a three weeks' tour of the mountains and then visits Cleveland. He opens in Chicago under Shook and Palmer." In a Shakespearean reference, the same issue announced on a separate page: "Mr. James O'Neill, the popular actor and affable gentleman, became a Benedict last Thursday." After the performances in Chicago, at the end of August and beginning of September, they went on to San Francisco.

page 78   to Orient, Long Island

A clipping in the Harvard University Theater Collection from the Springfield Republican, "James O'Neill Actor Is Dead" (circa August 12, 1920), declares "Previous to locating in New London he spent his summers at Orient, L. I."

page 78   Brennan and Sheridan cousins
             Thomas Brennan was Ella's maternal uncle by marriage and one of his
             married daughters was a Sheridan.
page 79   "good company." "He was prosperous."
             Long Day's Journey, 137.
page 79   "Thomas J. Quinlan died"
             The newspaper is dated May 26. Thomas Quinlan must have died on the
             26th, but a record in the Probate Court of Quyahoga County gives the date
             of Thomas Quinlan's death as "the 25th day of May 1874."
page 80   "It pained me." "Doctor Lyman's reports"
             Letter of December 20, [1926], SL, 227. Eugene O'Neill had spent a day or
             so at Shelton when it had just been set up and was still fairly primitive —
             probably the source of Edmund Tyrone's hostility in the play to being sent
             to a state farm. By the time Edward Boulton was sent to Shelton in
             June 1926, it was much improved. Both letters to Teddy Boulton in SL (205,
             227) show that O'Neill strongly associated his own tuberculous struggle
             with that of Agnes's father at the time. No wonder then that years later he
             brought into his family play an association of Edmund's tuberculosis with a
             mortal TB of the father of the woman toward whom he feels guilt.
page 80   always looked "fashionable"
             I am quoting Thomas Dorsey Jr. from my interview with him April 6, 1955.
             All quotes by him throughout this work are from that interview.
page 80   magnificent yellow satin. "coming out in London"
             In my interview with her on June 26, 1961, Carlotta O'Neill told me of the
             dress and also of her marriage to Moffat. Later she showed me a large col-
             lection of photographs from which I might select those I wanted; luckily,
             the "coming out" photograph was among them.
page 80   March 31, 1911
             The date of Carlotta's marriage to Moffat is in the document she filed for
             divorce in 1914.
page 81   "shimmering" satin. to create a "bustle effect"
             Long Day's Journey, 115. Carlotta's coming-out dress was actually more elab-
             orate, with silk fringes and brocaded panels. O'Neill simplified it to make
             the lace a single, sharp impression for the theater audience.
page 81   "rheumatism" in her hands
             Long Day's Journey, 104, 116, 123, 171.
page 81   "Carlotta's arthritis bad." "in bed — arthritis"
             Work Diary, 2:433.
page 81   "has been having trouble"
             Work Diary, 2:341.
page 81   "Mother"
             So O'Neill told Carlotta in a letter of May 25, 1932, SL, 399.

page 82   "sleepless" nights worrying
        Work Diary, 2:343.

page 82   care of a trained nurse
        Carlotta's nurse was Maxine Edie. "Maxie" had cared for O'Neill at Merritt Hospital during his major illness when Carlotta returned to Sea Island, Georgia, to conclude the sale of their house there in February 1937. The *Work Diary* notes card games and automobile excursions with Maxie and Mrs. Dukes, the wife of O'Neill's physician. Maxine Edie became a friend of O'Neill and Carlotta, and there are notes of visits from her in the *Work Diary* on August 21 and 22, 1937, and March 1 and 6, 1938, 2:279–80, 298, 314.

page 82   "still too upset"
        Work Diary, 2:343.

page 82   "I have not been very well"
        From a letter of Carlotta O'Neill to Doris Alexander, May 5, 1962.

page 82   would get up at four o'clock
        "Story of the Native Daughter Whose Beauty Now Makes Her Famous," *San Francisco Call*, May 5, 1907. Nellie Tharsing had submitted her daughter's photograph for a beauty contest sponsored by the *San Francisco Call* and judged by a sculptor, Douglas Tilden, and two painters, Arthur F. Mathews and G. Cadenasso. When Hazel Tharsing won, Nellie told the reporter that Hazel had "never had anything but perfect credit marks in school," and that she had graduated from St. Gertrude's Academy of the Rio Vista Convent in June 1905.

page 82   suffered a nervous breakdown
        Carlotta O'Neill told me of her breakdown in an interview on June 26, 1961, at her apartment in the Carlton House, 680 Madison Avenue, New York City. Under the idea that "roughing it" would bring her out of her depression, she was sent with the family of a friend of hers, Eileen Pickel (consisting of her mother, father, and brother as well as Eileen) on a cattle roundup from Yosemite to Mexico. From that glorious trip on, Hazel (Carlotta) liked to think of herself as a great strong American outdoor girl.
        When she was interviewed in London on May 4, 1907, by Herbert Williams ("Miss Tharsing Is Interviewed in London," *San Francisco Call*, May 5, 1907), Hazel talked enthusiastically of the Cambridge–Oxford "field meet" in which three of her young male friends who were fellow Americans had won "leading events." Hazel added, "I was wildly excited. And I came home simply covered with American flags." She told Williams that she was studying French and German and working most of her time on developing her voice. "I am a big, strong girl, and if my voice proves good I may be able to make some return to my mother for all she has done for me."

Hazel ended by exclaiming, "Imagine the judges choosing me! I wonder what Mother said! I wish I were at home — at home in dear old California." When Hazel chose the stage name that she would live by forever after, "Carlotta Monterey," she wished to suggest by it an exotic Spanish-flavored grandeur that she partook of in her native state.

page 82   Carlotta was humorously indignant

Carlotta O'Neill told me of how her husband adapted her girlish desire to be a nun for Mary Tyrone in my interview with her on June 26, 1961. She revealed something of the sense of power she took on during those years of nursing an invalid by declaring to me, "The little thing had used it without telling me." In the same interview she referred to O'Neill reverently as "The Master."

page 82   any kind of professional career

Only working women or women who were proprietors of property were listed in city directories. If Mary Ellen Quinlan had done any kind of professional playing or teaching of piano in 1875–76 in Cleveland after her graduation, she would have been listed along with her mother and brother in the house on Woodland Avenue.

page 83   a finishing school in Paris

Carlotta (as Hazel Tharsing) attended the finishing school probably sometime between 1908 and her marriage to Moffat in March 1911, most likely during 1909–10. The name of the school remains something of a mystery, however. When Carlotta spoke of it to me in 1961, it sounded as if she were saying "Madame Yateson's." She said that when she was in the American Hospital in Paris later on, Eugene asked her if she knew where she was, for the hospital had been built on the site of the finishing school. He told her, "Madame Yateson is right underneath here." On the other hand, when Carlotta's daughter Cynthia talked of the finishing school to me (interview of July 16, 1962), the name seemed more like "Madame Yatesman's."

page 83   her daughter Cynthia believed

I interviewed Cynthia and her husband Roy Stram on July 16, 1962, at their home in Sausalito, California.

page 83   divorce was finalized in 1915

In the Judgment Book 112, Superior Court, Alameda County, page 40 (County Clerk's Office, Oakland), it is recorded that the marriage of John Moffat and Hazel Tharsing was dissolved in Open Court on August 27, 1915.

page 83   She toured with Lou Tellegen

The caption under a photograph of Carlotta Monterey in *Town and Country*, April 1, 1915, announces that Carlotta is playing Lucy Gallon in *Taking Chances* at the Thirty-ninth Street Theater: "Although she is an American girl, she comes to us from London, where she has been playing a small role in one of the musical productions of the season."

page 83   leading lady in *The Bird of Paradise*
            "San Francisco Girl Returns as Star in Beautiful Play," *San Francisco Bulletin*, November 12, 1915, reports that Hazel Tharsing is playing the leading role in *The Bird of Paradise* under the stage name Carlotta Monterey, which she chose "because it was typical of California—it breathed of the early days of the Golden State." According to the article, she prepared for the role of Luana by tanning herself to an "oriental shade" on the beaches of Southern California and by mastering the "most intricate of the Hawaiian dances."

page 83   Saxe Commins's wife
            Her professional name as a concert pianist was her maiden name, Dorothy Berliner.

page 84   "not work at all." "go on the road." "the middle-of-the-night"
            Carlotta Monterey, "Life on the Road," *Green Book,* November 1916.

page 84   she hated acting
            So Carlotta O'Neill told me in the interview of June 26, 1961.

page 84   a few little boys
            All under the age of twelve.

page 84   really a resurrection
            See my discussion of *Days without End* in my *Eugene O'Neill's Creative Struggle*, 203–4.

page 85   Our Lady Of Lourdes
            Long Day's Journey, 175.

page 85   the Holy House of Loreto
            McCandless, *Family Portraits*, 10.

page 85   Lourdes Lake. Our Lady's Grotto
            So they are called in prospectuses of Mount St. Vincent on the Hudson.

page 85   admiration for Mother Elizabeth
            A convert to Catholicism, Mother Elizabeth was proud of being a "lineal descendent of Dr. George Arnold, organist at Winchester Cathedral under Queen Elizabeth." McCandless, *Family Portraits*, 5.

page 85   Sister Martha. a "little cranky"
            Long Day's Journey, 171.

page 85   "Do you ever think"
            Letter of O'Neill to Joseph McCarthy, September 2, 1930, SL, 370.

page 85   curdled feelings over long years
            See the beginning of chapter 5 about Eugene's alimony payments to Agnes, which became a source of acrimony between them.

page 85   "lost heart." "devoid of ambition"
            Letter from James O'Neill (father) to the Reverend Andrew Morrissey, CSC, reproduced in Edward L. Shaughnessy, "Ella, James, and Jamie O'Neill," *The Eugene O'Neill Review*, Fall 1991, 52. Hereafter cited as Shaughnessy.

page 86   smashed his academic career
The question of Jamie O'Neill's expulsion from Fordham is discussed in chapter 11, on Jamie Tyrone.

page 86   receiving prizes and distinction
Shaughnessy, 56–58.

page 86   "dig down and get." $400 to buy. "lazily expecting"
Letter of O'Neill to Shane [June 12, 1934], SL, 437.

page 86   "you will have to learn"
Letter of O'Neill to Shane O'Neill [early October ? 1937], SL, 470.

page 86   "Don't you know"
Letter of O'Neill to Shane O'Neill, October 21, 1938, SL, 482.

page 86   "It is nonsense"
Letter of O'Neill to Shane O'Neill [early October ? 1938], SL, 481.

page 86   "How the devil." "you would rather start." "start at the top"
Letter of O'Neill to Shane O'Neill, August 22, 1939, SL, 492, 493.

page 87   "The whole point is"
Letter of O'Neill to Harry Weinberger, February 27, 1939, SL, 483.

page 87   Shane's "lazy weakness"
Letter of O'Neill to Harry Weinberger, November 12, 1937, SL, 472.

page 87   "All you did was get"
Long Day's Journey, 32, 36.

page 88   Supreme Court Justice Edward White
The New York Times of August 13, 1920, reporting attendance at the funeral of James O'Neill in New London on August 12, 1920, declared, "Among those who were present were Chief Justice Edward D. White of the Supreme Court of the United States and William Connor of New York, who was Mr. O'Neill's manager from 1890 to 1902."

page 88   "Gene took one look." "Terry and I put"
Hapgood, A Victorian in the Modern World, 398.

page 89   a celebration after the performance
For instance, the New York Dramatic Mirror reported on December 3, 1892, that during James O'Neill's engagement in Cleveland the week starting November 14, 1892, "friends who had first known James O'Neill when he was in the stock at Cleveland presented him with a gold-mounted cane." A week later in Pittsburgh, where O'Neill was playing in Fontenelle during the Thanksgiving holidays, he took part in "a quiet little banquet" with a number of other actors, including Wilson Barrett, Fred Warde, and Louis James, to plan a convention of actors each year aimed at advancing the profession.

When James O'Neill performed in their city, the local chapters of the Elks Club and the Knights of Columbus often feted him and his company after the show. Also, from time to time, James would put on benefit perfor-

mances for a chapter of one or another of these clubs. A few random ex-
amples from some of these events that happened to be reported may suffice
to demonstrate the mutual support of James to the clubs and theirs to him.
For instance, when James performed at Brooklyn, New York, in October 1892 (as reported in the *New York Dramatic Mirror* of October 15, 1892),
"A large party of James O'Neill's fellow-townsmen from New London paid
Brooklyn a visit last Thursday evening in order to see him in Fontenelle."
On May 11, 1893, in Lawrence, Massachusetts, James presented an evening
performance of *Monte Cristo* for the benefit of the local Elks Club. As the
New York Clipper described it, "Mr. O'Neill and his company were the
guests of the Elks during the day, and after the performance enjoyed a social session." In Haverhill, Massachusetts, on September 12, 1893, O'Neill
presented *Fontenelle* to a large audience; the *New York Dramatic Mirror* reported on September 20, 1893, that at the end, James "was presented by the
Elks with a large basket of flowers."

On February 2, 1897 (as reported in the *Mirror* of February 13, 1897), in
Kalamazoo, Michigan, "The Elks entertained the members of the James
O'Neill Company." When James opened his season on August 31, 1897, in
Norwich, Connecticut (as reported in the *Mirror*, September 11, 1897),
"A large delegation of Elks from New London, where Mr. O'Neill spends his
summers, attended the performance of The Dead Heart and afterward tendered the actor and a few of his company a supper. A magnificent basket of
flowers was also presented to Mr. O'Neill by members of the order." The
Mirror of March 14, 1903, reported, "James O'Neill was the guest of honor at
the banquet given by the St. Louis Lodge of Elks in Faust's Cabin Thursday
night. Mr. O'Neill has been a member of the Elks for twenty-two years. The
cabin was handsomely decorated and illuminated."

As early as December 16, 1882, when James was touring in *The American
King* (so the *New York Clipper*, December 23, 1882, reported) he gave, at
Indianapolis, Indiana, a special matinee and evening performance of *A
Celebrated Case*, a share in the receipts to go to Lodge 114 of the Knights
of Columbus. The Knights also often entertained James, and by the time
James Jr. had joined his company, invitations usually included father and
son. Many other clubs, such as the Forty Club of Chicago, invited James to
dinner parties. A letter of February 16, 1897, to Edward Freiberger of the
Forty Club by James in the Theater Collection, Harvard, refers to "pleasant hours spent with the members of the Forty Club" and accepts an invi-
tation to dinner in the following days. James was always ready to join in
Irish festivities and to cooperate with organizations of the City of Cincinnati where he began his stage career. For instance, on December 7, 1882,
James "attended the Clan-na-Gael ball on December 7, 1882 in Cincinnati
and on the eighth gave a Benefit performance of *A Celebrated Case* for the

Cincinnati Battery, Company F, First Regiment" (as reported in the *New York Clipper,* December 16, 1882).

page 90   "Drink hearty!"
           Long Day's Journey, 111, 130.

page 90   "It went sooner than"
           From my interview with Thomas Dorsey Jr. on April 6, 1955.

Chapter Nine. James Tyrone

page 92   "militate against his." "If the name 'O'Neill'"
           Clipping of a feature article signed Bud Brier, which is likely from a
           Boston newspaper, as James O'Neill is referred to as "an established Boston
           favorite." Undated, unlabeled (probably from some time the 1880s),
           Harvard Theater Collection.

page 92   March 5, 1894. *The O'Neill.* "Shane O'Neill"
           In the *New York Clipper,* March 10, 1894, there is a report of the production
           of *The O'Neill* as "originally acted at Baldwin's Theatre, San Francisco,
           California, March 5."
                In its February 10, 1894, issue, the *New York Dramatic Mirror* announced
           the coming production in San Francisco of *The O'Neill* and reported that
           James O'Neill met William Greer Harrison and asked him to write the play
           for him several years beforehand in New York at a dinner where Harrison had
           given as an "after-dinner effort one of the speeches that is now embodied in
           the play." Both the original speech and the play are in blank verse.

page 92   "read and reread"
           Long Day's Journey, 11.

page 93   "a year or so after"
           Ibid., 117.

page 93   Manley Mallett
           James O'Neill's sister Anastasia's grandson (Eugene's second cousin),
           Manley W. Mallett, made these notes on the O'Neills on November 12,
           1974. See Louis Sheaffer, "Correcting Some Errors," in John H. Stroupe,
           editor, *Critical Approaches to O'Neill* (New York: AMS Press, 1988).

page 94   "at ten years old!"
           Long Day's Journey, 148.

page 95   as a rooming house keeper
           William J. O'Neill showed up with the other O'Neills, as did the two ma-
           chinists later. To find other roomers, one would have to go through every-
           one in the directory for home address.

page 95   Mary's son Edward
           Eugene O'Neill's letter to the editors of the *San Francisco Research Mono-
           graphs,* January 15, 1940 (SL, 497), tells them that he "knew little" of his

father's brothers and sisters. "He had two older brothers, I think. I remember him saying one brother served in the Civil War—an Ohio regiment, I suppose—was wounded, never fully recovered and died right after the war."

page 95   "exchanged the trade"

In James O'Neill's own account in his "Personal Reminiscences," *Theatre Magazine*, 1917, 338cf, he tells how as a boy he grew up in Cincinnati. "It was a favorite saying of my father that if he had ten sons every one of them would be brought up to a trade. Little faith put he in professions: a good honest trade was his idea of the best equipment he could bestow upon his children, and so at an early age I was apprenticed to a machinist." Then, recalling his first years as an infant in Kilkenny, Ireland (actually his recollections from a visit to Kilkenny in the summer of 1887), he continued, "Somehow the clank of iron, the ring of the hammer, the heavy glow of the forge seemed unattuned to the romance of Kilkenny's mossy towers where walked the shadowy ghosts of Congreve, Bishop Berkeley, of Dean Swift and Farquhar, Irishmen all, who wore their college gowns in and out of the grassy quadrangle of the venerable seat of learning that is Kilkenny's boast. Not without paternal expostulation, therefore, I exchanged the trade of machinist for the 'Profession' of clothier." This, of course, was not true, as his father had deserted the family before they left Buffalo. James O'Neill was always careful to protect his family from negative publicity.

While working in his brother-in-law's store in Norfolk, Virginia, he became, James said, "an established gallery god" at the Norfolk Theater. "I believe I had a subconscious assurance—the promise of a sublime, possibly ridiculous faith—that I should be an actor one day, although no possibility seemed more remote. However, what's an Irish lad without his dream?"

page 96   "I carried you in"

Elizabeth Murray's letter was reproduced in the *New York Tribune*, May 26, 1918. If there is an error in the newspaper report of the godmother, Ann Connors, and the correct name is Connor, she might well have been someone related to Will Connor, a great friend of James and Ella O'Neill as well as James's manager.

page 97   not pay the "terrible expense"

Robins Diary, July 15, 1882, Fales.

page 98   "because he had many extraordinary"

So O'Neill said in his response on January 15, 1940, to the questions from the researchers for the W.P.A. Monograph on James O'Neill, SL, 497.

page 98   "Mr. O'Neill argues you have"

Letter of Elizabeth Robins to her father (C. E. Robins), November 9, 1882, Fales.

page 98   "full of whiskey." "thrown money"

Long Day's Journey, 146.

page 98 "liberal, giving according"
Fred R. Wren wrote a series titled "Reminiscences of an Old Actor," for the Sunday magazine section of a newspaper. The reminiscences of James O'Neill appeared on July 21, 1907. I found it, unlabeled, in the Robinson Locke Scrapbook on James O'Neill in the Theater Collection of the New York Public Library. Hereafter cited as Wren.

page 98 "a soft hearted man"
See Croswell Bowen, *The Curse of the Misbegotten*, 38.

page 98 "life is really worth living"
From James O'Neill, "A Christmas Eve Experience," in the Christmas 1896 number of the *New York Dramatic Mirror*, in which he tells of going to the assistance of a poor little girl who mistook him for a Catholic priest and brought him to her dying mother. James O'Neill brought both a doctor and a priest to her and arranged for care of the orphan child.

page 99 "He never forgets a face"
Chicago Chronicle, February 28, 1897.

page 99 "gave freely to those"
Jerome A. Hart, *In Our Second Century: From an Editor's Note-Book* (San Francisco: Pioneer Press, 1931), 419.

page 99 "Harbour town." "Mr. O'Neill was"
New London Day, August 10, 1920.

page 99 "started a subscription"
New York Dramatic Mirror, October 15, 1892. The accident to the teamster had occurred on October 1.

page 99 donation of fifty dollars
"The Actor's Fund Benefit," *Chicago Herald*, April 4, 1882. I found this article in volume 3 of five bound volumes of clippings from Cincinnati and Chicago newspapers during the 1880s labeled "American Theatre" in the Theater Collection of the New York Public Library. Hereafter cited as "American Theatre."

page 99 a "personal contribution"
So James O'Neill's "cheque," which had been received "the other day," was noted in the *New York Dramatic Mirror*, February 10, 1894.

page 99 James O'Neill donated twenty-five
New York Dramatic Mirror, January 8, 1887. Richard Hooley, the theater manager, and Edwin Booth, the great star, both gave fifty dollars to the monument for the Actor's Fund cemetery plot. Typical of James O'Neill, he gave generously but not conspicuously so.

page 100 Benefit of the Catholic Asylum
A notice of the performance "on Thursday afternoon" appeared in the *Spirit of the Times*, October 28, 1876, p. 316.

page 100 for the theater ushers
New York Clipper, June 9, 1894.

page 100   Benefit of Madame Modjeska
New York Dramatic Mirror, May 13, 1905.

page 100   "snared." "Not I who have"
Letter of O'Neill to Brooks Atkinson, August 16 [1931], SL, 392.

page 101   "grand little place." "Reminds me." "some roots"
Letter of O'Neill to Saxe Commins, July 26, 1948, Princeton.

page 102   kept his carriage and horses
Asked in 1896 whether he was adopting the recent fad of the bicycle, James
O'Neill replied, "No, I don't ride a bicycle. A horse is good enough for me,
and the drives about my Summer home in New London are too delightful to
be set aside for a passing fancy." *New York Dramatic Mirror*, May 30, 1896.

page 102   Monte Cristo Cottage
Later, less informed New Londoners attributed the name — erroneously it
seems — to the much larger house James built farther upriver on the same
piece of land some years afterward. For instance, the *New London Day* of
August 10, 1920, the day of James O'Neill's death, announced incorrectly
that he "made his home at the Monte Cristo cottage in Pequot Avenue."
When the shabby remains of this larger house were made into a monument
to Eugene in recent years, that error was innocently repeated by the people
in charge, and now the erroneous name of the larger house is echoed
widely in O'Neill studies.

page 102   scenery of his new play *Fontenelle*
The *New York Dramatic Mirror*, for June 4, 1892, reported that James
O'Neill had awarded the contract for the design of *Fontenelle's* scenery to
Hugh L. Reid, "the Fifth Avenue Artist," and that "Arthur Wright, the well
known carpenter and mechanic of Philadelphia, is now at work in the theater of New London, Connecticut, supervising the building of the scenes
and effects. Mr. O'Neill is residing at New London this summer, and the
scenery will be painted there by Mr. Reid and his assistants."

page 102   building a more commodious house
City directories have led to some confusion by critics in dating when the
new house was built. Some have been led astray by the fact that, from 1885
to 1900, city directories noted James O'Neill as living at 134 Pequot Avenue,
which is the address for the entire original property: the original farmhouse and all its land. Only in 1900 does the second house appear in the
municipal directory separately numbered as 325 Pequot Avenue. New Londoners today would have a hard time envisioning what the place looked
like in the 1890s, since for many decades Pequot Avenue has been lined
with one house after another, just like any other city block. But, according
to people I interviewed in 1955, in the 1890s all that stood there was the
farmhouse and barn. The second house appeared in about 1894 (piecing
together various sources), quite a distance from the farmhouse and built on

the foundation of an outbuilding where the farmer sold produce. Otherwise, as far as one could see all around were just trees and greenery and the water. Not another building in sight. And since both houses remained on the single, original property, and no other full-time resident occupied the little house, there was no immediate reason to invent a second address. That is why there is no number for the new house in the directory before 1900.

page 102   *I'd Like to Do It Again*
New York: Farrar and Rinehart, 1931, 23–25.

page 103   "God is certainly good"
So Will Connor said in his interview on the accident in the *New York Dramatic Mirror*, August 31, 1895.

page 103   the waters of Long Island Sound
Apparently, when the Whites later sold the house, they sold separately the lot of the beach on the other side of Pequot Avenue where the new owner built a concrete bunker. Unfortunately, the original beauty of the outlook has thereby been sacrificed — the final devastating destruction of what had once been a charming home in a lovely rural setting.

page 103   it was "modesty"
As early in his career as January 27, 1884, a list of clichés associated with famous actors such as "Edwin Booth — Bad Support" and "John McCullough — Geniality," made James O'Neill's "Modesty." From a newspaper clipping in "American Theatre" 5:263. Recalling James O'Neill as "America's favorite romantic actor," Augustus Thomas declared that O'Neill was "as modest and lovable at the height of his popularity as he continued to the day of his recent death." Augustus Thomas, *The Print of My Remembrance* (New York: Scribner's, 1922), 134. In "James O'Neill Points a Moral for Young Actors," the *New York Telegraph* of December 30, 1905, declared that James O'Neill "is no longer a mere actor; he is an institution;" yet "with all his success and all his wealth James O'Neill is one of the plainest and simplest men that ever walked the boards."

page 103   "No, I haven't got a pig"
From "Bringing an Old Play Up to Date: A Talk with James O'Neill," unlabeled clipping of March 15, 1904, in the Robinson Locke Scrapbook on James O'Neill, Theater Collection, New York Public Library.

page 104   "beautiful home in New London"
Fred R. Wren, "Reminiscences of an Old Actor," July 21, 1907, in the Robinson Locke Scrapbook on James O'Neill in the Theater Collection of the New York Public Library.

page 104   "your father would never"
Long Day's Journey, 44.

page 104   perfectionism in dress. "fashionable" and "elegant"
Thomas Dorsey Jr. spoke of Ella O'Neill as "fashionable" and "elegant."
Bessie Sheridan, daughter of Ella's first cousin Mary Sheridan, told me (in
an interview of April 3, 1955) that Ella O'Neill was "the loveliest looking
woman I ever saw. She dressed beautifully, which helps."

page 104   The wife of Eugene's cousin Philip Sheridan
Philip was a brother of Bessie and, like her, a grandson of Bridget Quinlan's
sister Elizabeth Brennan. I spoke with Mrs. Sheridan by telephone in the
fall of 1962.

page 104   home beside the sea
In his poem "Glints of Them," published in the *New London Telegraph*,
October 19, 1912, the year in which *Long Day's Journey into Night* is set,
Eugene celebrated his "gold summer days" in New London summers with
their sound of the sea, their "bright green lawns," and the "cool shade" un-
der their "great trees." *O'Neill Poems*, 24.

David Karsner, who interviewed Eugene O'Neill in Maine in July 1926,
reported that the playwright had told him, "His father had a large and comfortable house at New London, Connecticut, near the sea, and Eugene har-
bors some beautiful memories of his later youth spent there." Karsner, 114.

page 104   June 30 and July 1
Work Diary, 1:104.

page 104   became hopelessly lost
Carlotta O'Neill told me of this visit in my interview with her on June 26,
1961.

page 105   to overtake it
Dorothy White told me that when she and her husband bought the house,
there were school desks and chairs bolted to the floor in the tower room on
the upper floor, suggesting that it received hard treatment as a school of some
sort before it became a residence again with the purchase by the Whites.

page 105   Judge Thomas E. Troland
I interviewed Judge Troland on April 5, 1955.

page 106   "He believed in"
The postmaster was J. F. Mahan. *New London Day*, August 12, 1920.

page 106   Louis Morrison had lost
James O'Neill explained that this was not true: "Morrison did not have two
hundred dollars invested in the whole thing." *New York Dramatic News*,
April 9, 1881.

page 107   James's "season." "One of the results"
New York Dramatic Mirror, June 12, 1886.

page 107   "A grand surprise"
Letter of O'Neill to Eugene O'Neill Jr. [January 8?, 1932], SL, 394. As to
Eugene O'Neill's joke about "those cows" perishing, the ranch raised steers
for the meat market, not cows for dairy products.

page 107   "Chattanooga craze for"
New York Clipper, February 5, 1887. James O'Neill performed in
Chattanooga on February 3.

page 107   "James O'Neill is a firm"
July 8, 1893.

page 107   "bought a valuable piece"
June 13, 1896. "Improved" property had buildings on it.

page 108   "the local agency"
Brooks Atkinson, "O'Neill Off Duty," New York Times, October 8,
1933.

page 108   the finest automobiles
In the same letter of August 16, 1931, in which Eugene O'Neill tells Brooks
Atkinson that his father always bought him the "classiest rowboats to be
had," he also says that "we sported the first Packard car in our section of
Connecticut," SL, 392.

page 108   a major investor. "important role." "Six weeks ago"
A clipping from a Philadelphia newspaper (from about December 4, 1909,
when James O'Neill opened there in The White Sister at the Lyric Theater)
declared that James O'Neill is a "shrewd business man, and is one of the
few wealthy men of the stage. Only recently he engaged in commercial
business in New York which is said to be doing well." Clipping in "James
O'Neill," Robinson Locke Collection of Dramatic Scrapbooks, New York
Public Library, Theater Collection.

page 108   "I don't know if I am"
Letter of O'Neill to his parents, Christmas Day, 1909, SL, 20.

page 109   "had once been shanghaied"
Dale Kramer, Heywood Broun: A Biographical Portrait (New York: Current
Books, 1949), 95–96.

page 109   "thrown away, squandered." "developing into"
Letter of O'Neill to George Tyler December 9, 1920, Princeton.

page 110   "Your dear daddy's"
Letter of George Tyler to O'Neill, December 13, 1920, Princeton.

page 110   "Dorsey was suing"
Louis Sheaffer, O'Neill: Son and Artist (Boston: Little, Brown, 1973), 77.
Hereafter cited as Sheaffer II.

page 110   the "cursed Sassenach"
In a letter to his agent Richard Madden, September 24, 1932, about his
British royalties, O'Neill joked, "If James O'Neill of Monte Cristo fame
heard that I ever gave the cursed Sassenach the slightest break he'd come
back from the grave and bean me with a blackthorn! My, but didn't he love
them!" Library, Dartmouth College, New Hampshire.

page 110   "more balled up"
Letter of O'Neill to Kenneth MacGowan, SL, 189.

page 110   "valued at a quarter"

                Long Day's Journey, 144.

page 111   "broken, unhappy." "wrecked my father's." "made a bad." "seared on my brain"

                Letter of O'Neill to George Tyler, December 9, 1920. Tyler Papers, Princeton.

page 111   "had thrown away"

                Basso, 34.

page 111   "Your dear father's"

                Letter of George Tyler to O'Neill, December 13, 1920, Tyler Papers, Princeton.

page 111   "exaltation." "their own hopeless." "because any victory"

                Mullett, 118.

page 112   both innocent and guilty

                The Tyrones are innocent because they have had no intention to harm each other, and because they are themselves victims of the forces out of the past that have driven them to harmful decisions. They are guilty because without their actions, the harm would never have come about.

page 112   "its deep pity"

                From O'Neill's dedication in *Long Day's Journey* to Carlotta, July 22, 1941.

page 112   the part of Edmund Dantes

                The role was offered to James O'Neill because Charles Thorne, originally cast in the starring role, had been taken with his final illness at this time. On tour with his own company and then delayed by snow, James reached New York only three days before the opening of *Monte Cristo*, with no time to learn the long, complicated role. As a result, he was panned on opening night. The critics declared he was representing Edmund Dantes as a "north of Ireland sailor." As James himself recalled, "The critics were right that time. I was bad. I knew it. But I got at the play with hammer and tongs. I rehearsed all day in my rooms. By the end of the week the play was going well." The improvement overcame the initial disappointment, ultimately making the play a success with both critics and playgoers. Ada Patterson, "James O'Neill—the Actor and the Man," *Theatre*, April 1908.

page 113   percentage of the box-office take

                In the *New York Dramatic Mirror*, December 1, 1883, James O'Neill declared, "You know I receive a salary from Mr. Stetson, and have an interest in the profits." The *Mirror* of May 10, 1884, reported that James would again star in *Monte Cristo* next season. "It is mooted that he will have a share in the profits instead of a salary. As he had $600 a week this season, Stetson is probably making a wise move." In the *Mirror* for October 3, 1885, James's manager, E. E. Zimmerman, was announcing that "Monte Cristo has been doing a really marvellous business since the season opened," and Zimmerman was announcing that John Stetson "thinks he made a mistake when he sold out his interest in the play so cheap." The price was $2,000.

page 113   "a lemon that had"
J.B.C., "James O'Neill Recalls Boston Memories," *Boston Transcript*, October 20, 1913.

page 113   September 1893 to June 1894
James O'Neill also performed a week of William Greer Harrison's Irish drama *The O'Neill* or *The Prince of Ulster* starting March 5, 1894, in San Francisco. But as the *New York Dramatic Mirror*, March 17, 1894, commented: "To fit it for the road and general dramatic representation [the play] will have to be considerably changed." San Francisco was Harrison's home-town and the crowded theater at his play's opening was, the *Mirror* said, "composed almost exclusively of society people and club men, friends of the author." From quotes of the play's blank verse in a newspaper, the *Mirror* of February 10, 1894, had decided that Harrison's verse was by no means Shakespeare. "But it is patriotic" (of Ireland, that is).

page 114   "sterling" play. "did all he could"
New York Dramatic Mirror, May 23, 1891, and May 9, 1891.

page 114   "the financial state." "money hand over"
New York Dramatic Mirror, May 23, 1891. James O'Neill thought the choice of New York for the opening was also to blame, partly because New York critics would be hostile to a Philadelphia author and partly because they preferred "buffoonery." James O'Neill decided that "New York is the town of towns for fads, skits, and horse-play."

page 114   "full of fine opportunities"
So the *New York Dramatic Mirror*, July 4, 1891, reported from an interview at the Coleman House with Sanford A. Cohen (who was managing O'Neill's company with William F. Connor) and James O'Neill, who had just listened with a "party of O'Neill's friends" to a reading by one of the authors.

page 115   "a new romantic drama"
New York Dramatic Mirror, May 21, 1892.

page 115   "Standing Room Only"
When, for instance, *Fontenelle* opened in Chicago on March 12, 1893, the *Mirror* of March 18 reported as of March 13, "James O'Neill opened to the capacity of Hooley's last evening with his new play, Fontenelle, which was enthusiastically received. The orchestra was forced under the stage and hundreds were turned away. Mr. O'Neill had a call after every act and three after the third act."

page 115   "upon taking up." "doing remarkable business." "still Mr. O'Neill"
Letter of William F. Connor to William Seymour on November 4, 1892, Seymour Collection, Princeton. The "legitimate" referred primarily to Shakespearean tragedies and the plays of Sheridan Knowles and Edward

Bulwer-Lytton, as they had been introduced to the London public by the actor William Macready in the first half of the nineteenth century and had been played frequently thereafter.

page 115 "In the many times." "from upper gallery"
Augusta Herald, April 19, 1907.

page 116 to star Edmund Breese
New York Clipper, July 19, 1902. On September 13, 1902, the *New York Dramatic Mirror* announced that "James O'Neill enjoyed a novel experience on September 3, when he saw, for the first time in his career, his own characters, Edmund Dantes and Comptes de Monte Cristo enacted by his successor, Edmund Breese. Mr. O'Neill viewed the performance at Willimantic, Connecticut."

page 116 "the most successful." "The answer, of course"
Letter of O'Neill to Robert G. Dawes, June 3, 1940, SL, 505.

page 116 "Yes, I am going back"
Untitled article dated June 3, 1905, in "James O'Neill," Robinson Locke Collection of Dramatic Scrapbooks, New York Public Library, Theater Collection.

page 117 "There's many a star"
Indianapolis News, October 5, 1908.

page 117 "look" and "live." "allows his own"
Kansas City Post, September 17, 1908.

page 117 "same charms." "Must say that"
This comes from a reprint of "How James O'Neill Saw Life at 60 Years of Age," from the *New York Morning Telegraph*, many years later in the August 14, 1920, issue of the *New London Day*.

page 118 "Tragedy deals with"
New York Dramatic Mirror, June 24, 1899.

page 118 "Yes, and I ought to." "I suppose you." "the technique of"
"Weaning the Public from Monte Cristo," *New York Dramatic Mirror*, February 2, 1895.

page 119 "Take some wood"
Alexander, *The Tempering of Eugene O'Neill*, 65. O'Neill also spoke in 1924 of the fact that "I was practically brought up in the theater — in the wings — and I know all the techniques of acting. I know everything that every one is doing from the electrician to the stage hands. So I see the machinery going round all the time." "Eugene O'Neill Talks of His Own and the Plays of Others," *New York Herald Tribune*, November 16, 1924.

page 119 "most popular actor." "Everyone loved him"
New London Day, August 12, 1920.

page 119 "You can certainly boast"
Letter of Agnes O'Neill, March 4, 1920 (Correspondence). Eugene O'Neill had written Agnes on March 2 that his father was "doomed." "I'm all

broken up and begin to cry every time the meaning of it all dawns on me"
(Correspondence).

Chapter Ten. Mary Tyrone

page 121   "was the fourth"
There is no way to know for sure whether Eugene O'Neill remembered the
number four or simply made it up at the moment. As already noted, O'Neill
rarely used numbers in his plays and where he did in this one, as in the case
of his father's wages and age as an apprentice metal worker, he checks out
to be historically accurate.

page 121   "He never forgets"
By 1897 Eugene O'Neill no longer traveled with his parents, as he was
boarding at Mount St. Vincent.

page 123   "Mr. O'Neill and his family"
New York Dramatic Mirror, May 21, 1892. The *Mirror* for June 12,
1886, quotes James O'Neill's manager Zimmerman as saying Mr. O'Neill
will spend the summer at his home in New London, Connecticut."
The summer of 1887, the O'Neills were in Europe. They were back
for the summer of 1888 and the *Mirror* for April 27, 1889, reports "James
O'Neill left town Monday for his country seat at New London, Connecticut."

page 123   "his farm near Bound Brook"
The farm was located in an area later incorporated as the town of Zion.
From time to time the O'Neills used the farm for short visits from New York
or New London. See, for instance, Eugene O'Neill's letter to Marion
Welch [early September 1905], SL, 15.

page 123   "He has some very old." "write him often"
Shaughnessy, 50.

page 123   "Mrs. O'Neill's health"
Ibid., 52.

page 124   "an indomitably united front"
Letter of O'Neill to Eugene O'Neill Jr., May 7, 1945, SL, 569.

page 124   "A large delegation"
This was in the *Dramatic Mirror* of September 11, 1897. It also reported that
James O'Neill had had a "painful accident" on that opening night when
his foot was burned by the wadding from a gun fired in the Bastille scene.
"Although in great pain, Mr. O'Neill finished the performance."

page 125   "His mother brought him"
Hector Charlesworth, "City Teacher Given Credit by Miss Anglin,"
Toronto Globe, February 18, 1943.

page 125   "one of the largest"
New York Clipper, August 19, 1899.

page 125   a full-rigged ship

O. W. Boyd, "Scenic Art," *Dramatic Magazine*, Chicago, November 15, 1900, 110–11. See also "Mademoiselle Mephisto's Anecdotes," *New York Clipper*, December 1, 1900.

page 126   "lease in pocket." "four blocks off on 64th"

"Mademoiselle Mephisto's Anecdotes," *New York Clipper*, November 3, 1900. In this report the journalist scrambled the facts, making 68th Street the mistaken address and 64th Street the correct one. In a letter to me January 4, 1955, Brother Berard, FSC, principal of the De La Salle Institute, 160 West 74th Street, New York 23, New York, told me that Eugene O'Neill's home address when he entered the school in the middle of September 1900 was given as "8 West 68th Street." So it would seem that 68th Street was the correct address. I corrected the *Clipper* quotation accordingly.

page 126   "I spent the summer"

Rochester Post Express, September 18, 1913. As James O'Neill concluded the interview—speaking of his wife's not knowing what was the matter with him—, "I didn't more than half know myself, but when came this opportunity in Joseph and His Brethren, I knew it was the call of the stage. It was irresistible, and I answered it—and I don't look unhappy, do I?" Tyler had offered him the part of Jacob, but James asked also for that of Pharaoh because he did not want to wait around idle after the first act until the last act, where Jacob makes his only appearances.

page 126   "James O'Neill, the actor"

The *New London Day* had a Twenty-five Years Ago column, which, in 1937, cited events of 1912. From this, one learns that on November 29, 1912, "Eugene O'Neill, son of the actor, James O'Neill, was ill at the family home in Pequot Avenue and faced necessity of an operation." On December 1, Eugene was reported to be "seriously ill of pleurisy at the family home." The closing of the house was retold in the column for December 10, 1937.

page 127   "signs at the right." a "good case." "is in excellent"

Dr. Miller described Eugene O'Neill as a "young man in whom Ferrand is interested." Gaylord Farm archives.

page 127   good for Ella

The only possible hint of trouble for Ella O'Neill came in James O'Neill's letter (Gaylord Farm archives) to Dr. Lyman on learning that Eugene would be released from Gaylord on June 3, 1913. James asked if Eugene were "so thoroughly cured that no one—not even his ailing mother—can become infected with tuberculosis by living in the same house and eating at the same table with him." The "ailing" probably did not refer to addiction, for James was clearly planning to bring Ella to New London, which he would not have done if she were taking drugs. Also in 1913 Ella was in her midforties and may have been going through menopause.

page 127   she had pleaded in vain

Ella's doctor at that time was Eugene's friend, Dr. Ganey, and most likely it was he who refused her prescriptions for morphine. When I interviewed him in 1955—unlike most people who recalled her charm—Dr. Ganey recalled her to me as a "cold woman"—which she certainly would have been to him had he humiliated her and rejected her pleas during the agony of withdrawal symptoms.

page 127   Worry over him

In the midst of her own troubles, Ella O'Neill asked Louise Bryant to find Eugene early in 1917 so that he could be sobered up and returned to creative work.

page 127   "Most of the P. M."

SL, 98–99.

page 128   "He was a very good"

This undated letter of Ella O'Neill to Agnes O'Neill (Yale), comes a little before Christmas of 1919, for Ella sends it with some stockings as a "little remembrance for Christmas" and asks her what books Eugene would like for Christmas.

page 128   "lecture" letter. "I've never in"

Letter of O'Neill to Agnes O'Neill, January 22, 1920, SL, 106.

page 128   "prompts his kindness"

Fales.

page 128   "quite seriously injured"

Ella was in fact not badly hurt.

page 128   who had been driving

So the New York Clipper of January 27, 1883, reported, but almost all their other facts in this account are wrong.

page 129   Grace made her debut

That was at Springfield, Massachusetts, according to the New York Clipper, September 11, 1886. The Clipper of September 18 reported that O'Neill played to standing room only.

page 129   "very pretty and clever"

This description of Grace Raven in the Spirit of the Times appeared on May 9, 1891, in a review of The Envoy. The New York Dramatic Mirror of that date reported: "Grace Raven looked comely and gave a coquettish interpretation to the part of Marie Perotti."

page 129   South Bend, Indiana. "deafening applause"

Shaughnessy (49) quotes from the Notre Dame school magazine Scholastic, May 7, 1887, 561–62, a notice of this visit.

page 129   "Grace Raven, who has"

From an interview with James O'Neill in the New York Dramatic Mirror, May 23, 1891.

page 129   "I remember that one"
SL, 192.

page 130   he was nine years old. Salsbury's Troubadours
"Nate Salsbury Dead," *New York Dramatic Mirror*, January 3, 1903. Most of
my facts on Salsbury's life come from this article.

page 130   "Jim, did you ever expect this"
Salsbury's joke rests on the fact that a "heavy" man's role in drama was usually to try to foil the romance of the hero, rather than to have a romance
himself and produce a family and children, as Salsbury had.

page 130   a friendship with his widow
An undated note from James O'Neill to William Seymour in the Seymour
Collection, Princeton, must have come after Nate Salsbury's death. In it
James O'Neill introduces to William Seymour "Miss Chubb of whom
I spoke to you recently. She is a friend of the Salsbury family and anything
you can do for her will be greatly appreciated by me."

page 130   "tried to locate"
The editors of SL, 166, identify Milton Salsbury, Nate's son, erroneously, as
"O'Neill's cousin."

page 130   they were divorced. "his figure" so "erect"
Sarah Truax, *A Woman of Parts: Memories of a Life on Stage* (New York:
Longmans, Green, 1949). For Sarah Truax's marriage problems see 141, 156;
for association with James and Ella O'Neill, 138–39.

page 131   entertaining others together
Extant evidence indicates that James O'Neill included his wife in all his invitations wherever he could. For instance, the *New York Dramatic Mirror* on
May 4, 1889, reported that "James O'Neill and James L. Carhart were initi-
ated last Sunday into the mysteries of the Actor's Order of Friendship." Perhaps Ella met Carhart then or soon after for, writing to Carhart from New
London, June 19, 1889, James O'Neill concluded his letter, "Mrs. O'Neill
joins me in best wishes for your success." She seems also to have met
Edward L. Freiberger of the Forty Club. In a letter to him of March 19, 1897,
James O'Neill told him, "Mrs. O'Neill thanks you in advance for the auto-
graphs promised her." Both letters are in the Theater Collection, Harvard.

page 131   "I am going to New London"
Seymour Collection, Princeton.

page 131   "You see, she never"
Letter of George Tyler to O'Neill, December 13, 1920, Tyler Papers,
Princeton.

page 131   "noble women of our profession"
James O'Neill wrote this letter to Harrison Grey Fiske, his friend and editor
of the *New York Dramatic Mirror*, in response to an editorial in the journal
on the men in opposition to the Fund Fair. In his letter, O'Neill points out
his "surprise and indignation that members of our profession . . . can so

far forget the vast amount of good the Fund has already done and whose further doing is only limited by its treasury . . . to openly denounce and defame its organizers and promoters." O'Neill's letter was published in the March 26, 1892, *Mirror*. One of the objectors was the Chicago theater manager, J. H. McVicker, who said he was against any scheme calculated to place in a false position the young lady members of the dramatic profession. Others opposed were J. Wesley Rosenquest, Joseph Arthur, W. E. Sinn, Marcus Mayer, Marc Klaw, John H. Russell, Maurice Barrymore, William M. Donlevy, James M. Hill, Ben Teal, A. L. Erlanger, and Thomas B. Mc-Donough. In the March 12, 1892, *Mirror*, Fiske said, "We shall pass over Mr. Maurice Barrymore's published remarks. He exclaims of the Fair, 'Pah! it makes me sick.' A man who is sick deserves our sympathy. He is not responsible for what he raves while delirious."

page 132 "his fixed habit"

The *New York Dramatic Mirror* reported on March 3, 1906, that James O'Neill "has made the discovery that Columbia, South Carolina has a town clock that strikes the hours literally by hand. 'Two men,' he says, 'are on the municipal salary list, engaged by the year, at twelve hour shifts, to strike the hours on a bell in the town hall.'"

page 132 enjoyment of gourmet dining

When in New York, the O'Neills dined often at the very best. An anecdote published in the *Dramatic Mirror* of January 5, 1895, says that James O'Neill met a "distinguished looking gentleman" in the piazza in front of his hotel at Lake Como in Italy on his last trip there, who knew him as "Monte Cristo." O'Neill could not recall where he had met the "polished stranger." Finally, after two days, he realized that the charming gentleman was a waiter who had often served him at Delmonico's.

James's only known trips to Europe are those of the summers of 1887—when apparently he went only to England and Ireland—and of 1906, but there may have been one or two between the first and 1895, for there are other anecdotes that place him in Europe at the Chateau d'If.

page 132 "My aunt, Loretto Ritchie"

Letter of Marion McCandless to me, January 6, 1955.

page 132 received from George Tyler

Marion McCandless had forgotten the name, calling him Ryder, but she recognized the correct Tyler when I gave it to her in my reply.

Chapter Eleven. Jamie Tyrone

page 133 "old sorrow"

So O'Neill called *Long Day's Journey* in his dedication of the play to Carlotta of July 22, 1941. See the full text of the dedication in the notes to chapter 13.

page 133   *The Great God Brown*

For an account of how Eugene O'Neill worked out his feelings toward his brother Jamie in *The Great God Brown* see chapter 3, Doris Alexander, *Eugene O'Neill's Creative Struggle: The Decisive Decade 1924–1933* (University Park: Pennsylvania State University Press, 1992), 59–79.

page 134   "sit back like a lazy"

Long Day's Journey, 32.

page 134   "Withdrawn by request"

Fordham archives.

page 134   "James O'Neill had no slightest"

This episode is from an unlabeled clipping (apparently from a magazine) in the Robinson Locke Scrapbook for James O'Neill, New York Public Library. Since Jimmy Byth was O'Neill's advance man and press agent at the date of the clipping, December 7, 1907, he was likely also the author of the statement.

page 135   "Jamie has made"

Gelb II, 167.

page 135   "Mr. O'Neill and his son"

This episode is from a clipping of August 17, 1902, unlabeled in the Robinson Locke Scrapbook on James O'Neill, New York Public Library.

page 136   an "immense drawing card"

New York Clipper, November 22, 1902.

page 136   "seriously ill." "We had to close"

Ada Patterson, "Eleanor Robson—From Debutante to Star," *Theatre Magazine*, undated, circa October 1905, clipping in the Robinson Locke Scrapbook, Eleanor Robson, volume 2, New York Public Library.

page 138   "fine of method"

R.B.H., "The remarkable Revival of 'The Two Orphans,' at the Amsterdam Theatre," *Broadway Weekly*, circa March 28, 1904, undated clipping in the Robinson Locke Scrapbook on Grace George, volume 2, New York Public Library.

page 138   "courtly, fine, and finished"

New York Dramatic Mirror, November 5, 1904. This was a review of the Chicago performance that opened on October 31.

page 138   "much like his father"

Florida Times, February 25, 1906.

page 139   "a riotous single"

Douglas Gilbert, *American Vaudeville: Its Life and Times* (New York: Whittlesey House, 1940), 347.

page 140   second road company

Both companies of *The Traveling Salesman* melodrama were very successful. Reports of the second company in the *New York Dramatic Mirrors* and

Clippers of those years are invariably either "audience pleased," capacity house, or "Standing Room Only." By September 6, 1911, the *New York Dramatic Mirror* spoke of "James O'Neill, Jr., who, if he is seen much longer in the cast of The Traveling Salesman, will suffer from the Monte Cristo blight of his father." Jamie usually received good reviews, if only as a generalization about the subordinate actors in the cast. For instance, the *New York Dramatic Mirror* of November 20, 1909, declared that the play at San Francisco (November 1–13) was "very much enjoyed as indicated by the frequent laughter and applause" of "large sized" audiences. James O'Neill, listed as one of the subordinate players, came in for their praise for having assumed their roles "admirably."

page 140   what he found at hand
Thomas Dorsey Jr. told me he heard James O'Neill tell Jamie at one point, "Jimmy, all you know is what I tell you."

page 140   "for the company." "the only thing he knew"
This episode is described in "Mademoiselle Mephisto's Anecdotes," *New York Clipper*, May 14, 1903.

page 141   "reckless waste." "across the board"
Ibid.

page 141   "a breeder of race horses"
Letter of O'Neill to Marion Welch [early September 1905], SL, 15.

page 141   "They started to talk horses"
See Kyle Crichton, "Mr. O'Neill and the Iceman," *Collier's*, October 26, 1946. I have put together Eugene O'Neill's statement late in life about the coachman his father hired who owned some racehorses and knew Al Weston with the fact that not long after, James O'Neill was renting his farm at Bound Brook to a breeder of horses as mentioned in Eugene's letter to Marion Welch of 1905, to arrive at the idea that James must have gone into partnership with his coachman who owned racehorses. These were certainly the years of Eugene's interest in racing. In another letter to Marion Welch, SL, 14, he tells her that when visiting Saratoga he "visited the racetrack and won some money on the 'ponies.'"

page 142   "bit of news." "He hasn't had a drink"
SL, 162.

page 142   "If it takes my snoring"
Long Day's Journey, 21.

page 142   "She would not hear." "stab you in." "the gate"
Long Day's Journey, 173, 166, 159.

page 143   "how fat and beautiful"
Ibid., 17, 20.

page 143   "fat girl in a hick." "women but whores"
Ibid., 160, 163. In the Yale University edition of *Long Day's Journey*, the line of Jamie Tyrone, "God bless you, K.O." (167) should read, as it does

in the manuscript, "God bless you, Kid. (His eyes close. He mumbles.) That last drink—the old K.O." Of course, "K.O." is short for "Knock Out."

Chapter Twelve. Edmund Tyrone

page 144   profession of wholesale grocer
Much of the material on Eugene O'Neill's family on his mother's side and on his wife Agnes's father (Edward Boulton) has already been broached in chapter 8, "The False in the True," and may be referred to, with its notes, as backup for this discussion.

page 144   "a very favorable case"
See the letter of Dr. James Alexander Miller to Dr. David Lyman, December 17, 1912, Gaylord Farm archives.

page 145   Hutchins Hapgood testified
This account of Eugene O'Neill's drinking was broached in chapter 8, "The False in the True."

page 145   Malcolm Cowley told me
Cowley and Eugene O'Neill both used the bootlegger Spanish Willie during the early 1920s to supply them with Prohibition whiskey. The occasions when O'Neill was so drunk that Cowley had to put him to bed (which Cowley told me of in a long interview) took place when O'Neill would stay in Cowley's Greenwich Village apartment during visits to New York from his house at Ridgefield, Connecticut.

page 145   "drunk himself into a coma"
Wallace quoted by Cowley to the Gelbs. Gelb I, 543.

page 145   James O'Neill never drank
James O'Neill's drinking was discussed in chapter 8, "The False in the True."

page 145   excluded mention of that first marriage
For instance, an early "autobiographical note" at Yale by Eugene O'Neill tells of Princeton and his work in a mail-order house "for a year and a half" but says nothing of his marriage to Kathleen.

page 146   tensions, conflicts, and shifting alliances
In a manuscript labeled "N.L. play. 'A Long Day's Journey.' Gen. notes," Eugene O'Neill wrote out a list of "Shifting alliances in battle," which include "Father, two sons versus Mother; Mother, two sons versus Father; Father, younger son vs. Mother, older son; Mother, younger son vs. Father, older son; Father & Mother vs. two sons; Brother vs. Brother; Father vs. Mother."

page 146   Elizabeth Murray
The letter from Eugene's old nurse at birth was reprinted in the *New York Tribune*, May 26, 1918.

page 146   a rebirth into a rich

In a letter to Dr. Lyman attached to the 1914 Question Sheet from Gaylord Farm, Eugene O'Neill spoke of the sanitorium as "the place I was reborn in" and added that his "second birth was the only one which had my full approval." Gaylord Farm archives.

page 147   "a good man, in the best." "the great affection"

SL, 131.

page 147   "old sorrow." "in blood"

From O'Neill's dedication to *Long Day's Journey*. See the complete dedication in the notes to chapter 13.

Chapter Thirteen. The Black Widow

page 149   finished the second draft

Work Diary, 2:390.

page 149   "Publication shall not take place"

SL, 575.

page 149   "is to be published"

SL, 589.

page 149   his "darling Carlotta"

See *Inscriptions: Eugene O'Neill to Carlotta Monterey O'Neill*, edited by Donald Gallup (New Haven: privately printed, 1960; in the collection of Yale University Library), particularly those O'Neill wrote to her in 1940, 1941–43, 1946, 1948, 1949, 1951, 1952.

page 149   they were to break the seal

Harvey Breit, "In and Out of Broadway," *New York Times*, February 19, 1956.

page 150   she then talked with Donald Gallup

John Chapman, "The Seven Haunted O'Neills," *Sunday News*, December 16, 1956, quotes Mrs. O'Neill as saying that when she asked the librarian if he knew where she could publish, he said, "Certainly. I'm sure the Yale University Press will publish it."

page 150   newspapers all over

See, for instance, the *Hartford Times*, June 21, 1955. Mrs. O'Neill gave Yale the American and Canadian publication rights, the income to be "used for the upkeep of the Eugene O'Neill Collection in the Library, for the purchase of books on the drama, and for Eugene O'Neill scholarships in the Yale Drama School."

page 150   only five thousand copies

Breit, "In and Out of Broadway."

page 150   interview with Seymour Peck and Brooks Atkinson

Peck published part of the interview in "Talk with Mrs. O'Neill," *New York Times*, Sunday, November 4, 1956. My copy of the whole taped interview came from one in Croswell Bowen's possession.

page 150   "Eugene reads Long Day's." "Eugene leaves"
            Work Diary, 2:416–17. O'Neill abbreviated the names with first initials in
            the original.
page 151   "I'm glad you continue"
            SL, 526.
page 151   "twenty-five years after"
            SL, 589.
page 151   behalf of Karl Ragnar Gierow
            Harry Heintzen, "O'Neill's Last Premiere," *This Week,* January 29, 1956.
page 151   "A few weeks before." "carrying out one"
            Louis Sheaffer, "Swedish Specialty: O'Neill's 'Journey.'" *New York Herald
            Tribune,* Sunday, May 13, 1962.
page 151   announced July 1, 1956
            Lewis Funke, "News and Gossip of the Rialto," *New York Times,* July 1, 1956.
page 151   He was "stunned." "What money she could"
            Emory Lewis, "Journey Uptown with O'Neill," *Cue,* November 3, 1956, 13.
page 152   award of a Pulitzer prize
            "Fourth Pulitzer for O'Neill," *Newark Evening News,* May 7, 1957. Nothing
            shows more decisively how conventional and timid the juries for the
            Pulitzer prizes in drama were than the titles of the four plays of O'Neill that
            received prizes compared to the glittering array of his titles that were over-
            looked. One suspects that the fact that O'Neill was dead had as much to do
            with their selection of *Long Day's Journey into Night* as its excellence.
            Of the other three prizes he received, two were for his early, least experi-
            mental works, *Beyond the Horizon* and *Anna Christie.* The third was for his
            great commercial success, *Strange Interlude* (in part as a gimmick with its
            dinner break). Never-awarded plays among his more daring works were *The
            Emperor Jones, The Hairy Ape, Desire Under the Elms, The Great God
            Brown, Mourning Becomes Electra, Ah, Wilderness!,* and *The Iceman
            Cometh.* Of course, success of a first performance was always a requirement
            for their choices, and *The Iceman Cometh* was not successful until the sec-
            ond production by Quintero.
page 152   compromises of the commercial theater
            In a letter to Lee Simonson, [May? 1934], SL, 435, writing of the "inevitable
            compromises and distortions of production" in show business, O'Neill
            declared, "Bucking it always drives me to secret inner rages and hatred
            which exhaust my spiritual vitality. I take my theater too personally,
            I guess — so personally that before long I think I shall permanently resign
            from all production and confine my future work to plays in books for
            readers only."
page 152   "with a thick white handkerchief"
            Long Day's Journey, 13.

page 152   "O'Neill had confided to me"
George Jean Nathan, "Eugene O'Neill's Notable Tragedy," *New York Journal American*, November 8, 1956.

page 153   "the four haunted Tyrones"
The complete dedication reads as follows: "For Carlotta, on our 12th Wedding Anniversary:

    Dearest: I give you the original script of this play of old sorrow, written in tears and blood. A sadly inappropriate gift, it would seem, for a day celebrating happiness. But you will understand. I mean it as a tribute to your love and tenderness which gave me the faith in love that enabled me to face my dead at last and write this play—write it with deep pity and understanding and forgiveness for *all* the four haunted Tyrones.

    "These twelve years, Beloved One, have been a Journey into Light—into love. You know my gratitude. And my love!

    "GENE, Tao House, July 22, 1941."

page 153   "Essentially, *Long Day's*"
Brooks Atkinson, "Tragedy Behind a Tragic Masque," *New York Times*, February 19, 1956.

page 153   "the finest of all." "how these critics"
John Chapman, "Did O'Neill Have Right to Write It?," *New York News*, December 30, 1956.

A Moon for the Misbegotten

Chapter Fourteen. The Epitaph

page 157   "This can be strange"
October 29, 1941, *Work Diary*, 2:421.

page 157   "Dolan play"
Floyd, 372. Sheaffer II, 529.

page 157   "Moon of the Misbegotten"
November 3, 1941, *Work Diary*, 2:421.

page 157   "A Moon for the Misbegotten"
On November 12, 1941, *Work Diary*, 2:422, O'Neill noted, "change title to above—much more to point."

page 158   "glued to the radio." "determined to finish." "too much war." "little done"
December 7, 10, 23, 26, *Work Diary*, 2:424–25.

page 158   "Christ, Father, it's nice"
Eugene O'Neill, *A Moon for the Misbegotten* (New York: Random House, 1952), 39. Hereafter cited by title only.

page 159   *The Great God Brown*
See Alexander, *Eugene O'Neill's Creative Struggle*, 63–72, for O'Neill's treatment of Jamie in *The Great God Brown*.

page 159   letter from Mrs. Libbie Drummer
Sheaffer II, 83–85.

page 159   "saw I was drunk." "It was as if"
A Moon for the Misbegotten, 147, 150.

page 160   "in a drunken stupor." "broken up"
Sheaffer, II, 86, 87.

page 160   "You have the power"
Welded, Random House, 2:473.

page 160   "the dawn was grey"
Ernest Dowson, "Non Sum Qualis Eram Bonae Sub Regno Cynarae."

page 161   "The Lay of the Singer's"
O'Neill Poems, 38–39.

page 161   "the aftermath that poisons." "too many nights"
Ibid., 119, 120.

page 161   "dual mother image"
The title of chapter 7 of Carl Jung, *Psychology of the Unconscious,* translated by Beatrice M. Hinkle, M.D. (New York: Dodd, Mead, 1916), is "The Dual Mother Role." O'Neill always said he found Jung "extraordinarily illuminating." Letter to Barrett Clark, Clark, 136.

page 161   in "order to be born." "terrible mother." for the play."
Ibid., 251, 390, 405, 423.

page 162   "freedom and rebirth." "devil mother." "storms and calms." "out in death." "heart has borne"
The Calms of Capricorn: A Play, developed from O'Neill's scenario by Donald Gallup with a transcription of the scenario (New Haven: Ticknor & Fields, 1982), 135–36, 138, 141.

page 162   "at new low." "short shift." "fades out." "bad night, prostate." "Parkinson's bad"
See June 14, July 2, 8, 14, 17, 1942, also July 12, 17, 29, also most of July and August, *Work Diary,* 2:438–43, cf. See also note in Chapter 5 regarding the various diagnoses for O'Neill's neurological illness.

page 163   "no go—decide will"
December 13, 1942, ibid., 2:453.

page 163   "really written"
January 3, 1943, ibid., 2:455.

page 163   "constant strain"
January 31, 1943, ibid., 2:457.

page 163   "destroying old stuff"
See January 24, 28, February 21, 22, 23, cf.

page 163   "May you have your wish"
A Moon for the Misbegotten, 177.

Index to Literary Works
of Eugene O'Neill

Anna Christie, 16

Bound East for Cardiff, 32, 40, 45, 48–49
Bread and Butter, 29

"Calms of Capricorn, The," 162
Chris Christopherson, 7

Days without End, 53, 54
Dynamo, 53, 55

Emperor Jones, The, 16, 47
Exorcism: A Play of Anti Climax, 16, 17, 18, 22

Great God Brown, The, 133, 159

Hairy Ape, The (play), 20
"Hairy Ape, The" (story), 20, 23
Hughie, 2

Iceman Cometh, The: anarchist friends as characters, 29–44; betrayal and treachery theme, 36–37, 38, 42–43; Byth incorporated into story, 16–28; Carlotta O'Neill's permission for production, 149; death theme, 48, 57–58, 68, 93, 198–99n (57); Donald Vose as basis for character, 37, 38–42; errors made during first run, 62–64; guilt theme, 97; Oban character, 12, 13, 14; O'Neill's ambivalence toward father, 12–13; O'Neill's description of ideas and characters, 7–15, 59–61, 67, 172nn (11, 12); pipe dreams theme, 28, 54, 55, 64, 68; suicide as climax, 15

"Lay of the Singer's Fall, The" (poem), 161
Lazarus Laughed, 58
Long Day's Journey into Night, 1–2; alcoholism, 87–88, 90; appreciation by Eugene O'Neill Jr., 150–51; Carlotta O'Neill's permission for production, 149–50; confined time scale, 3; critical reviews, 153; day symbolism, 67, 68; differences from O'Neill's life, 3–4, 146–48; father's disappointment in James Jr., 87, 91, 133–34; guilt and innocence theme, 97, 112, 144–45; initial titles, 68; O'Neill's clause regarding time of publication, 149; O'Neill's lack of family history, 78–80; O'Neill's use of family events, 3, 70–91, 92, 93–105, 153; pipe dreams theme, 68;

Long Day's Journey into Night (cont.)
publication announced, 150; weather
symbolism, 69; wedding gown of
Mary Tyrone, 70–71, 80–81

Moon for the Misbegotten, A: O'Neill's
notes, 157–58, 163; setting and
characters, 161
More Stately Mansions, 161–62
Mourning Becomes Electra, 53, 104

Strange Interlude, 54
Straw, The, 54

Tale of Possessors Self-Dispossessed, A, 54
"Tomorrow" (story), 23–24, 26, 27, 28
Touch of the Poet, A, 2

"Web, The" (story), 23
Welded, 50, 160
Work Diary, 58, 81, 82, 162–63

Index

References to notes include the page number on which the note occurs, with the page number to which the note refers in parentheses following. All references to O'Neill are to Eugene unless otherwise specified.

Actor's Fund Fair (1892), 99
Adams, Albert (Al, the policy king), 9, 10–11, 12, 13, 14–15, 45, 171n (11)
Adams, Albert J. (son of Al Adams), 11
Adams, Lawrence (son of Al Adams), 10, 14
Adams, Louis (son of Al Adams), 11–12
Adams, Walter (son of Al Adams), 11
Adventures of Gerard, The (play), 137
Ah, Wilderness!, 48
Allen, Viola, 139
American King, The (play), 106, 122
Anarchist Forum for Current Topics (Ferrer Center), 31
anarchist movement: Donald Vose's betrayal, 34–35, 36, 187n (38); meaning in the early twentieth century, 29, 182n (29); O'Neill's relationship, 29–44. See also Ferrer School (New Jersey; also known as Modern School)
Anarchist Woman, An (Hapgood), 42
Anglin, Margaret, 125
Arbeiterzeitung (anarchist paper), 30
Archibold, Frank, 18
Ash Can School of painting, 29

Ashe, Beatrice, 31, 45, 48, 50, 51, 67, 88, 145, 160
Atkinson, Brooks, 150, 152, 153
Audrey (play), 136, 137

Baker, George Pierce, 8, 14
Barrymore, John, 139
Barrymore, Lionel, 139
Basso, Hamilton, 111
Bellew, Kyrle, 138
Bellows, George, 29, 30
Berkman, Alexander, 35
Bird of Paradise, The (play), 84
Blemie (Silverdene Emblem; O'Neill's dog), 68
Bobo, Dr., 47
Boer War, 26, 27, 47, 55, 180–81n (26)
Booth, Edwin, 72, 118
Boulton, Agnes (O'Neill's second wife): alimony payments, 53; O'Neill's divorce, 53; O'Neill's drinking, 8–9, 127, 128; O'Neill's guilty feelings for her, 145; report of O'Neill's suicide attempt, 17, 20, 22
Boulton, Teddy (Edward), 80, 144
Boyce, Neith, 40

Brennan, Elizabeth (O'Neill's great aunt), 77–78, 209–10n (77), 210n (78)
Brennan, Lillian, 135
Brennan, Thomas (husband of Elizabeth Brennan), 78
Brittain, Henry L., 8
Brown, Harry, 76
Burns, William J., 34, 35
Byth, James Findlater: appearance, 24–26; death, 22–24, 28; friendship with O'Neill, 21–22; knowledge of Boer War, 25–27; publicity articles, 24–25, 134

Carleton, Henry Guy, 118
Carlin, Terry: denial of testimony by Donald Vose, 35–36; drinking, 49, 88; friendship with O'Neill, 40, 189–90n (40); model for Slade character, 38–39, 41, 42–44, 57, 59, 60
Cerf, Bennett, 149, 151
"Christmas Eve Experience, A" (James O'Neill), 98, 219n (98)
Christopherson, Chris (O'Neill's roommate), 7–8, 21, 22, 25
Ciprico, George M., 106
Circle in the Square Theater (Greenwich Village), 63
Cohan, George M., 48
Commins, Saxe, 36, 40, 41
Connor, William F., 102, 103, 110, 119, 130, 135, 136
Connors, Anne, 96
Cook, George Cram, 40
Corbett, Gentleman Jim, 103
Cowley, Malcolm, 145
Crichton, Kyle, 18
Croke, Jack, 47, 48
Cushman, Charlotte, 72

Davis, Owen, 102–3
De La Salle Institute, 125, 126

DePolo, Harold, 142
Dillman, Bradford, 152
Dodge, Mabel (Dodge Luhan), 32, 40
Don Carlos de Seville (play), 118
Dorsey, Thomas, Jr., 88, 90, 102, 105, 122, 139
Dorsey, Thomas, Sr., 88, 98, 105, 110, 122
Dowling, Eddie, 62
Dowson, Ernest, 159, 160
Driscoll, J., 20–21, 25
Drummer, Libbie, 159–60
Duce, H. C., 26
Dumas, Alexandre, 112, 116
Dunnock, Mildred, 151

Eastman, Max, 44
Eldridge, Florence, 152
Elks Club, 89, 215–17n (89)
Ellsworth, Mark, 116
Ely, Israel C., 94
Emerson, Loretto Ritchie, 77, 132
Envoy, The (play), 114, 129
Evarista, Sister Mary (Daisy Green), 77

Farrand, Livingston, M.D., 127
Fay, Elfie, 139
Fechter, Charles, 112, 113
Fellner, Eugene, 118
Ferrer School (New Jersey; also known as Modern School), 30, 31, 37, 182n (30). See also anarchist movement
Fitzgerald, Eleanor, 35
Fontenelle (play), 77, 208n (77)
Fordham Monthly, The (literary magazine), 158
Forrest, Edgar, 25
Francesca da Rimini (play), 118
Freiligrath, Ferdinand, 33
Friedmann, Herman, 136

Gallup, Donald, 150
Garden Restaurant, 7, 8

George, Grace, 138
Gierow, Karl Ragnar, 151
Gilbert, Claude, 116
Gladiator, The (play), 118
Glaspell, Susan, 40
Goldman, Emma, 30, 33, 34, 36, 38–39, 40; Havel's reaction to her, 32; Vose family, 35, 37, 42
Green, Daisy (Sister Mary Evarista), 77

Hamilton, Alfred (Alfie), 74, 75, 76, 97, 206–7n (73)
Hamilton, Gilbert Van Tassel, 13
Hapgood, Hutchins, 35, 40; accounts of Havel, 31, 32, 33; accounts of O'Neill's drinking, 88, 145; books, 41–42; friendship with Carlin, 39, 43
Harrison, William Greer, 92
Havel, Hippolyte, 30, 31, 32, 33, 39
Hawthorne, Louise, 75
Helburn, Theresa (Terry), 22, 58, 63
"Hell Hole" (*Iceman Cometh* location), 7, 8–9, 28, 45, 50, 145
Henri, Robert, 29, 30
Home Colony (Washington), 35
Honor of the Humble, The (play), 136
Hooley, Uncle Dick, 72, 74
Hooley's Parlor Home of Comedy, 72, 74, 75, 76, 129
Hopkins, Arthur, 7
Howard, Bronson, 118
Hudson Dusters gang (New York), 45, 46

Illington, Margaret, 138
Ireland, Ed, 29

James, Louis, 138
Jenkins, Kathleen (O'Neill's first wife), 8, 16, 18, 48, 108, 145
John Golden Theater, 62
Jones, Anne (O'Neill's aunt), 95
Jones, James, 95, 96

Jung, Carl, 62, 161, 238n (161)

Keefe, Ed, 29
Kemp, Harry, 39–40
Knights of Columbus, 89, 215–17n (89)
Krafft-Ebing, Baron Richard von, 30

Langner, Lawrence, 57, 60, 62
Larsen, Hanna Astruf, 8
Liebler and Company, 18, 21, 22, 109, 136, 138
Little, Richard M., 24, 27
Luhan, Mabel Dodge, 32, 40
Luxemburg, Rosa, 42
Lyman, David, M.D., 80, 127

MacGowan, Kenneth, 50, 63
Maeder, Frank, 107
Malden, Karl, 151
March, Fredric, 152
Marshall, E. G., 64
Martin Beck Theater, 62
Marx, Karl, 36
McCandless, Marion, 132
McCarthy, Joseph, 85
McGinley, Arthur (Art), 9, 13, 49, 50
McGinley, John, 9
McNamara, James B., 34
McNamara, John, 34
Merman, Ethel, 151
Meserve, Donald Vose. *See* Vose, Donald
Mielziner, Jo, 151
Miller, James Alexander, M.D., 127, 144
Millionaire, The (play), 122
Minor, Robert, 36, 37
Moffat, John (Scotty), 80, 83
Monte Cristo (play): bit parts played by O'Neill, 19; first performances by James O'Neill, 115–16, 224n (112); O'Neill on negative effect on father's career, 12, 111, 117

Monte Cristo Cottage, 102, 123, 220n (102)

Monterey, Carlotta. *See* O'Neill, Carlotta Monterey (née Hazel Tharsing; O'Neill's third wife)

Morris, Clara, 138

Morrison, Louis, 106

Morrissey, Rev. Andrew, 85

Morton, George, 75

Mother Earth (anarchist monthly), 30, 33, 34, 35, 38, 40, 41

Mount St. Vincent, 84, 124, 125

Mullen, Edward, 18

Mullett, Mary B., 111

Murray, Elizabeth, 96, 146

Musketeers, The (play), 125

Nagle, John G., 25

Nathan, George Jean, 50, 55, 62, 152; O'Neill's suicide attempt, 20, 22, 25, 28

Neilson, Adelaide, 72

Nietzsche, Frederich, 58

Nobles, Milton, 99

O'Neill, Agnes. *See* Boulton, Agnes (O'Neill's second wife)

O'Neill, Alfred Hamilton. *See* Hamilton, Alfred (Alfie)

O'Neill, Anastasia (James O'Neill's sister), 93, 95

O'Neill, Carlotta Monterey (née Hazel Tharsing; O'Neill's third wife): basis for Mary Tyrone, 80–86, 120; nervous breakdown, 82, 212–13n (82); O'Neill's literary executor, 149–53; visit to O'Neill's childhood home, 105

O'Neill, Edmund (O'Neill's dead brother), 93

O'Neill, Edward (O'Neill's grandfather), 93–94

O'Neill, Edward (O'Neill's uncle), 95

O'Neill, Ella (O'Neill's mother). *See* O'Neill, Mary Ellen (Ella; née Quinlan; O'Neill's mother)

O'Neill, Eugene, Jr. (O'Neill's son), 49, 107, 150–51

O'Neill, Eugene Gladstone (Gene): ambivalence toward father, 12–13; attitude toward anarchist movement, 29–44; boyhood interest in horses, 141–42; dark outlook after tuberculosis diagnosis, 146; gold-prospecting in Honduras, 108–9; guilty feelings as key autobiographical fact, 80–81, 144–45; inheritance from father's estate, 110–11; interest in Irish history, 92–93; Ivy League experiences, 12, 13, 86, 134, 173n (13); knowledge of Al Adams, 171n (11); Nobel Prize award, 58; periodical alcoholism, 87–88, 127–28; Pulitzer prizes, 152, 236n (152); "son of Monte Cristo," 12, 172n (12); suicide attempt, 15, 16, 28; theatrical training, 119; unfinished cycle of plays, 54, 196n (54), 203n (67); *Work Diary*, 58, 81, 82, 162–63

O'Neill, James (O'Neill's father): acquaintanceship with Al Adams, 11; acting career, 89, 112–14; apprenticeship to machine shop, 94–96; benefit performances, 89, 215–17n (89); bouts of panicky austerity, 97–98; boyhood reminiscences, 95, 218n (95); "A Christmas Eve Experience," 98, 219n (98); courtship of and marriage to Ella Quinlan, 70–72, 75, 78, 82, 121, 130–32; drinking, 87–88; friendship with Nate Salsbury, 129–30; investments, 105–10, 168n (8); opinion on playwriting, 118; opinion on power of tragedy, 117–18; personality, 9–10, 98–102, 121; relationship with Nettie

Walsh, 72–77, 206–7n (73), 207n (74); touring experience, 83

O'Neill, James, Jr. (Jamie; O'Neill's brother): acting career, 108, 134–39; alcoholism, 8, 88, 90, 139, 159–60; disappointment to father, 139–40; female conquests, 137, 139, 143, 159–60; gambling, 140–41, 142

O'Neill, John (O'Neill's godfather; machinist), 96

O'Neill, Margaret. *See* Platz, Margaret (Maggie; James O'Neill's sister)

O'Neill, Mary Ann (O'Neill's grandmother), 94–95, 96

O'Neill, Mary Ellen (Ella; née Quinlan; O'Neill's mother): drug addiction, 120–21, 121–22, 125–27, 128, 146, 229n (127); elegance, 104; friends, 76–77, 128–29; marriage, 70–71, 74–75, 78, 82, 121, 130–32; mastectomy, 122, 127; scandal over Nettie Walsh, 76; support of husband's acting career, 89

O'Neill, Richard (O'Neill's uncle), 94

O'Neill, Shane (Earl of Tyrone, King of Ireland), 92–93

O'Neill, Shane (O'Neill's son), 85–87

O'Neill, William (machinist), 94, 96

O'Neill, William J. (clerk), 95

O'Neill or The Prince of Ulster, The (play), 92

Otis, Harrison Gray, 34

Pearl Harbor, 158

Peck, Seymour, 150, 152

Perkins, David F., 153

Phillips, Mrs., 159

Pitts, J. A., 94

Platz, Margaret (Maggie; James O'Neill's sister), 121

Platz, Paul Alwyn, 121

Post, Guy Bates, 130

Quinlan, Bridget, 77, 78, 209–10n (77), 210n (78)

Quinlan, Mary Ellen. *See* O'Neill, Mary Ellen (Ella; née Quinlan; O'Neill's mother)

Quinlan, Simon, 74

Quinlan, Thomas Joseph, 70, 71, 77, 78, 79–80, 144

Quinlan, William Joseph, 78, 79, 144, 210n (78)

Quintero, José, 63, 149, 151

Radcliffe, Minnie, 124, 125

Random House, 149, 150

Raven, Grace, 129

Reed, Charles H., 75

Reed, John, 23, 36, 40

Reuters, 25, 26

Revolt (weekly magazine), 30–31, 33, 34, 35, 36, 39

Rippin, Jessica, 67

Robards, Jason, 152

Robins, Elizabeth, 75, 76, 97

Robinson, Boardman, 36

Robson, Eleanor, 136–37

Sage, William E., 73

Salsbury, Milton, 130

Salsbury, Nate, 107, 129–30

Sam, Vilbrun Guillaume, 47, 48

Samuels, Rachel, 130

Sayler, Oliver, 33

Schmidt, Matthew, 34, 35, 36, 37, 38, 40

Scott, Sir Walter, 48

Seaman, Alfred Hamilton (Pop), 72, 73, 74, 75, 96

Sheridan, Mrs. Philip, 122

Sheridan, Philip, 104

Simmons, Zachariah, 10

Sisk, Robert, 53

Smith, Joe, 46, 47

Spirnaugle, Ambrose, 79
SS *Ikala*, 7
St. Mary's Academy, 82, 85
Steffins, Lincoln, 35
Stetson, John, 112, 113, 128
Stevens, Earl, 108–9
Stokes, W. E. D., 9, 10, 12
Swedish Royal Dramatic Theater, 151
Sweeney, Charles, 21, 23
Swinburne, Algernon, 159

Tammany Hall (New York), 45
Tharsing, Hazel, 82. *See also* O'Neill,
    Carlotta Monterey (née Hazel
    Tharsing; O'Neill's third wife)
Tharsing, Nellie, 82
Theater Guild, 55, 57, 62, 63, 149
Thomas, Augustus, 118
Thompson, Charlie, 19
Thus Spake Zarathustra (Neitzsche), 58
Tierney, Sister Mary Leo, 129
Toohey, John Peter, 109
Traveling Salesman, The (play), 108, 140,
    232–33n (140)
Troland, Thomas E., 105
Truax, Sarah, 130, 131
Tucker, Benjamin, 29, 39
Two Orphans, The (play), 72, 138
Tyler, George, 7, 101, 109, 111, 132

Voice of the Mighty, The (play), 9
Vorse, Mary Heaton, 46, 47
Vose, Donald, 34–35, 36, 187n (38)
Vose, Gertie, 34, 35, 37, 41, 42

Wallace, Tom, 45, 47
Walsh, Ann, 72–73
Walsh, Nettie, 72–73, 75, 76–77, 97,
    206–7n (73), 207n (75)
Walsh, Rev. Thomas E., 123
Warner, Charles, 138
Warren, James C., 17, 18
Weinberger, Harry, 87
Welch, Marion, 9
West, Lillian, 76–77
Wharf Theater (Provincetown), 30
When Greek Meets Greek (play), 125
White, Dorothy, 103
White, Edward, 88
White, Lawrence, 103
White Sister, The (play), 109, 139–40
Winther, Sophus Keith, 58
Woolcott, Alexander, 109
Worm, A. Toxen, 21, 177n (21)
Wren, Fred, 98, 99, 121

Young, Art, 32

Zimmerman, Edward, 107

Other Books by Doris Alexander

The Tempering of Eugene O'Neill

Creating Characters with Charles Dickens

Eugene O'Neill's Creative Struggle: The Decisive Decade, 1924–1933

Creating Literature out of Life: The Making of Four Masterpieces